ZAGATSURVEY®

2006/07

CHICAGO RESTAURANTS

Including
Milwaukee

Chicago Editor: Alice Van Housen

Milwaukee Editor: Ann Christenson

Coordinator: Jill Van Cleave

Editor: Daniel Simmons

Published and distributed by
ZAGAT SURVEY, LLC
4 Columbus Circle
New York, New York 10019
Tel: 212 977 6000
E-mail: chicago@zagat.com
Web site: www.zagat.com

Acknowledgments

We thank Bill Rice, Brenda and Earl Shapiro, Steven Shukow and Tom Van Housen. We are also grateful to our associate editor, Emily Parsons, and editorial assistant, Kelly Stewart, as well as the following members of our staff: Maryanne Bertollo, Reni Chin, Larry Cohn, Andrew Eng, Schuyler Frazier, Jeff Freier, Natalie Lebert, Mike Liao, Dave Makulec, Robert Poole, Thomas Sheehan, Joshua Siegel, Carla Spartos, Sharon Yates and Kyle Zolner.

Contents

About This Survey

Here are the results of our *2006/07 Chicago Restaurant Survey,* covering 1,023 establishments as tested, and tasted, by 4,842 local restaurant-goers. To help you find Chicago's best meals and best buys, we have prepared a number of lists. See Most Popular (page 9), Top Ratings (pages 10–15), Best Buys (page 16) and 42 handy indexes.

This marks the 27th year that Zagat Survey has reported on the shared experiences of diners like you. What started in 1979 as a hobby involving 200 of our friends rating NYC restaurants has come a long way. Today we have over 250,000 active surveyors and now cover dining, entertaining, golf, hotels, resorts, spas, movies, music, nightlife, shopping, theater and tourist attractions. All of these guides are based on consumer surveys. They are also available by subscription at zagat.com, and for use on PDAs and cell phones.

By regularly surveying large numbers of avid customers, we hope to have achieved a uniquely current and reliable series of guides. More than a quarter-century of experience has verified this. In effect, these guides are the restaurant industry's report card, since each place's ratings and review are really a free market study of its own customers. This year's participants dined out an average of 3.2 times per week, meaning this *Survey* is based on roughly 804,000 meals. Of these 4,800-plus surveyors, 44% are women, 56% men; the breakdown by age is 12% in their 20s; 28%, 30s; 21%, 40s; 22%, 50s; and 17%, 60s or above. Our editors have synopsized our surveyors' opinions, with their comments shown in quotation marks. We sincerely thank each of these people; this book is really "theirs."

We are especially grateful to our Chicago editor, Alice Van Housen, a freelance writer and editor; to our Chicago coordinator, Jill Van Cleave, a cookbook author and food consultant; and to our Milwaukee editor, Ann Christenson, the dining critic for *Milwaukee Magazine.*

**Finally, we invite you to join any of our upcoming *Surveys* –
to do so, just register at zagat.com.** Each participant will receive a free copy of the resulting guide when it is published. Your comments and even criticisms of this guide are also solicited. There is always room for improvement with your help. Just contact us at chicago@zagat.com.

New York, NY
July 12, 2006

Nina and Tim

Nina and Tim Zagat

What's New

This year, Chicagoans let out their belts a few notches thanks to a host of restaurant newcomers, then used their napkins to dry farewell tears for some old favorites.

Considerable Comings: Debuts included more sushi spots than you can poke a chopstick at (Agami, Hachi's Kitchen, Mizu, Sushi Ai), a fiesta of upscale Mexican and Nuevo Latino arrivals (Carnivale, Cuatro, Olé Olé, Zapatista) and a big serving of small-plates purveyors (del Toro, Fixture, Quartino, X/O Chicago). Also, a couple of impressive New York names elbowed their way into town (David Burke's Primehouse, Il Mulino). Looking ahead, Tru's Tramonto/ Gand power pair will expand with Osteria di Tramonto and Tramonto's Steak & Seafood in Wheeling, and Miami heat will hit town via Douglas Rodriguez's De La Costa, while Blackbird fans are buzzing over unconfirmed rumors that Paul Kahan plans to sire a gastropub.

Regrettable Goings: It was curtains for some classics, including Chilpancingo, Las Bellas Artes, Leo's Lunchroom, 302 West, Trader Vic's and Trio/Trio Atelier, as well as some surprisingly short-lived pedigreed newcomers such as Acqualina, A Milano Italian Grill and Charlie's on Leavitt. But a deluge of dismay over The Berghoff's closing was followed by Wiener-schnitzel whiplash when the born-again Berghoff Cafe bowed scant months later.

The Ban Wagon: The Chicago City Council rolled out phase one of its smoking ban, partially precluding puffing to the relief of many (and chagrin of a few); taverns and restaurant bars were given 2.5 years to comply before the last butt is snuffed out. And fatted fowl honked with relief when the council banned foie gras sales, though some chefs and foodies were crying foul at press time.

Cream of the Cream City Crop: Meanwhile up north, Milwaukee winers-and-diners descended on Downtown to welcome a hip, handsome Asian (Sake Tumi), an elegant New American (Envoy) and two red-meat meccas (Carnevor, Yanni's). Elsewhere, the East Side's Bosley on Brady (seafood/steakhouse) and the Third Ward's Holiday House (Eclectic) showcase sophistication without pretension.

Money Matters: The average cost of a Chicago meal is now $33.75, up an annualized 3.3% from last *Survey*'s $31.64 and above the national average of $32.21. No wonder, then, that 69% of surveyors spent more in restaurants than they did two years ago. Still, cost ain't keeping 'em home: 44% eat out as often, while 39% report increased patronage of The Windy City's world-class eateries.

Chicago, IL
Milwaukee, WI
July 12, 2006

Alice Van Housen
Ann Christenson

subscribe to zagat.com

Ratings & Symbols

Name, Address, Phone Number & Web Site

Hours & Credit Cards

Zagat Ratings

F	D	S	C
▽ 23	9	13	$15

Tim & Nina's ◗ 🅢 ⊄

456 E. Chicago Ave. (Division St.), 312-555-3867; www.zagat.com

Hordes of "unkempt" U of C students have discovered this "never-closing" "eyesore", which "single-handedly" started the "deep-dish sushi pizza craze" that's "sweeping the Windy City like a lake-effect storm"; "try the eel-pepperoni-wasabi-mozzarella or Osaka-Napolitano pies" – "they're to die for" – but bring cash, since "T & N never heard of credit cards or checks."

Review, with surveyors' comments in quotes

Top Spots: Places with the highest overall ratings, popularity and importance are listed in BLOCK CAPITAL LETTERS.

Hours: ◗ serves after 11 PM
🅢 closed on Sunday

Credit Cards: ⊄ no credit cards accepted

Ratings are on a scale of **0** to **30**.

F	Food	D	Decor	S	Service	C	Cost
23		9		13		$15	

0–9 poor to fair	**20–25** very good to excellent	
10–15 fair to good	**26–30** extraordinary to perfection	
16–19 good to very good	▽ low response/less reliable	

Cost (C): Reflects our surveyors' average estimate of the price of a dinner with one drink and tip and is a benchmark only. Lunch is usually 25% less.

For newcomers or survey write-ins listed without ratings, the price range is indicated as follows:

I	$25 and below	**E**	$41 to $65
M	$26 to $40	**VE**	$66 or more

Chicago's Most Popular

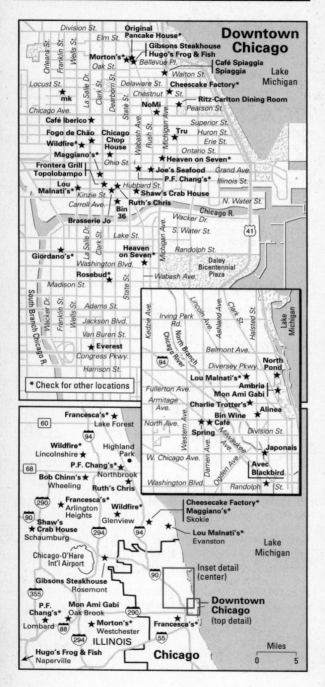

Downtown Chicago

Division St.
Elm St.
Original Pancake House*
Oak St.
Gibsons Steakhouse
Hugo's Frog & Fish
Morton's* Bellevue Pl.
Café Spiaggia
Spiaggia
Walton St.
Lake Michigan
Locust St.
Delaware St.
Chestnut St.
Cheesecake Factory*
mk
Chicago Ave.
NoMi
Pearson St.
Ritz-Carlton Dining Room
Café Iberico
Superior St.
Fogo de Chão
Huron St.
Tru
Wildfire* **Chicago Chop House**
Erie St.
Maggiano's
Ontario St.
Ohio St.
Heaven on Seven*
Frontera Grill
Topolobampo
Joe's Seafood
Grand Ave.
P.F. Chang's*
Illinois St.
Lou Malnati's*
Hubbard St.
Shaw's Crab House
Kinzie St.
Carroll Ave.
Ruth's Chris
N. Water St.
Bin 36
Chicago R.
Brasserie Jo
Wacker Dr.
S. Water St.
Lake St.
Randolph St.
Heaven on Seven*
Giordano's*
Washington Blvd.
Daley Bicentennial Plaza
Rosebud*
Madison St.
Wabash Ave.
Adams St.
Jackson Blvd.
Van Buren St.
Everest
Congress Pkwy.
Harrison St.

*** Check for other locations**

Irving Park Rd.
Belmont Ave.
North Pond
Diversey Pkwy.
Lou Malnati's*
Ambria
Fullerton Ave.
Mon Ami Gabi
Charlie Trotter's
Alinea
Armitage Ave.
Bin Wine
North Ave.
Café Spring
Japonais
W. Chicago Ave.
Avec
Blackbird
Washington Blvd.
Randolph St.

Francesca's*
Lake Forest
Wildfire*
Lincolnshire
Highland Park
P.F. Chang's*
Northbrook
Bob Chinn's
Wheeling
Ruth's Chris
Francesca's*
Arlington Heights
Wildfire*
Glenview
Cheesecake Factory*
Maggiano's*
Skokie
Shaw's Crab House
Schaumburg
Lou Malnati's*
Evanston
Lake Michigan
Chicago-O'Hare Int'l Airport
Inset detail (center)
Gibsons Steakhouse
Rosemont
Downtown Chicago (top detail)
P.F. Chang's*
Lombard
Mon Ami Gabi
Oak Brook
Morton's*
Westchester
Francesca's*
ILLINOIS
Hugo's Frog & Fish
Naperville
Chicago

Miles
0   5

Most Popular

Each surveyor has been asked to name his or her five favorite places. This list reflects their choices.

1. Charlie Trotter's
2. Tru
3. Frontera Grill
4. Wildfire
5. Morton's Steak
6. Gibsons Steak
7. mk
8. Topolobampo
9. Everest
10. Joe's Seafood/Steak
11. Ambria
12. Maggiano's
13. Spiaggia
14. Shaw's Crab House
15. Alinea
16. NoMI
17. Blackbird
18. Rosebud
19. Fogo de Chão
20. Hugo's Frog & Fish
21. Francesca's
22. Original Pancake*
23. Mon Ami Gabi
24. Cheesecake Factory
25. Giordano's
26. P.F. Chang's*
27. Café Iberico
28. Chicago Chop Hse.*
29. Spring
30. Lou Malnati Pizza
31. North Pond
32. Avec
33. Heaven on Seven
34. Ruth's Chris Steak
35. Bin 36/Bin Wine
36. Ritz-Carlton Din. Rm.*
37. Brasserie Jo
38. Japonais
39. Bob Chinn's Crab
40. Café Spiaggia*

It's obvious that many of the restaurants on the above list are among Chicago's most expensive, but if popularity were calibrated to price, we suspect that a number of other restaurants would join the above ranks. Given the fact that both our surveyors and readers love to discover dining bargains, we have added a list of 80 Best Buys on page 16. These are restaurants that give real quality at extremely reasonable prices.

* Indicates a tie with restaurant above

Top Ratings

Excluding places with low voting.

Top Food

29 Carlos'
28 Le Français
   Les Nomades
   Tru
   Alinea
   Tallgrass
   Arun's
   Ambria
27 Topolobampo
   Charlie Trotter's
   Everest
   Vie
   Spring
   Barrington Bistro
   Oceanique
   Ritz-Carlton Din. Rm.
   Blackbird
26 Courtright's
   Frontera Grill
   Spiaggia

   Mirai Sushi
   Avenues
   mk*
   Isabella's Estiatorio
   Gabriel's
   Seasons
   Va Pensiero
   Crofton on Wells
   Sushi Wabi
   Le Titi de Paris
   Joe's Seafood/Steak
   Salbute
   Agami
   Morton's Steak
   Kevin
   NoMI
   Le Lan
   Bistro Banlieue
   Naha
25 Avec

By Cuisine

American (New)
28 Alinea
27 Charlie Trotter's
   Vie
   Spring
   Blackbird

American (Traditional)
25 Seasons Café
24 Bongo Room
   Lawry's Prime Rib
23 Wildfire
   West Town Tavern

Asian (misc.)
26 Kevin
   Le Lan
24 Shanghai Terrace
23 Yoshi's Café
   Opera

Barbecue
23 Fat Willy's
22 Twin Anchors
   Ribs 'n' Bibs
21 Merle's Smokehouse
   Hecky's

Cajun/Creole
21 Heaven on Seven
   Wishbone
20 Pappadeaux Seafood
19 Dixie Kitchen
   Davis St. Fishmarket

Chinese
24 Lao Sze Chuan
23 Happy Chef Dim Sum
   Chen's Chinese
   Emperor's Choice
22 Evergreen

Coffee Shops/Diners
23 Original Pancake
   Manny's
   Orange
22 Lou Mitchell's
21 Milk & Honey

Eclectic
25 Moto
   Lula
23 Aria
   Victory's Banner
   Orange

French (Bistro)
- **27** Barrington Bistro
- **26** Bistro Banlieue
- **25** D & J Bistro
  Retro Bistro
- **24** Chez François

French (New)
- **29** Carlos'
- **28** Le Français
  Les Nomades
  Tru
  Tallgrass

Greek
- **22** Roditys
  Pegasus
- **21** Santorini
  Greek Islands
  Artopolis Bakery

Hamburgers/Hot Dogs
- **25** Hot Doug's
- **22** Superdawg Drive-In
  Al's #1 Beef
- **21** Pete Miller Sea/Steak
- **20** Wiener's Circle

Indian
- **23** India House
- **22** Tiffin
  Gaylord Indian
  Indian Garden
- **21** Vermilion

Italian
- **26** Spiaggia
  Gabriel's
  Va Pensiero
- **24** Café Spiaggia
  Coco Pazzo

Japanese
- **26** Mirai Sushi
  Sushi Wabi
  Agami
- **25** Kuni's
  Heat

Mediterranean
- **26** Isabella's Estiatorio
  Naha
- **25** Avec
  Scylla
- **24** Pita Inn

Mexican
- **27** Topolobampo
- **26** Frontera Grill
  Salbute
- **24** Salpicón
- **23** Cafe 28

Middle Eastern
- **24** Pita Inn
- **23** Maza
- **21** Tizi Melloul
  Turquoise
- **20** Kabul House

Nuevo Latino
- **23** Cuatro
- **22** Nacional 27
  Mas
  Carnivale
- **21** Vermilion

Pizza
- **24** Lou Malnati Pizza
  Art of Pizza
- **22** Aurelio's Pizza
  Pizza D.O.C.
  Pizzeria Uno/Due

Seafood
- **27** Spring
  Oceanique
- **26** Avenues
  Joe's Seafood/Steak
- **25** Scylla

Small Plates
- **25** Avec
  Green Zebra
- **23** Maza
  BOKA
- **22** X/O Chicago

Spanish/Tapas
- **23** La Tasca
  Mesón Sabika
  Café Iberico
- **22** Twist
  Cafe Ba-Ba-Reeba!

Steakhouses
- **26** Morton's Steak
- **25** Chicago Prime Steak
  Chicago Chop Hse.
  Gibsons Steak
- **24** Capital Grille

Top Food

Thai
28 Arun's
22 Thai Pastry
   Spoon Thai
21 Vong's
20 Ruby of Siam

Vegetarian
25 Green Zebra
   Lula
24 Ethiopian Diamond
23 Maza
   Victory's Banner

By Special Feature

Breakfast
26 Seasons
   NoMI
25 Seasons Café
   Lula
24 Bongo Room

Brunch
27 Ritz-Carlton Din. Rm.
26 Frontera Grill
   Seasons
25 Magnolia Cafe
   North Pond

Business Dining
28 Le Français
   Les Nomades
   Alinea
27 Topolobampo
   Charlie Trotter's

Child-Friendly
24 Bongo Room
   Lawry's Prime Rib
   Lou Malnati Pizza
23 Original Pancake
   Manny's

Hotel Dining
28 Ambria
   Belden-Stratford
27 Ritz-Carlton Din. Rm.
   Ritz-Carlton
26 Avenues
   Peninsula
   Seasons
   Four Seasons
   Va Pensiero
   Margarita Inn

Late Dining
26 Agami
25 Avec
   Michael
   Seasons Café
   Gibsons Steak

Meet for a Drink
26 Frontera Grill
   mk
   Joe's Seafood/Steak
   NoMI
25 one sixtyblue

Newcomers/Rated
26 Agami
25 Michael
24 Custom House
23 Cuatro
   Brazzaz

Newcomers/Unrated
   Berghoff Cafe
   David Burke Prime
   Di Pescara
   Il Mulino New York
   Quartino

People-Watching
27 Spring
   Blackbird
26 Mirai Sushi
   mk
   NoMI

Winning Wine Lists
29 Carlos'
28 Le Français
   Les Nomades
   Tru
   Alinea

Worth a Trip
29 Carlos'
   Highland Park
28 Le Français
   Wheeling
   Tallgrass
   Lockport
27 Vie
   Western Springs
26 Courtright's
   Willow Springs

subscribe to zagat.com

Top Food

By Location

Andersonville/Edgewater
24 Ethiopian Diamond
    M. Henry
23 Francesca's
22 Jin Ju
    Speakeasy

Bucktown
25 Scylla
24 Think Café
23 Coast Sushi
    Café Absinthe
    Hot Chocolate

Chinatown
24 Lao Sze Chuan
23 Happy Chef Dim Sum
    Emperor's Choice
22 Evergreen
    Phoenix

Gold Coast
26 Spiaggia
    Seasons
    Morton's Steak
    NoMI
25 Seasons Café

Greektown
22 Roditys
    Pegasus
    Butter
21 Santorini
    Greek Islands

Lakeview/Wrigleyville
24 Tango Sur
    Art of Pizza
23 Chen's Chinese
    Yoshi's Café
    Cafe 28

Lincoln Park
28 Alinea
    Ambria
27 Charlie Trotter's
25 North Pond
24 Sai Café

Little Italy
24 RoSal's Kitchen
23 Francesca's
22 Al's #1 Beef
    Tuscany
    Chez Joël

Loop
27 Everest
26 Morton's Steak
24 Nick's Fishmarket
23 Palm, The
    Aria

Market District
26 Sushi Wabi
25 Moto
    one sixtyblue
23 Starfish
    Red Light

River North
27 Topolobampo
26 Frontera Grill
    Avenues
    mk*
    Crofton on Wells

Streeterville
28 Les Nomades
    Tru
27 Ritz-Carlton Din. Rm.
24 Capital Grille
23 Saloon Steak

Suburbs
29 Carlos'
28 Le Français
    Tallgrass
27 Vie
    Barrington Bistro

Uptown/Lincoln Square
26 Agami
25 Magnolia Cafe
23 Bistro Campagne
22 Thai Pastry
    Pizza D.O.C.

West Loop
27 Blackbird
25 Avec
24 Meiji
23 La Sardine
22 Nine

Wicker Park
27 Spring
26 Mirai Sushi
24 Bongo Room
23 Bob San
    Francesca's

Top Decor

27 NoMI
Tru
Ritz-Carlton Din. Rm.
Seasons
Signature Room
North Pond
Alinea
Spiaggia
26 Everest
Agami
Lobby, The*
Les Nomades
Ambria
SushiSamba rio
Shanghai Terrace
Avenues
RL
Japonais
Custom House
Zealous

25 Courtright's
Charlie Trotter's
Carnivale
Le Français
Seasons Café
Tizi Melloul
Spring
Carlos'
Canoe Club
24 Pump Room
Cité
Atwater's
Nine
Le Colonial
mk
X/O Chicago
Atwood Cafe
one sixtyblue
Arun's
Le Titi de Paris

Outdoors

Athena
Cafe Ba-Ba-Reeba!
Feast
Meritage Cafe
Mesón Sabika
Park Grill

Pegasus
Puck's at MCA
Smith & Wollensky
SushiSamba rio
Tavern on Rush
Timo

Romance

Ambria
Avenue M
Bistro Campagne
BOKA
Café Absinthe
Everest

Geja's Cafe
Il Mulino New York
Le Colonial
Spring
Tizi Melloul
Va Pensiero

Rooms

Alinea
Carnivale
Custom House
Il Mulino New York
Japonais
Marché

NoMI
North Pond
Ritz-Carlton Din. Rm.
RL
Saltaus
Shanghai Terrace

Views

Cité
Courtright's
Everest
Fulton's
NoMI
North Pond

Park Grill
Riva
Seasons
Signature Room
Spiaggia
Tasting Room

Top Service

28 Alinea
Ritz-Carlton Din. Rm.
Tru
Carlos'
Les Nomades
Le Français
27 Charlie Trotter's
Seasons
Ambria
Everest
26 Arun's
Avenues
Courtright's
Moto
NoMI
Gabriel's
Seasons Café
25 Spiaggia
Shanghai Terrace
Isabella's Estiatorio
Tallgrass*
Va Pensiero
Topolobampo
Le Titi de Paris
Spring
Joe's Seafood/Steak
mk
24 Capital Grille
Brazzaz
Morton's Steak
Barrington Bistro
Café la Cave
Fogo de Chão
Oceanique
Le Lan
Scylla
Naha
Buona Terra
Ritz-Carlton Café
Sal & Carvão

Best Buys

Top Bangs for the Buck

1. Cereality Cereal
2. Superdawg Drive-In
3. Potbelly Sandwich
4. Hot Doug's
5. Margie's Candies
6. Wiener's Circle
7. Gold Coast Dogs
8. Mr. Beef
9. Al's #1 Beef
10. Pita Inn
11. Julius Meinl Café
12. Cold Comfort Cafe
13. Victory's Banner
14. Milk & Honey
15. Original Pancake
16. Art of Pizza
17. Irazu
18. Aurelio's Pizza
19. Penny's Noodle
20. Lou Mitchell's
21. Breakfast Club
22. Pompei Bakery
23. Toast
24. M. Henry
25. Orange
26. Nookies
27. My Pie Pizza
28. Tre Kronor
29. Pasta Palazzo
30. Bongo Room
31. Billy Goat Tavern
32. Aladdin's Eatery
33. Ann Sather
34. Artopolis Bakery
35. Medici on 57th
36. Flo
37. Hai Yen
38. Uncommon Ground
39. Duke of Perth
40. Kitsch'n

Other Good Values

Akai Hana
A La Turka
Andies
Bagel, The
Bandera
Best Hunan
Big Bowl
Boston Blackie's
Café Iberico
Cheesecake Factory
Club Lucky
Cyrano's Bistrot
D&J Bistro
Dave's Italian
Davis St. Fishmarket
Dining Rm. at Kendall
erwin cafe & bar
Fonda del Mar
Francesca's
Froggy's French
Greek Islands
Hot Tamales
La Crêperie
Las Tablas
Maggiano's
Maiz
Matsuya
Old Jerusalem
Parthenon
P.F. Chang's
Reza's
Riques
Rose Angelis
Shiroi Hana
Tango Sur
Thai Classic
Thai Pastry
Timo
Village, The
West Town Tavern

Chicago
Restaurant Directory

Adelle's   25   22   23 $36
1060 College Ave. (bet. President St. & Stoddard Ave.),
Wheaton, 630-784-8015; www.adelles.com
A "delightful" "little spot", this "pretty, cozy" Wheaton
New American "fills a need" in the Western Suburbs with
"hearty yet innovative" "comfort food done well" and offered at a "value price", not to mention a staff that provides "excellent attention to customers"; monthly wine
dinners, live jazz on Thursday nights and "great outdoor
dining" are additional incentives.

Adobo Grill   21   19   20 $32
1610 N. Wells St. (North Ave.), 312-266-7999
2005 W. Division St. (Damen Ave.), 773-252-9990
www.adobogrill.com
Pleased patrons of this "mid-scale Mexican" pair in Old
Town and Wicker Park praise the "quality" fare with "bold
flavors" and "a nice variety of Latin specialties" ("don't look
for tacos or burritos"); the "party atmosphere", "especially
on weekends", is "fun" to some, "noisy" to others, and while
the "killer" "custom-made guacamole", "potent margaritas" and "impressive tequila list" are widely praised, ban-
ditos bemoan that they "seem to be the standouts."

AGAMI ●   26   26   23 $38
4712 N. Broadway (Leland Ave.), 773-506-1854
"Incredibly fresh", "flavorful sushi that really pops in your
mouth" as well as "inventive" signature dishes are served
by a "friendly staff" at this Uptown Japanese; "fish on a
video screen" are part of "over-the-top" "underwater" decor that "Jules Verne would envy", and the "fashionable
bar area" offers an "excellent selection of sake."

Akai Hana   21   12   18 $26
3223 W. Lake Ave. (Skokie Blvd.), Wilmette,
847-251-0384
North Suburban sushi stalwarts "crowd" this "reliable",
"family-friendly" Japanese in Wilmette that "keeps it simple" with "solid", "bargain"-priced fare in a "low-key",
"strip-mall location" and a staff that "means well"; snipers
see it "getting tired", though, saying the service is "mixed",
the "food hasn't kept up with their escalating prices" and
the "cheesy decor" "wasn't even an afterthought."

Aki Sushi ●   –   –   –   M
2015 W. Division St. (Damen Ave.), 773-227-8080
Wicker Park's short-lived Touch of Sushi has morphed into
this latest Japanese contender in the modern maki mael-
strom offering a menu dominated by fresh 'fusion' rolls
(with only a few teriyaki cooked selections); laid-back
lounge music, candlelight and a rock garden with koi pond
set the mood, which is easily enhanced by the swanky
sake-cocktail options.

Aladdin's Eatery   17 12 15 $14
614 W. Diversey Pkwy. (Clark St.), 773-327-6300;
www.aladdineatery.com
Charmed champions of this Lincoln Park "treasure" cheer for its "quick", "cheap, healthy Middle-Eastern" eats from a "huge menu" with lots of "vegetarian options", adding that "you can't beat the prices"; still, antis assert that the decor "doesn't draw people in" and insist that the "average cuisine", though "not bad", "isn't exactly what [they] would ask the genie to conjure up."

A La Turka   20 19 19 $25
3134 N. Lincoln Ave. (Belmont Ave.), 773-935-6447;
www.alaturkachicago.com
"Savor the flavors" of "a trip to Turkey without leaving Chicago" at this "funky", "dim" Lakeview lair, where the "authentic" food is "tasty" and "well prepared", the "Zorba-like owner is charming" and the "beautiful belly dancers" (Thursday–Sunday nights) are "amazing"; so even if "service can be spotty", it all adds up to "a fun evening of Turkish food, culture and atmosphere" "at a reasonable price" – "with hookahs to boot!"

Alice & Friends   ∇ 20 9 15 $16
Vegetarian Cafe ⊠
5812 N. Broadway (Ardmore Ave.), 773-275-8797
This "unpretentious" Uptown Asian draws plums for its "interesting selections" of "healthful, delicious" vegetarian and vegan fare, including "unbeef, unchicken and whatever other unmeat is available" ("good desserts" too), but earns lemons for its so-so service and "low-budget decor" dominated by "spooky TV-evangelism" videos that seem to "run on perpetual loop"; N.B. no alcohol service, and no BYO.

ALINEA   28 27 28 $168
1723 N. Halsted St. (bet. North Ave. & Willow St.), 312-867-0110;
www.alinearestaurant.com
Soaring scoring supports the "sheer genius" of chef-owner Grant Achatz and the "astonishing flavors" of his "fabulous" "experimental" New American cuisine at this Lincoln Park "thrill ride" that "engages all of your senses" and "expands your concept of fine dining"; the space is "lovely, understated and serene", the nearly 700-bottle wine list is "superb" and the "polished service" (ranked No. 1 in Chicagoland) is damn near "perfect"; be prepared, though, as this "surreal" "journey" will be "loooong" and "ungodly expensive" – though "worth it."

Allen's - New American Café ⊠   24 20 23 $50
217 W. Huron St. (bet. Franklin & Wells Sts.), 312-587-9600;
www.allenscafe.com
Allen Sternweiler's River North New American "still pleases" with seasonal sustenance that's "inventive but

not too busy" and a menu that "satisfies meat eaters and seafood lovers alike" ("especially" the "excellent game" dishes); factor in an "eclectic wine list", "great service" and a "clean modern setting" that's "casual but upscale", and it's "one of the classier options in the area."

Al's #1 Italian Beef
22 | 7 | 15 | $9
169 W. Ontario St. (Wells St.), 312-943-3222 ●
1079 W. Taylor St. (Aberdeen St.), 312-226-4017 ⊠
1600 W. Lake St. (bet. Lombard & Rohlwing Rds.), Addison, 630-773-4599
551 W. 14th St. (Division St.), Chicago Heights, 708-748-2333
Lincolnwood Town Ctr., 3333 W. Touhy Ave. (McCormick Blvd.), Lincolnwood, 847-673-2333
10276 S. Harlem Ave. (103rd St.), Oak Lawn, 708-636-2333 ⊠
33 S. Northwest Hwy. (bet. Euclid & Prospect Aves.), Park Ridge, 847-318-7700
7132 183rd St. (Harlem Ave.), Tinley Park, 708-444-2333
www.alsbeef.com

"Are your cholesterol and sodium dangerously low?" – then visit this "quintessential" "Chicago legend", a "cheap-eats" chain spun off from the 1938 "Taylor Street original" that's cheered for Italian beef "sandwiches so juicy there's no neat way to eat them" (plus "delicious burgers and sausages, and even better fries"); "lacking" service and "non-existent" decor don't deter the "crowds", though some who swear the kitchen's "getting a little skimpy on the meat" say they "don't get why it calls itself #1."

Amarind's
▽ 25 | 15 | 19 | $24
6822 W. North Ave. (Oak Park Ave.), 773-889-9999
"Gorgeous presentations" and a "good variety" of "imaginative", "fresh" Thai fare at "extremely reasonable" prices please patrons of this "casual", "unpretentious" "jewel" on the cusp of Oak Park that's "worth the trip" to the Far West suburbs; N.B. a bargain prix fixe lunch (Tuesday–Friday) and free parking lot sweeten the pot.

Amber Cafe
24 | 19 | 20 | $44
13 N. Cass Ave. (Burlington Ave.), Westmont, 630-515-8080
Western Suburban locals feel "lucky" to have this "excellent" "seasonal" New American "gem" in Westmont with "a real Downtown feel", "inviting atmosphere" and "well-priced wine list", even if it's "still figuring some things" out – including service that seesaws from "warm" to "disappointing"; P.S. the "beautiful patio" is "a nice place to sit out in the summer."

AMBRIA ⊠
28 | 26 | 27 | $79
Belden-Stratford Hotel, 2300 N. Lincoln Park W. (Belden Ave.), 773-472-5959; www.leye.com
Lincoln Park's "perennial favorite" "splurge destination" "has had a shot of energy" from "new chef" Christian

Eckmann, whose "outstanding" Spanish-tinged New French cuisine exhibits "interesting, well-executed modern twists"; the "expert" staff's "unobtrusive service" includes "outstanding wine pairings" ("personable" "sommelier Bob Bansberg is a gift"), and the "dark-wood" paneling, "fresh flowers" and "tuxedos" make for "*très romantique*" dining – even if the "staid", "civilized" experience spells "stuffy" to some; P.S. "don't forget your jacket or your wallet."

American Girl Place Cafe 12 | 21 | 19 | $28 |
American Girl Pl., 111 E. Chicago Ave. (Michigan Ave.), 312-943-9400; www.americangirlplace.com

Home of "charming tea parties for girls big and small" and shows in the adjacent theater, this "enchanting" Gold Coast "kiddie cutie" is a "dream"-come-true, making "great memories" for little ones in "mommy training" (there's even "booster chairs for the dolls"); the "setting is a trip" and almost everyone's "happy and excited to be there" – so what if the "overpriced" Traditional American food is "enough to make one pray for boys"; P.S. "at least they serve alcohol" (wine and beer only).

Andies 18 | 15 | 18 | $21 |
5253 N. Clark St. (Berwyn Ave.), 773-784-8616 ◗
1467 W. Montrose Ave. (Greenview Ave.), 773-348-0654
www.andiesres.com

The "good-size portions" of "fresh, flavorful" Middle Eastern cuisine (including "many vegetarian options") are "a great value" at this "reliable" duo of "casual" "standbys" that regularly draw "crowds"; raters who rank them "run-of-the-mill" regret their "ho-hum atmosphere", uneven service (though the "delivery is dependable") and "inconsistent" kitchens, claiming they "might be better if they did fewer things well"; N.B. the Andersonville location serves a brunch buffet and is open later than Uptown.

Angelina Ristorante 20 | 18 | 20 | $27 |
3561 N. Broadway (Addison St.), 773-935-5933

Within the "cozy neighborhood" confines of this "romantic" "little storefront" in Wrigleyville, "surprisingly authentic" Southern Italian fare is offered at "reasonable prices" along with "earnest" "service by the adorable Boys Town set" (plus "now they deliver"); inversely, indifferent in-putters infer it's "inconsistent"; P.S. the Sunday "champagne brunch is a great deal."

Anna Maria Pasteria 19 | 19 | 19 | $27 |
4400 N. Clark St. (Montrose Ave.), 773-506-2662

"Sisters Anna and Maria" do "homey", "hearty" Italian food that's "solid, if not spectacular", and "fairly priced" at this "cute" Uptown "neighborhood spot" that draws a "good mix of straights, gays, singles and families"; regulars also appreciate the "friendly service" and credit the siblings for doing a "nice job relocating" in 2005 from their former Wrigleyville digs (hence the rising Decor score).

Ann Sather
19 | 13 | 18 | $16

5207 N. Clark St. (Foster Ave.), 773-271-6677
929 W. Belmont Ave. (Sheffield Ave.), 773-348-2378

Ann Sather Café
3411 N. Broadway (Roscoe St.), 773-305-0024
3416 N. Southport Ave. (Roscoe St.), 773-404-4475
www.annsather.com

You "can't beat the buns" – cinnamon, that is – at this "nothing-fancy" Traditional American–Swedish sisterhood of "solid" full- and cafe-service "standbys" that are "buzzing on weekends" with fans of their "hugely substantial" "family" or "hangover" breakfasts and brunches (only the Belmont Aveue location serves dinner), even if detractors declare them "bland" and "tired"; N.B. alcohol service is BYO, and not allowed at the Andersonville branch.

Antico Posto
23 | 20 | 21 | $30

Oakbrook Center Mall, 118 Oakbrook Ctr. (Rte. 83), Oak Brook,
630-586-9200; www.leye.com

Boosters boom "*buono!*" for this "cute", "classy" and "relaxing" West Suburban Italian "tucked away in Oakbrook Center", where an "attentive staff" delivers "fresh, delicious" fare from a "varied menu" paired with "a wine list for all occasions" and followed by "great tiny dollar desserts" – all in all, it's "better than expected from a mall restaurant."

Arco de Cuchilleros
19 | 14 | 17 | $27

3445 N. Halsted St. (Newport Ave.), 773-296-6046

Amigos of this "overlooked" Spanish spot "hidden" "in the heart of Boys Town" enjoy sampling its 40-plus menu of "reliably delicious", "cheap tapas" along with "sangria on the patio" (there's also a small Iberian wine list); opposers, though, "say *adios* to" what they call "uninteresting" edibles, "sketchy service" and "cramped quarters."

Aria
23 | 23 | 24 | $50

Fairmont Chicago Hotel, 200 N. Columbus Dr. (South Water St.),
312-444-9494; www.ariachicago.com

Friends of this New American–Eclectic eatery in the Fairmont Chicago Hotel maintain that its "menu is like a trip around the world", its wine list is "well thought out" and its "service has improved" of late; the "posh" Loop location is set up for "sleek comfort", with "a bit of space between you and your dining neighbors", and "the bar is good for cozy dessert and drinks"; N.B. they offer a children's menu.

Army & Lou's
∇ 19 | 14 | 16 | $18

422 E. 75th St. (Martin Luther King Dr.), 773-483-3100;
www.armyandlous.com

Supporters swear that "soul food could be defined with a picture of this community fixture" on the Far South Side, a "favorite" for "generous portions" of "down-home" Southern sustenance such as the signature short ribs and peach cobbler, all at "reasonable prices" and served by "the sweetest waitresses"; P.S. live jazz "every Friday night" is an added incentive.

Art of Pizza, The   24 | 6 | 16 | $13 |
3033 N. Ashland Ave. (Nelson St.), 773-327-5600
Pie-sanos praise this Lakeview lair as one of the best pizza joints in town, sighing that they "cannot live without the fabulous buttery, crispy crust" of its "excellent" thin version or the "secret sauce" that made its "delish deep dish" "famous" in Chicagoland; true, the "strip-mall storefront" has "no decor to speak of", hence aficionados "always do delivery" – indeed, some say they've "never been inside."

Artopolis Bakery, Cafe & Agora ●   21 | 17 | 17 | $18 |
306 S. Halsted St. (Jackson Blvd.), 312-559-9000;
www.artopolischicago.com
A "wonderful little fusion of a bar and coffee shop", this Greektown Greek-Med makes "marvelous", "lighter-than-average" sandwiches and salads and "beautiful desserts" available for "sit-down or takeout"; it's a "hip" hang that's "fun" and "friendly", hence Hellen-ophiles "can spend all afternoon here" enjoying the "good people-watching" – and the "late service is a godsend" (midnight weekdays, 1 AM on weekends).

ARUN'S   28 | 24 | 26 | $88 |
4156 N. Kedzie Ave. (bet. Belle Plaine & Berteau Aves.), 773-539-1909; www.arunsthai.com
Arun Sampanthavivat's "completely inventive", "customized" 12-course tasting-only menu of "transcendental" Thai is tantamount to "edible art", "served with care and courtesy" in a "simply" "elegant gallery" setting with a "great wine cellar"; sure, it's "tucked in an industrial/residential neighborhood" on the Northwest Side, but it's "as good as the best in Thailand" and "a whole lot easier to get to", even if it "can seem wildly expensive" – in other words, "make sure this is on your 'things to do before I die' list."

a tavola 🚫   23 | 18 | 23 | $43 |
2148 W. Chicago Ave. (bet. Hoyne Ave. & Leavitt St.), 773-276-7567; www.atavolachicago.com
Connoisseurs of Northern Italian flavors favor this "secret", "quiet" "romance-and-fine-dining" destination "hidden in plain sight" in Ukrainian Village for its "small menu" of "sophisticated" savories (such as its "famous risotto" and gnocchi that are like "little pillows of heaven"); "minimal", "elegant" decor and a "knowledgeable", "attentive staff" round out the experience.

Athena ◑　　　　　　　19　20　19　$26
212 S. Halsted St. (Adams St.), 312-655-0000;
www.athenarestaurant.com
"The prices are right" at this "family-oriented" Greektown "standard" with a "nice staff" serving "tasty", "basic" Greek cooking; fans feel affection for the "fabulous garden" with its "skyline and stars" during summer (not to mention "winter indoors by the fireplaces"), but critics crow that the "crowds seem to overlook" faults with the fare just "for a chance to dine" "alfresco."

ATWATER'S　　　　　　21　24　22　$46
Herrington Inn, 15 S. River Ln. (State St.), Geneva, 630-208-7433;
www.herringtoninn.com
"Hidden" in the Herrington Inn, this "intimate" Suburban West spot offers a "romantic setting" with a "beautiful river view" (especially from the patio); the "creative" New French–New American cuisine is "great", especially "for hotel dining", and Sunday brunch is offered.

ATWOOD CAFE　　　　　21　24　21　$37
Hotel Burnham, 1 W. Washington St. (State St.), 312-368-1900;
www.atwoodcafe.com
"You feel like you're part of the city's architectural history" at this Traditional American "oasis" in the Loop's "landmark" Hotel Burnham, where a "big-city experience" is "crowded" into "tiny", "cramped" quarters (though "high ceilings" help) amid "magical" "Mad Hatter's Ball" decor; the "trendy comfort food" is offered with "solid service", so many "do lunch", "pre-theater" or a "State Street shopping stop", or perhaps "dine alfresco and enjoy the passersby."

Aurelio's Pizza　　　　　22　15　18　$16
Centennial Plaza, 1455 W. Lake St. (Lombard Rd.), Addison,
630-889-9560
1545 Western Ave. (south of Lincoln Hyw./14th St.),
Chicago Heights, 708-481-5040
1002 Warren Ave. (Highland Ave.), Downers Grove, 630-810-0078
13001 W. 143rd St. (Bell Rd.), Homer Glen, 708-645-4400
18162 Harwood Ave. (183rd St.), Homewood, 708-798-8050
17 W. 711 Roosevelt Rd. (Summit Rd.), Oak Brook, 630-629-3200
6543 W. 127th St. (Ridgeland Ave.), Palos Heights, 708-389-5170
601 E. 170th St. (South Park Ave.), South Holland, 708-333-0310
15901 Oak Park Ave. (Rte. 6), Tinley Park, 708-429-4600
www.aureliospizza.com
Additional locations throughout the Chicago area
Supporters salivate for the "different", "delicious thin-crust" pies with "sweet tomato sauce" and the "great antipasto salad" at these "favorite" "suburban staples"; traditionalists are true to the family-owned Homewood location (the others are franchises) with its "old-fashioned pizza-parlor decor", saying it offers "the best" chow in the chain (in-the-know "regulars ask for theirs cooked in the old oven").

AVEC ●
25 | 19 | 22 | $42

*615 W. Randolph St. (Jefferson St.), 312-377-2002;
www.avecrestaurant.com*

"The fabulous people" "squeeze into" this "must-dine"
Med small plate specialist for the "incredible flavors" of
Koren Grieveson's "fantasy" "peasant cuisine", paired
with an "eclectic, affordable wine list" and served by a
"knowledgeable staff"; its "metrosexual Paul Bunyan"
"wood-lined steam-room" setting with "table sharing" and
"bench seating" is "not for the anti-social", who lambaste
it as "loud" and "wildly uncomfortable", but extroverts
enthuse over the "hip" West Loop "scene"; P.S. "if only
they took reservations."

Avenue M ⊠
– | – | – | M

691-695 N. Milwaukee Ave. (Huron St.), 312-243-1133
Daniel Kelly (of the defunct d.kelly) cooks seasonal New
American fare with a steakhouse sensibility at this swanky
Near West newcomer with an intimate balcony and an
outdoor patio festooned with flowering trees and imported
grapevines; curtained off from the main dining room is a
late-night lounge designed to lure the pretty people.

AVENUES
26 | 26 | 26 | $88

*Peninsula Hotel, 108 E. Superior St. (bet. Michigan Ave. &
Rush St.), 312-573-6754; www.peninsula.com*
A trio of 26s conveys surveyors' praise for this "posh",
"gracious" River North New French–seafood sophisticate
where boulevardiers are buoyed by Graham Elliot Bowles'
"amazing tasting menus" and "innovative, avant-garde
presentations" – plus the "champagne cart pre-dinner is a
nice touch"; the "well-spaced" tables of its "luxurious"
Peninsula Hotel setting provide "beautiful views", and service strikes most as "impeccable" (though a smidge
"stuffy" to some); P.S. you might want to "come with an expense account or rich aunt."

Babylon Middle Eastern Kitchen
▽ 17 | 10 | 15 | $13

2023 N. Damen Ave. (McLean Ave.), 773-342-7482
Middle-Eastern meals at this casual, cafeteria-style
Bucktown BYO are a "tasty", "authentic" option for "quick
and cheap" dine-in, or "call in your order ahead of time"
and do takeout if you're not a fan of that "sandwich-shop
look and feel"; N.B. plans are in the offing to switch to table service, and the hookahs are history unless the outdoor dining area is open.

Bacchanalia ⊘
▽ 23 | 13 | 21 | $27

2413 S. Oakley Ave. (bet. 24th & 25th Sts.), 773-254-6555
"Mouthwatering" "homestyle" Northern Italian fare (order
"anything Vesuvio" and "make sure you have a cannoli")
is on the menu at this "down-to-earth" dining depot in the
Heart of Italy; the "nothing-special decor" seems "right

out of the un-cool '50s" (actually, the place opened in 1979), but "enormous portions" ensure "you'll go home with an entire meal in a doggy bag."

Bacino's   21 | 12 | 15 | $18
2204 N. Lincoln Ave. (Webster Ave.), 773-472-7400
118 S. Clinton St. (Adams St.), 312-876-1188 ⊠
www.bacinos.com
This pair of pie purveyors has its partialists, who peg it as their "local pick" for "great" "thin-crust" and "Chicago stuffed" pizza made from "fresh ingredients" (a special mention for the "heart-healthy spinach" version), plus they serve pasta too; P.S. as an "extra bonus", "the Lincoln Avenue location is especially close to the bars."

Bagel, The   18 | 11 | 16 | $16
3107 N. Broadway St. (Belmont Ave.), 773-477-0300
Westfield Shoppingtown, 50 Old Orchard Ctr. (Old Orchard Rd.), Skokie, 847-677-0100
www.bagelrestaurant.com
"If you're having a knish fit", consider this pair of "old-time delis" in Skokie and Lakeview for "big portions" of "nosh-worthy fare" such as "softball-size matzo balls" and "mish-mash soup" that "should be served with a snorkel"; fans find comfort in "decor and clientele reminiscent of Miami Beach in the '50s" and even service that ranges from "friendly" to "crabby", but grouches grump they "can't figure out why" these "inconsistent" "greasy spoons are so popular."

Balagio   ∇ 22 | 21 | 21 | $28
19917 S. LaGrange Rd. (La Porte Rd.), Frankfort, 815-469-2204
18042 Martin Ave. (Ridge Rd.), Homewood, 708-957-1650 ⊠
www.balagio-restaurant.com
South-siders say these are "satisfying" spots for a "pleasant, relaxing dining experience", with "huge portions" of "tasty" Italian eats ("you can easily share with a friend and still have leftovers") presented amid "beautiful decor" – and a "great piano bar" at the Homewood location; still, the charms of these "friendly" "neighborhood favorites" may be lost on non-locals; N.B. the Frankfort place has a pizza oven.

Ballo ◑   19 | 17 | 18 | $37
445 N. Dearborn St. (Illinois St.), 312-832-7700
Contributors converge on the "partylike atmosphere" at Alex Dana's (Rosebud) "flashy" River North ristorante, complete with "disco ball", "loud music" and "mob movies playing on plasma TVs"; whether the "hearty", "old-fashioned Italian" eats and "antipasto bar" are "surprisingly good" or "nothing to rave about", the scene "hot" or "cheesy", and the service "friendly" or "in-your-face" – maybe because

"you can't hear your waiter"– are your call; P.S. after dinner it "turns into a nightclub for late-night revelers."

Bandera 20 20 19 $30
535 N. Michigan Ave., 2nd fl. (bet. Grand Ave. & Ohio St.), 312-644-3524; www.houstons.com
Up "on the second floor of the Mag Mile", this Streeterville "comfort-food heaven" is "one of the best locations in town" for a retail respite, "business lunch" or "romantic" interlude over Southwestern-style Traditional American chow like "great rotisserie chicken", "huge salads" and "melt-in-your-mouth mashed potatoes", all of which are "cheap for this neck of the woods" – no wonder there are "loooong waits" at peak periods (though you can "eat at the bar"); P.S. "live jazz" is offered nightly.

Bank Lane Bistro ⊠ 23 18 20 $39
670 Bank Ln. (bet. Deerpath Rd. & Market Sq.), Lake Forest, 847-234-8802; www.banklanebistro.com
"Darling" and "discreet", this "little restaurant" that "looks out onto Lake Forest's beautiful, historic Market Square" is "one of the more romantic North Shore" options, with a "helpful staff" serving a "sophisticated but not pretentious menu" of "delicious" New American cuisine (try "the daily degustation with wine pairings"); P.S. summertime porch tables are a great way to enjoy this "refreshing choice."

Bar Louie ☾ 15 14 15 $19
3545 N. Clark St. (Addison St.), 773-296-2500
1704 N. Damen Ave. (Wabansia Ave.), 773-645-7500
5500 S. Shore Dr. (55th St.), 773-363-5300
226 W. Chicago Ave. (Franklin St.), 312-337-3313
47 W. Polk St. (Dearborn St.), 312-347-0000
1321 W. Taylor St. (Ashland Ave.), 312-633-9393
1520 N. Sherman Ave. (Grove St.), Evanston, 847-733-8300
22 E. Chicago Ave. (Washington St.), Naperville, 630-983-1600
14335 S. LaGrange Rd. (143rd St.), Orland Park, 708-873-9999
Louie on the Park ☾
1816 N. Lincoln Ave. (Clark St.), 312-337-9800
www.barlouieamerica.com
Barflies befriend this bevy of "casual" Traditional Americans as "pit stops" for "meeting friends", "ogling" others, enjoying "late-night dining" or just "hanging and watching a game" while snarfing an "interesting" "variety" of "good" "pub food" along with a "great beer selection"; still, skeptics swat at the "noisy" "chain"-sters' "uneven offerings" and "inconsistent service at the various locations."

BARRINGTON COUNTRY BISTRO 27 21 24 $42
Foundry Shopping Ctr., 700 W. Northwest Hwy. (Hart Rd.), Barrington, 847-842-1300; www.barringtoncountrybistro.com
Toques off to the "top-quality traditional bistro fare" (No. 1 in its category) and "excellent service" provided within a

"very pleasant country-French setting" overseen by a "gracious owner" at this "hidden gem", a "continual favorite" – its "inauspicious" Northwest Suburban "mall location" notwithstanding; P.S. "lunch is a special treat", and the Sunday prix fixe is a steal.

Basil Leaf Cafe   21 16 20 $24
2460 N. Clark St. (Fullerton Pkwy.), 773-935-3388;
www.basilleaf.com
Neighbors of this "cute", "friendly" Lincoln Park Northern Italian nod to its "wide selection" of "yummy pastas", "first-rate salads" and "fresh soups", all at "reasonable prices" and served in an "unpretentious" setting that "reminds [some] of Tuscany"; P.S. "it's fun to sit outside" on the "charming patio."

Bella Notte   23 17 21 $33
1374 W. Grand Ave. (Noble St.), 312-733-5136;
www.bellanottechicago.com
"Head west on Grand" to this "friendly", "family-run" "favorite" if you favor "huge portions" of "old-school Chicago Italian" ("great seafood pasta dishes", and "the stuffed bone-in filet is the bomb") in a "convivial" Near West "neighborhood place"; the only rift among raters is on the relative merits of the "flashier digs" over the "homey" forerunner (next door), but the jumping Decor score definitely supports the switch.

Benihana   19 16 20 $34
Fitzpatrick Hotel, 166 E. Superior St. (Michigan Ave.), 312-664-9643
747 E. Butterfield Rd. (Meyers Rd.), Lombard, 630-571-4440
1200 E. Higgins Rd. (Meacham Rd.), Schaumburg, 847-995-8201
150 N. Milwaukee Ave. (Dundee Rd.), Wheeling, 847-465-6021
www.benihana.com
Those who score these Japanese steakhouse staples as "sentimental favorites" find "fun" in the "circus" of "well-prepared", "reliable seafood-and-steak" teppanyaki "cooked at your table", adding you can "meet some interesting people" thanks to the "communal arrangement"; still, the unenthused, who find them more "tired" than "tried-and-true", "expect" more, maintaining "the projectiles should at least be tasty if they're being thrown at my head" – especially since you'll leave with "that just-fried smell."

Ben Pao   21 22 19 $31
52 W. Illinois St. (Dearborn St.), 312-222-1888; www.benpao.com
"Pillars and waterfalls" in a "glamorous" setting "put you in a mood for an exotic meal" at this "trendy" Lettuce Entertain You Chinese-"themed palace" in River North, where supporters savor "surprising twists" on Asian food, with "innovative preparations" of "fresh ingredients"; antis, however, allege that the "Americanized" and "expensive" "Disney[-esque] experience" is "disappointing all around."

Berghoff Cafe
– | – | – | M

17 W. Adams St. (bet. Dearborn & State Sts.),
312-427-7399

Berghoff Cafe O'Hare

O'Hare Int'l Airport, Concourse C, 773-601-9180
Fleisch und kartoffel fans heartbroken by the closure of
longtime Loop German The Berghoff can now rejoice over
weekday-only lunch at this new incarnation on the lower-
level of the old space, with a slightly modified cafeteria-
style menu that adds salad, sandwich and pasta options to
the classic Teutonic choices; the former main room upstairs is now a private event facility (The Century Room),
and the historic bar has reopened with a new name (17
West); N.B. the airport outpost has a shortened menu.

Best Hunan
21 | 13 | 17 | $23

Hawthorn Fashion Sq., 700 N. Milwaukee Ave. (Rte. 60),
Vernon Hills, 847-680-8855; www.besthunan.com
Friends feast on "good size portions" of "some excellent"
"traditional Chinese" dishes (and "lunch specials" that
"are a great value") at this "comforting" North Shore
Hunan-Mandarin mainstay where they "treat you like one
of the family"; still, some foes feel Shanghai-ed by what
they call "inconsistent" offerings.

Bêtise, A Bistro on the Lake
21 | 20 | 20 | $39

Plaza del Lago, 1515 Sheridan Rd. (Lake Ave.), Wilmette,
847-853-1711; www.betisebistro.com
"Light lunches", "casual dinners" and an "especially nice
Sunday brunch" constitute the "very good" bistro "cuisine
for the season" at this "local favorite", whose "quaint
French atmosphere" is also appreciated by native North
Shore-birds; still, faint praisers peg it as a "reasonable
choice" for "a quick meal, not a special meal", while liter-
alists lament that "'on the lake' is a little misleading – more
like in a mall."

Big Bowl Asian Kitchen
18 | 17 | 17 | $22

6 E. Cedar St. (State St.), 312-640-8888
60 E. Ohio St. (Rush St.), 312-951-1888
215 Parkway Dr. (Milwaukee Ave.), Lincolnshire,
847-808-8880
1950 E. Higgins Rd. (Rte. 53), Schaumburg, 847-517-8881
www.bigbowl.com
While "clearly a 'concept'" chain, this stir-fry setup is a
great "your-way" option for fans of "fast", "fresh-tasting
blends of Americanized Thai, Chinese and other Asian cuisines" plus "addictive" "fresh-made ginger ale" and "hi-
biscus iced tea" (it's "great for vegetarians" and "kids love
it"); longtime supporters insist its "back on track now that
it's an LEYE operation again" after some "corporate shuf-
fling", but those who "preferred the old menu" believe the
"bland" bowls "feel mass-produced."

Bijan's Bistro ◐   19 | 17 | 18 | $26 |
663 N. State St. (Erie St.), 312-202-1904;
www.bijansbistro.com
"Pop in for a warm welcome" at this River North "neighborhood bar with a bit more class" than some and a "good,
mixed" New American menu that satisfies "celebs", "locals" and "lots of industry people" who "go there when
they get off work"; it's especially valued for weekend
brunch and as a "late-night" "hangout" for "drunk vittles"
(the kitchen's open till 3:30 AM), even if "bistro is a bit of a
misnomer" – it's more in the "below-fine-dining-but-
above-coffee-shop category."

Billy Goat Tavern   15 | 11 | 14 | $12 |
Navy Pier, 700 E. Grand Ave. (Lake Shore Dr.), 312-670-8789
430 N. Lower Michigan Ave. (Illinois St.), 312-222-1525 ◐ ⇦
O'Hare Field Terminal 1, Concourse C, 773-462-9368
330 S. Wells St. (Van Buren St.), 312-554-0297 ⌧ ⇦
1535 W. Madison St. (Ogden Ave.), 312-733-9132 ⇦
309 W. Washington St. (Franklin St.), 312-899-1873 ⌧ ⇦
Among this herd of Traditional American "joints", the original "shrine" "down in the belly of the el" "under Michigan
Avenue" is a "dingy" "icon" with a "storied past" ("home
of the Cubs curse") offering a "salt-of-the-earth Chicago-
style" experience" famed for "paper-thin" "cheezborg-
ers" and "lousy" service; still, shrinking violets who keep
"waiting for the grill man to press a hamburger patty in his
armpit" suggest your "time and money are better spent
renting a video of the *Saturday Night Live* skit."

BIN 36   20 | 19 | 20 | $39 |
339 N. Dearborn St. (Kinzie St.), 312-755-9463
BIN WINE CAFÉ
1559 N. Milwaukee Ave. (Damen Ave.), 773-486-2233
www.bin36.com
"Hip" and "happening", these "swanky but approachable"
(and sometimes "noisy") River North and Wicker Park
New American–French bistro "scenes" feature "fun
flights" of "esoteric" *vins,* a "mind-boggling cheese list" and
"great appetizers" that are generally considered "better
than" the "unremarkable entrees", all served by staffers
who "actually know a little bit about the wines" – "all of
[which] can be purchased right there"; P.S. insiders assert
that the "mini-Bin" cafe may be "even more delightful."

Birch River Grill ⌧   – | – | – | M |
75 W. Algonquin Rd. (Arlington Heights Rd.), Arlington Heights,
847-427-4242
Upscale down-home eats issue from the 'American
kitchen' of this Northwest Suburban lodge from the team
behind Karma and Dine; if the hearty, moderately priced
offerings (e.g. Yankee pot roast, banana cream pie) don't
soothe diners, the comfy room with rustic wood-and-

leather accents, cushy banquettes and a stone fireplace certainly will; N.B. open for breakfast, lunch and dinner.

BISTRO BANLIEUE   26 20 23 $43
44 Yorktown Convenience Ctr. (bet. Butterfield Rd. & Highland Ave.), Lombard, 630-629-6560; www.bistrob.com
"Excellence in a discount strip mall" may seem like an oxymoron, "but once inside" this "elegant and comfortable" "hidden gem" in the West Suburbs, you'll find "authentic French bistro" comestibles (the "half portions" are "adequate" for some appetites) and a "well-versed staff"; P.S. the "private-feeling patio" is "splendid."

Bistro Campagne   23 21 21 $38
4518 N. Lincoln Ave. (bet. Sunnyside & Wilson Aves.), 773-271-6100; www.bistrocampagne.com
"Hearty, healthy" and "wonderful" "provincial French bistro" cuisine exhibiting chef-owner Michael Altenberg's "commitment" to "working with the best organic farms in the area" delights denizens of this "tiny" (some say "cramped") and "romantic" Lincoln Square "find" where the "beer list is as interesting as the wine list", the service "experienced" and "personable", and the "pretty" "patio transports you to the countryside" – in other words, it's "the kind of place you wish was a secret."

Bistro Kirkou   22 18 22 $45
500 Ela Rd. (Maple Ave.), Lake Zurich, 847-438-0200
"Creative combinations" of "delicious" French bistro fare, "friendly, efficient service" and a "gracious" host-owner (one of the house's "Le Titi de Paris alumni") make this "small, intimate" setting with multiple rooms, murals and a fireplace "one of the bright spots" in the Northwest Suburbs; still, naysayers nag it's "noisy" and "uninspired."

Bistro 110   20 19 19 $39
110 E. Pearson St. (bet. Michigan Ave. & Rush St.), 312-266-3110; www.bistro110restaurant.com
"For years" this "reliable" Gold Coast "crowd-pleaser" has been a "favorite" of Francophiles who find "comfort" in its "traditional" bistro cooking, including its "signature roasted garlic" ("just hand it over and no one will get hurt"); still, quoters quibble over whether it's "reasonable" or "overpriced", the ambiance is "quaint" or "fake" and the service "friendly" or *trop* "French" in "attitude", while other "disappointed" diners deem it "tired" and "touristy" because of its "prime" "off-Michigan" location.

Bistrot Margot   21 19 20 $37
1437 N. Wells St. (bet. North Ave. & Schiller St.), 312-587-3660
216 S. Washington St. (Jefferson Ave.), Naperville, 630-778-1944
www.bistrotmargot.com
"Authentic French bistro food" "done well" draws devotees to these dual locations – "Old Town residents are

lucky to have this as their neighborhood place", while the newer West Suburban spot is a "great addition to Naperville" – even if the "friendly service" can be "hit-or-miss" and the "romantic", "unpretentious" original's "distracting noise level" makes it "conversation-challenging" ("try to sit upstairs where tables are not on top of each other"); P.S. both offer outdoor dining and "great" Saturday–Sunday brunch.

Bistrot Zinc
20 | 20 | 20 | $36

1131 N. State St. (bet. Cedar & Elm Sts.), 312-337-1131
"Your classic neighborhood bistro" is a "quiet getaway" just "a few paces from the hubbub of Rush Street", where the "good take on standard" French food and "charming atmosphere" (including an "authentic zinc bar") serve up "a little bit of Paris in the Gold Coast"; P.S. contributors compliment the "outstanding child-friendly weekend brunch."

Bite
▽ 23 | 13 | 18 | $18

1039 N. Western Ave. (Cortez St.), 773-395-2483
Ukrainian Villagers tout the "tasty regular dishes" (including weekend brunch) plus "fancy specials" of Eclectic eats at this "out-of-the-way" outpost with "a grunge setting" and a staff that just might sport "the most body piercings per server in Chicago" – and all at a cost that "doesn't take a bite out of your wallet"; N.B. you can BYO from The Empty Bottle music club next door.

BLACKBIRD ⊠
27 | 20 | 23 | $57

619 W. Randolph St. (bet. Desplaines & Jefferson Sts.), 312-715-0708; www.blackbirdrestaurant.com
Make sure this "fabulously polished" West Loop "classic" is on your list for "pure tastes in a pure space" courtesy of chef Paul "'King' Kahan", whose "exquisite" New American cuisine employing "local, organic and unique ingredients" "makes you proud to be from Chicago"; the setting may be "stark" ("the whole white on white thing"), the "tables cramped" and the "din" "astonishing", but there's "plenty of eye candy", plus "consummately professional" service and "one of the highest-quality wine selections in the city, at all price ranges."

Blind Faith Café
19 | 14 | 17 | $19

525 Dempster St. (Chicago Ave.), Evanston, 847-328-6875; www.blindfaithcafe.com
A "vegetarian's delight" with "vegan choices too" (they serve eggs but no meat) in an "arty section of Evanston", this "homey" "'70s throwback" is "accommodating to additions/substitutions for a given diet", and loyalists "love the baked goods" from the in-house bakery and the "fresh smoothies"; still, some slam the "erratic service" and suggest it's "slightly overpriced" "for health food"; P.S. "for self-service, sit in the front cafe area."

Block 44 ☒   – | – | – | M |
4363 N. Lincoln Ave. (Montrose Ave.), 773-868-4404
The Lincoln Square space once occupied by Acqualina is now home to this moderately priced New American done in a tasty palette of tamarind, butter and chocolate, with curved walls, leather chairs and a mahogany bar; grazers can order the '44 menu', a sampling of four dishes paired with wines, and the global wine list can be similarly enjoyed in flights and by the half- or full-glass pour.

Bluefin   21 | 18 | 16 | $32 |
1952 W. North Ave. (Milwaukee Ave.), 773-394-7373;
www.bluefinsushibar.com
A "head-turning crowd" gathers for "always-good sushi" "with some inventive rolls" and "great lunch specials" at this "dark" Bucktown Japanese that some swear by as a "date spot"; other fin-atics disagree, though, declaring they've "had better for the price" and sinking the service as "spotty" – perhaps accounting for its rating plunge.

Blue Water Grill   22 | 23 | 20 | $48 |
520 N. Dearborn St. (Grand Ave.), 312-777-1400;
www.brguestrestaurants.com
This "trendy" New American "East Coast transplant" and "sophisticated watering hole" in River North's "old Spago space" is a "New York–style" "scene" where "the focus is on unique seafood preparations" (special mention for the "sushi and raw oyster bars"); "cool drinks", an "amazing Sunday brunch" and a "nice jazz bar upstairs" also win praise from the "hip yet diverse crowd", though sticklers would still "throw this one back" for a "contrived" concept, "disjointed" service and "expense-account prices."

BOB CHINN'S CRAB HOUSE   23 | 13 | 19 | $36 |
393 S. Milwaukee Ave. (Dundee Rd.), Wheeling, 847-520-3633;
www.bobchinns.com
"They crank it out" at this "fun" North Suburban "fresh-fish" "factory" and mai tai "madhouse", serving "seafood by the ton" in a "tacky", "cavernous" "picnic setting"; "crab lovers" who "survive the wait" to savor its 100-plus options and "monster salad bar" maintain it's "a mind-blower for out-of-towners" (with an "awesome kids' menu" too), but grumps grade it "greasy, pricey" and "noisy", noting they "don't like getting the bum's rush" – though if you "go at lunch, [they're] not as crazy to get you out the door."

Bob San ◗   23 | 18 | 20 | $34 |
1805 W. Division St. (Wood St.), 773-235-8888;
www.bob-san.com
Bob Bee's "hip but relaxed" sister to Sushi Naniwa scores with "excellent", "creative" Japanese "cooked and raw fish" and generally "good service" offered amid a "real", "funky" Wicker Park "neighborhood vibe"; it's peopled

with "singles, couples and young families", many of who enjoy the outdoor dining option, even if buzzkills bet there are "some better values out there."

Bogart's Charhouse　　　21 18 19 $35
18225 Dixie Hwy. (183rd St.), Homewood, 708-798-2000
17344 Oak Park Ave. (171st St.), Tinley Park, 708-532-5592
"The first thing you see is the meat cooler and BBQs flaring" at these similar but separately owned South and Southwest Suburban steakhouses praised by "Humphrey Bogart fans" for purveying "great steaks for the price" and "free table salads" within an "atmosphere that puts you right in the middle of Casablanca"; pickier eaters pronounce the pair "pleasant" and "a good choice if you're in the neighborhood", but "not worth a special trip."

BOKA　　　　　　　23 22 22 $46
1729 N. Halsted St. (North Ave.), 312-337-6070;
www.bokachicago.com
"Finally, a good pre-theater spot that you'd actually visit even when you don't have Steppenwolf tickets" fawn flatterers of this Lincoln Parker's "creative" small and large plates (from a seasonal New American "menu that changes all the time"), "attractive staff" and "sophisticated", "high-energy" "date" environment; hecklers, however, hiss about "hype for not a lot of substance", noting it "can be noisy" and "prices are a little steep", but all agree it has "one of the best outdoor seating areas."

Bongo Room　　　　24 17 17 $18
1470 N. Milwaukee Ave. (Honore St.), 773-489-0690
1152 S. Wabash Ave. (Roosevelt Rd.), 312-291-0100
Delighted drummers who "dream about" the "interesting pancake options" arrive "early to get a seat" for the "indulgent" weekend brunch at this "Wicker Park standard" with a "varied and delicious" Traditional American menu that's "worth every penny and calorie", adding "if you don't want to wait an hour" try the "great" South Loop location; that said, jaded jurists wonder "what are all of those people waiting for?"; P.S. "lunch can be surprisingly busy" too (they don't serve dinner).

Boston Blackie's　　　19 13 16 $18
164 E. Grand Ave. (St. Clair St.), 312-938-8700
120 S. Riverside Plaza (bet. Adams & Monroe Sts.),
312-382-0700 ⊠
222 E. Algonquin Rd. (Tonne Dr.), Arlington Heights, 847-952-4700
405 Lake Cook Rd. (Rte. 43), Deerfield, 847-418-3400
Hubbard Woods Plaza, 73 Green Bay Rd. (Scott Ave.),
Glencoe, 847-242-9400
www.bostonblackies.com
You "need a big mouth" for the "juicy, delicious", "gut-stuffing burgers" at these "classic" Traditional American

city and suburban "joints" that loyalists laud as "dependable stops" for "good, cheap eats" in a "no-frills", "retro" "sports-bar" atmosphere; still, bummed beef eaters aren't lining up for what they call "serviceable food", "variable" service and an annoying "à la carte" price structure – "with surcharges for basic extras that should be included."

BRASSERIE JO　　　　　22 | 21 | 20 | $40
59 W. Hubbard St. (bet. Clark & Dearborn Sts.), 312-595-0800; www.brasseriejo.com
As its steady scoring since last *Survey* suggests, this Lettuce Entertain You River North 10-year-old remains a "favorite" for fans of its "nicely presented", "delicious" Brasserie "comfort food", "extensive beer and wine list" and locale that's "like walking into a 1940s-era Paris" boîte ("large and noisy, as it ought to be"); still, contrarians contend "there are better" examples with "better prices" and "wish the service were as good as the food"; P.S. the sidewalk cafe is "dog-friendly."

Brazzaz　　　　　　　23 | 21 | 24 | $57
539 N. Dearborn St. (Grand Ave.), 312-595-9000; www.brazzaz.com
"Go hungry" but "pace yourself" at this "modern", "elegant" "carnivores' heaven" serving 20-ish varieties of unlimited "grilled protein" with an "unbelievable salad bar" of "warm and cold foods"; eaters enthuse it's an "expense-account outing" that "should be called 'pizzazz' for the sharp and fun experience it delivers", making it a "nice addition to the Brazilian steakhouses that have proliferated in the River North area"; N.B. lunch is less than half the cost of dinner.

Breakfast Club, The ⊘　　　19 | 12 | 18 | $14
1381 W. Hubbard St. (Noble St.), 312-666-3166; www.chicagobreakfastclub.com
"The 'morning after' crowd" makes its way to this "breakfast nook" "hidden down by the rail tracks" in West Town for "tasty diner-style food" served amid "homey" "pink decor" that reminds some of "eating at grandma's" – especially if the old gal was known for giving "brusque service" and making you "bring cash"; N.B. name notwithstanding, lunch is also served.

Brett's Café Americain　　　20 | 17 | 18 | $26
2011 W. Roscoe St. (Damen Ave.), 773-248-0999; www.brettscafe.com
Many Roscoe Villagers value this "underappreciated", "neighborhoody", "cozy storefront" for its "fresh", "innovative [New] American menu", including a "bargain prix fixe dinner" offered before 6:30 PM and a "delightful brunch" with an "irresistible", "huge basket of homemade breads and jams"; still, sensitive sorts say that the staff's

"bad attitude" – especially the "grumpy", "loud" management "that barks at customers and servers alike" – "spoils the experience" (at least the "outdoor seating is sweet").

Bricks　　　　　　　　21 | 14 | 17 | $19 |
1909 N. Lincoln Ave. (Wisconsin St.), 312-255-0851;
www.brickspetaluma.com
"As underground as its underground location", this Lincoln Park parlor serves "gourmet" "thin-crust pizzas" in a "groovy" atmosphere with "fun servers", "reasonable pricing" and a "strong beer" list – though the "cavernous" confines are "cozy" and "relaxed" to some raters, "dark" and "dank" to others.

Brioso　　　　　　　　19 | 14 | 18 | $27 |
4603 N. Lincoln Ave. (Wilson Ave.), 773-989-9000
Touters of this "trendy" Lincoln Square taqueria appreciate its "fun", "friendly" feel and "hearty" fare, saying its "interesting" "Nuevo-Mexican" meals are "Americanized, but in a good way"; detractors declare the fare "not authentic", though, and decry the "minimal decor", but all agree the drinks are "highly recommended" – as is the outdoor cafe.

Bruna's Ristorante　　　▽ 23 | 13 | 19 | $31 |
2424 S. Oakley Ave. (24th Pl.), 773-254-5550
Heart of Italy habitués get a "warm" reception at this "old-world Italian" "throwback to a great old neighborhood"; there's "nothing innovative or new here" but" it's "a reliable red-sauce house" that's like a "walk down memory lane" to "grandma's in Palermo" – especially if her place "needs a face-lift."

Buona Terra Ristorante　　24 | 20 | 24 | $28 |
2535 N. California Ave. (Logan Blvd.), 773-289-3800;
www.buona-terra.com
This "lovely little storefront" in Logan Square "welcomes" with "delicious and unpretentious [Northern] Italian food" (a "combination of specialty dishes and old favorites"), "thoughtful service" and "good wine at reasonable prices", all "in a comfortable environment" with murals, "exposed-brick walls" and a garden; P.S. the "Thursday night prix fixe is an amazing bargain."

Butter ⊠　　　　　　　22 | 21 | 21 | $53 |
130 S. Green St. (Adams St.), 312-666-9813;
www.butterchicago.com
Butter lovers melt for chef Ryan Poli's "innovative" New American cuisine, which reveals his "commitment to sustainable ingredients", at this "sleek" and "trendy" Greektowner that's "fast becoming an 'in' spot" ("positive energy" and "pretty things abound"); foes, though, fret it's "all over the map" and "tries a little too hard to be hip", adding that the "small portions do not justify the high price tag."

Cab's Wine Bar Bistro
22 │ 19 │ 23 │ $38

430 N. Main St. (Duane St.), Glen Ellyn, 630-942-9463;
www.cabswinebarbistro.com

"Solid" New American cuisine "well-prepared" by a chef
"with an eye for taste and beauty" and served within an
"elegant yet cozy" setting by an "unpretentious staff" that
"makes great wine picks" has confreres calling a cab and
heading for this "welcoming" West Suburban "find";
N.B. periodic wine dinners are an added draw.

Café Absinthe
23 │ 21 │ 22 │ $42

1954 W. North Ave. (Damen Ave.), 773-278-4488

"Creative", "diverse" seasonal New American fare and a
"very good wine selection" make the heart grow fonder for
aficionados of this "old favorite", who aver it's "aging
gracefully" in its "secret" ("entrance through the alley")
Bucktown digs; "decadence meets urban chic" within the
"minimalist setting" replete with "rustic brick walls" and
an "open kitchen", but even converts caution it can be
"loud" and the seating "a little crowded."

Cafe Ba-Ba-Reeba!
22 │ 19 │ 19 │ $30

2024 N. Halsted St. (Armitage Ave.), 773-935-5000;
www.cafebabareeba.com

It's "always" a "lively" "party" at this longtime Lincoln Park
"crowd-pleaser" that "preceded the [small-plates] craze by
years", where pleased *patróns* "share" "super choices"
from a "huge menu" of "delish" Spanish snacks – not to
mention the "hearty" weekend brunch and "addictive sangria"; still, tart tipsters testify it's a "tapas tourist trap"
that's "resting on its laurels", adding it's "not cheap" when
you tally the total; P.S. "in the summer, try to get a table on"
the "great patio."

Café Bernard
21 │ 17 │ 20 │ $36

2100 N. Halsted St. (Dickens Ave.), 773-871-2100;
www.cafebernard.com

It "feels like home" but "tastes like Paris" at this "friendly"
French bistro, a "best-kept secret" in Lincoln Park for
more than three decades, where the "honest", "hearty"
cooking is "reasonably priced", paired with a "thoughtful,
value-oriented wine list" and served in "quaint", "comfortable" digs that are especially appealing "if you're not in-
terested in hype"; P.S. "you can get the same menu around
back at the [Red] Rooster [wine bar] for less cash."

Cafe Bolero
21 │ 17 │ 17 │ $25

2252 N. Western Ave. (bet. Belden Ave. & Lyndale St.),
773-227-9000; www.cafebolero.com

"Down-to-earth Cuban cooking" and 110 varieties of rum
delight denizens of this "cozy", "no-frills" Bucktown
cucina; "what it lacks in decor it makes up for" with its "inexpensive", "homestyle staples" and "friendly staff", plus

"there's often live music to give you a flavor of [island] life"; P.S. "nice outdoor seating" too.

Cafe Borgia ▽ 25 13 22 $30
17923 Torrence Ave. (179th St.), Lansing, 708-474-5515; www.cafeborgia.com
"You can taste that everything is made fresh" at this "small" South Suburban Northern Italian favorite that "feels like a trattoria in Italy" thanks to "outstanding food" and "friendly service"; in fact, the only liability, locals lament, is that since Lansing is largely "devoid of good restaurants" (and this one doesn't take reservations) there are often "long lines"; P.S. it's "especially fun to visit in the summer when the patio is open."

Cafe Central 23 18 21 $36
455 Central Ave. (bet. Linden & St. Johns Aves.), Highland Park, 847-266-7878; www.cafecentral.net
Make for this "small, intimate" "medium-priced Carlos'" spin-off if you crave "creative", "hearty [French] bistro fare" complemented by a "colorful room and staff" (owner "Debbie [Nieto] makes you feel right at home"); most cafe-goers consider it a "top-notch choice for semi-elegant" North Shore "neighborhood" dining, though a contingent claims it can be "crowded, noisy, uncomfortable" and "a bit pricey for what you get"; P.S. "summertime means south-facing tables under umbrellas" on the sidewalk.

Café des Architectes 22 23 20 $42
Sofitel Chicago Water Tower, 20 E. Chestnut St. (Wabash Ave.), 312-324-4063; www.sofitel.com
Wayfarers say *"oui oui"* to this "chichi" "gem" in the Gold Coast's Sofitel Chicago Water Tower, where the "sharp", "stunning" interior is "architecturally one of the finest environments" extant, and dining "outdoors is almost like eating in a park"; the "creative", seasonal New French–Med "food is as good as many restaurants costing much more", and is available for breakfast, weekend brunch, lunch and dinner – plus the attendants are "attentive"; N.B. free valet parking is provided at night.

CAFÉ IBERICO ● 23 15 16 $26
739 N. LaSalle St. (bet. Chicago Ave. & Superior St.), 312-573-1510; www.cafe-iberico.com
It gets "as crowded and noisy as Pamplona's running of the bulls" at this River North small-plate arena resembling a "huge Spanish university cafeteria", where a "mostly young crowd" willingly weathers "long waits" (no reservations Friday–Saturday) to "drink addictive sangria, feast on" "great-tasting", "authentic" dishes and "make friends with surrounding tables"; critics concede it's "cheap" but complain "you get what you pay for", adding "service could be better" and the "no-frills decor" is "bland."

Café la Cave   24 | 23 | 24 | $51

2777 Mannheim Rd. (bet. Higgins Rd. & Touhy Ave.), Des Plaines, 847-827-7818; www.cafelacaverestaurant.com

"Old-fashioned Continental" "fine dining" with "waiters in tuxedos" makes this "one of the better" "special-occasion" "bets for the [O'Hare] area"; it's "right out of the '60s" (it "will remind you of a Sinatra movie set, baby!") but stalwarts who find "romance" in the "room with the cozy fireplace" or "the original cave" swear it "stands the test of time" – though less nostalgic New Agers negate it as "a bit stuffy for the 21st century."

Café le Coq   23 | 22 | 20 | $38

734 Lake St. (Oak Park Ave.), Oak Park, 708-848-2233

"Coq a doodle doo!" announce adherents of this "upscale French bistro", a "classy place" serving Steve Chiappetti's "tasty" "traditional" dinners and a "very good Sunday brunch" along with "a fun wine list" within a "charming" Oak Park "storefront space"; fence-sitters, though, feel they're "still waiting for [their] first great dish", find the coop "cramped" and say service is "indifferent" on occasion, quipping "perhaps that gives it an air of authenticity."

Cafe Matou   22 | 19 | 21 | $40

1846 N. Milwaukee Ave. (bet. Leavitt St. & Oakley Ave.), 773-384-8911

Feline friends of this "funky", "out-of-the-way" Bucktown "neighborhood winner", whose name translates as 'tom cat', "purr" over chef-owner Charlie Socher's "consistently interesting and well-prepared" "classic French" food with "sublime sauces" from a "menu that changes often" (plus "exceptional specials"), not to mention the "lovely wine selection"; even so, a litter of catty commenters contends service goes "south" on "off nights."

Cafe Pyrenees   21 | 19 | 19 | $36

Adler Square Shopping Plaza, 1762 N. Milwaukee Ave. (Buckley Rd./Rte. 137), Libertyville, 847-362-2233; www.cafepyrenees.com

Satisfied scribes see "solid" "simple everyday French" bistro eats at "reasonable prices", especially the "good lunch deals", and an "attentive staff" at the new Libertyville locale of this "diamond in the rough"; optimists opine it "hasn't lost any of the charm of its old location" in Vernon Hills (plus now it "has a bar"), but pessimists purport that it "seems like just a regular restaurant" now, judging it just "not as good as it used to be" – hence the ratings dip.

Cafe Selmarie   21 | 16 | 18 | $21

4729 N. Lincoln Ave. (Lawrence Ave.), 773-989-5595; www.cafeselmarie.com

The "European mood" is "so authentic you want to pay in euros" at this "kid-friendly" "neighborhood treasure" and "dessert oasis" table-ing "tasty meals" of New American "comfort foods" (eager eaters "get up early" for its "champion of breakfasts"); the location "on the fountain park in Lincoln Square" provides "perfect people-watching", and "summer nights are magic" on the "charming" patio.

CAFÉ SPIAGGIA   24   22   23 $48
980 N. Michigan Ave., 2nd fl. (Oak St.), 312-280-2750;
www.cafespiaggia.com
"If you don't want to wear a tie or go bankrupt, but do want great Italian comfort food" with a "well-chosen wine list to match", head to this Gold Coast "oldie but goldie" ("Spiaggia's little sister") that's "ideal" "for a quick bite" for "business" folk, "super shoppers" or even "when eating solo"; it's a "fun, relaxed place", even if the "eclectic setting" has an "awkward" layout and service is either "pretentious" or has "personality", depending on your point of view.

Cafe 28   23   19   20 $29
1800-1806 W. Irving Park Rd. (Ravenswood Ave.), 773-528-2883;
www.cafe28.org
For a "first date" or "gathering" "with a group", this "classy" Lakeview "favorite" yields "yummy Cuban" and Mexican meals (including an "amazing brunch") made from "the freshest ingredients" and accompanied by "fabulous mojitos"; "on quiet nights, it's a symphony", but it's "a cacophony on busy weekends" when "crowds pack the place" – and the sometimes "slow service" combined with a "no-reservations" policy means you should "expect long waits."

Caliterra Bar & Grille   23   19   21 $49
Wyndham Chicago, 633 N. St. Clair St. (Erie St.), 312-274-4444;
www.wyndhamchicago.com
A "pleasant surprise" awaits voyagers who venture to this Streeterville venue with a "refined, distinctive menu" of "spot-on", "wine-friendly" Cal-Ital cuisine and one of "Chicago's best cheese carts"; supporters surmise "some of the locals think it's just a 'hotel dining room' and miss out on a great experience", asserting "if it weren't hidden on the second floor [of the Wyndham Chicago] it would be packed every night."

Campagnola   23   20   22 $39
815 Chicago Ave. (Washington St.), Evanston, 847-475-6100;
www.campagnolarestaurant.com
"Combinations of organic and wholesome ingredients" make for "creative, interesting" fare at this "friendly" "outpost for unique Italian dining", an "upscale" "North Shore treasure" where a "thoughtful wine selection" and "service with a delicate touch" are also offered in a "cozy", "understated atmosphere"; P.S. its "outdoor dining is a welcome treat in warmer months."

Canoe Club
19 | 25 | 17 | $35

15200 S. 94th Ave. (151st St.), Orland Park, 708-460-9611;
www.thecanoeclubrestaurant.com

It's "like a high-budget beach movie" – complete with "palm trees" and "live sharks" – at this "island-friendly" New American installation serving what swayed survey-ors say is "some of the freshest seafood in the South Suburbs", all washed down with "great tropical drinks"; the tide is out, however, for voters who veto the vittles as "variable", say the service is "so-so" and judge the "gym-nasium"-sized Hawaiian setting "cute" "until you try to hold a conversation."

Cape Cod Room
21 | 21 | 21 | $52

Drake Hotel, 140 E. Walton Pl. (Michigan Ave.), 312-787-2200;
www.thedrakehotel.com

The seas part for this "clubby" Streeterville seafood "standby" "with a maritime theme", "a welcome anachro-nism in food and service style" if you're a "sucker for red-check tablecloths", "Bookbinder soup" "served with a side of sherry" and "Dover sole deboned as it should be"; critics, however, crab that this "classic" is "coasting", snapping "service is not their strong point" and quipping "the only thing that has changed in [73] years is the prices."

Capital Grille, The
24 | 23 | 24 | $55

633 N. Saint Clair St. (Ontario St.), 312-337-9400;
www.thecapitalgrille.com

Lobbyists laud this "loud, lively" Streeterville meatery as an "excellent chain steakhouse" where you can or-der a "juicy, tender" "dry-aged steak" (though purists would prefer it "if they served Prime beef" rather than Choice) and "more than a few fish options", backed by an "oenophile's dream wine list" and "out-of-this-world" pineapple martinis; with "polished service" from a staff that does "plenty of sucking up, which is needed given the high prices", it has all "the trappings of a fine power-dinner locale."

CARLOS'
29 | 25 | 28 | $89

429 Temple Ave. (Waukegan Ave.), Highland Park, 847-432-0770;
www.carlos-restaurant.com

A "memorable evening" awaits visitors to this 25-year-old North Shore "treasure", a "fine-dining" "temple on Temple Avenue" that's ranked No. 1 for Food among Chicagoland restaurants on the strength of its "superb", "very creative" New French fare, which is accompanied by a "fantastic wine list" and served by a "staff that knows when to be friendly and when to be reserved"; the feel is "formal yet extremely comfortable, with cozy booths and soft lighting", making it a "great celebration place" – "if you can afford it"; N.B. jackets required.

Carlucci   19   18   18 $36

1801 Butterfield Rd. (I-355), Downers Grove,
630-512-0990
250 Marriott Dr. (Milwaukee Ave.), Lincolnshire, 847-478-0990;
www.carlucci-lincolnshire.com
Riverway Complex, 6111 N. River Rd. (Higgins Rd.), Rosemont,
847-518-0990
www.carluccirestaurant.com

These fraternal twins in Rosemont and Downers Grove
fare solidly for "straightforward and satisfying" Northern
Italian and "imaginative, well-seasoned specials" (though
"lunch is where the real bargains are"); still, testy tipsters
testify that this twosome of "transplants" "will never measure up to the [bygone] original" "in Lincoln Park", observ-
ing the output is "ordinary" and the "service uneven" (plus
"busy" can mean "noisy"); N.B. the Lincolnshire location
is no longer in the family.

Carmichael's   22   18   21 $41
Chicago Steak House ◗

1052 W. Monroe St. (bet. Morgan St. & S. Aberdeen St.),
312-433-0025; www.carmichaelsteakhouse.com

West Loop surveyors peg this as "primarily a neighborhood place" for "great steaks" "prepared exactly to your
liking", as well as other "tasty" "standard steakhouse
fare" and a "reasonably priced wine list", served in an
"open, casual atmosphere" with a "fabulous outdoor patio";
moderates maintain it has "nothing distinctive" to offer,
though, except its "proximity to the United Center."

Carmine's ◗   21   18   20 $39

1043 N. Rush St. (bet. Bellevue Pl. & Cedar St.), 312-988-7676;
www.rosebudrestaurants.com

To allies, this gregarious Gold Coast offshoot of the Rosebud
family tree is a "hot spot" for "gargantuan" heaps of
"honest-to-goodness Italian" "pasta and other delights"
delivered in a "hopping" house where nightly "entertainment is a plus" – enjoying "brilliant live piano" within or
"eating outside to watch all the action" on Rush Street; even
antis who argue that the food is "not fabulous" and the
prices are "above average" grant it's "good for tourists."

CARNIVALE   22   25   19 $40

702 W. Fulton St. (Halsted St.), 312-850-5005;
www.carnivalechicago.com

"Fun, loud and colorful describe the room, clientele and
staff" at this wild West Loop "warehouse" where "exciting" Nuevo Latino menu items meet "enormous", "eye-
popping" environs, "another amazing visual masterpiece"
from Jerry Kleiner (Marché, Red Light); "at the moment"
it's "the best party in town", even if it's "expensive for what
it is", "service could use a little work" and the noise level
can be "almost painful."

Carson's Ribs
20 | 13 | 17 | $30

612 N. Wells St. (Ontario St.), 312-280-9200
200 N. Waukegan Rd. (bet. Deerfield & Lake Cook Rds.),
Deerfield, 847-374-8500
www.ribs.com
"Finger-licking" loyalists love these City and North Suburban bastions of American BBQ for "great messy ribs" with the "zesty" "special house sauce" (and "don't neglect" the "two-inch pork chops" or "au gratin potatoes that are worth a trip on their own"); still, others are unimpressed by what they call the "kitchen's uneven results"; N.B. ratings may not reflect the "aging" Downtown location's recent remodeling and menu updates.

Catch 35
23 | 21 | 21 | $43

Leo Burnett Bldg., 35 W. Wacker Dr. (bet. Dearborn & State Sts.),
312-346-3500
35 S. Washington St. (bet. Benton & Van Buren Aves.),
Naperville, 630-717-3500
www.catch35.com
A catchword for these "inventive" Asian-inspired seafood sisters is "keeper" claim converts "hooked on" their "oh-so-fresh fish and the various ways it's prepared" (and an "interesting wine list"); the "pre-theater" and "expense-account business crowd" can afford the "power prices" at the Loop original (if the "'80s decor" feels too "corporate", try the "congenial, crowded piano bar"), and the West Suburban site attracts a "trendy Naperville scene" – that said, doubters dub them "not exceptional."

Cereality Cereal Bar & Cafe ⌷
16 | 16 | 18 | $8

100 S. Wacker Dr. (Monroe St.), 312-506-0010; www.cereality.com
The "faddish" "fun" makes "you feel like a kid" at this "clever" Loop "fave" where "efficient" counter staffers in "pajamas (that's right, folks: pajamas)" bowl over surveyors with a "unique" menu of "fabulous cereal concoctions" served in a "zippy" space with "great outdoor river seating"; some soggy skeptics "want to scream 'oh, grow up already'", but it's still Chicagoland's Best Bang for the Buck – after all, "you can afford it even if you're still on an allowance"; N.B. they're crunching away on an Evanston branch.

CHARLIE TROTTER'S ⌷
27 | 25 | 27 | VE

816 W. Armitage Ave. (Halsted St.), 773-248-6228;
www.charlietrotters.com
"A religious experience" "worth a mortgage payment" awaits at this Lincoln Parker, the "epitome of [New] American gastronomy" and our Most Popular Chicagoland restaurant, where customers are "dazzled" by "brilliant" chef Charlie Trotter's daily changing menu (with "fantastic pairings" from an "exceptional wine cellar") and "cosseted" by a "masterfully courteous and knowledgeable" staff; a few find the "formal" feel "churchlike" and the

whole experience a bit "precious", but most maintain it's "absolutely sublime"; P.S. "for the ultimate, get a reservation at the kitchen table."

CHEESECAKE FACTORY   19 | 19 | 17 | $25
John Hancock Ctr., 875 N. Michigan Ave. (bet. Chestnut St. & Delaware Pl.), 312-337-1101 ◗
Oakbrook Center Mall, 2020 Spring Rd. (bet. Harger Rd. & 22nd St.), Oak Brook, 630-573-1800
Woodfield Mall, 5 Woodfield Mall (Frontage & Golf Rds.), Schaumburg, 847-619-1090
Westfield Shoppingtown, 374 Old Orchard Ctr. (Skokie Blvd.), Skokie, 847-329-8077
www.thecheesecakefactory.com
The "cheesecake lives up to the hype" at these "kid-friendly" city and suburban "crowd-pleasers" that are "remarkably consistent" for their "ridiculously large" Traditional American menus, "absurd waits" and "portions for giants", though some chastisers chide them as "cheesy", "cookie-cutter" "contributors to America's expanding waistline" that are "oversized", "overwhelming" and "overrun with tourists"; P.S. "lucky" Streeterville diners can "snag an outdoor table" on Michigan Avenue.

Chef's Station   23 | 18 | 21 | $42
Davis Street Metro Station, 915 Davis St. (Church St), Evanston, 847-570-9821; www.chefs-station.com
Commenters commute to this haute hideaway "at the intersection of creative and casual" in Evanston for "great quality" New American dining with an "excellent wine list" (the "prix fixe meal with wine flight is a terrific value"); less enthusiastic eaters equivocate over "uneven service" and "quirky", "un-hip decor", but all agree you can "have a lovely summer" meal on the patio.

Chen's Chinese & Sushi   23 | 20 | 20 | $23
3506 N. Clark St. (Addison St.), 773-549-9100; www.chenschicago.com
Aficionados appreciate the "new twists on Chinese" and Japanese fare – including "low-fat options" and "excellent sushi" – made with "high-quality ingredients" at this "fun place" with a "hip", "modern setting" that makes it "look more expensive than it is" ("it's hard to believe you're eating just a block from Wrigley Field"); P.S. the "fast delivery guys" are so "quick" they seem to "arrive before you hang up the phone."

Chestnut Grill & Wine Bar ◗   ▽ 15 | 18 | 18 | $37
200 E. Chestnut St. (Mies van der Rohe Way), 312-266-4500
"Great piano bar entertainment seven nights a week" appears to be the most popular aspect of this Streeterville New American with a "supper-club menu"; lukewarm let-

terists suggest it's "good for a light meal if you're visiting the MCA" or as a place to "bring your 'affair'", but nutcrackers consider the food "not special" and the service "disinterested", claiming neither "lives up to the promise of an otherwise inviting spot."

Chez François ⊠ | 24 | 20 | 21 | $43 |

14 S. Third St. (State St.), Geneva, 630-262-1000;
www.chezfrancoisrest.com

"Warm, amiable and authentic in setting, service and cuisine", this "quaint", "quiet" "gem in the Fox Valley" just may be "the closest" West Suburbanites "can find to a truly French dining experience"; its "wonderful", "unfussy" "bistro fare" is a "great value" ("especially the fantastic prix fixe lunch"), the "Tuesday evening half-price wine is fantastic" and "don't miss the jazz trio that plays on Friday nights."

Chez Joël | 22 | 18 | 19 | $37 |

1119 W. Taylor St. (Racine Ave.), 312-226-6479;
www.chezjoelbistro.com

"France comes to Little Italy and triumphs" testify touters of this "surprise" French find featuring "fresh", "quality bistro dining" "in the middle of the spaghetti belt"; expansive eaters say the "cute" space is "sometimes a little *too* cozy" (i.e. "very cramped"), but those who find it "comfortable" – especially the "beautiful backyard patio" – are "thankful" that "it's not that well known."

CHICAGO CHOP HOUSE | 25 | 20 | 22 | $54 |

60 W. Ontario St. (bet. Clark & Dearborn Sts.), 312-787-7100;
www.chicagochophouse.com

A "heavy hitter" "in a city that knows meat", this "quintessential Chicago steak joint" and "ol' boys club" in River North "is rich in tradition – and you can taste it in the food" (including "wonderful prime rib") not to mention see it in the "historical" setting with "tin ceilings", "old Chicago photos" and other "memorabilia", as well as a "great bar area with old-time drinks made the way they should be made"; P.S. "men with white collars" like to "expense this one."

Chicago Diner | 19 | 14 | 18 | $18 |

3411 N. Halsted St. (Roscoe St.), 773-935-6696;
www.veggiediner.com

"Homemade goodness without the flesh" sustains supporters of this "earthy" Lakeview "institution" with a "diner feel" that serves both "unique and traditional" vegetarian "comfort food" ("breakfast like mom used to make"), "bakery items", "vegan shakes" and organic wines and beers – though faulting feeders feel the "food sounds better on the menu than it tastes in real life"; P.S. the "outdoor garden is a nice place to sit in the summer."

Chicago Firehouse　　　　18 21 19 $40
1401 S. Michigan Ave. (14th St.), 312-786-1401;
www.chicagofirehouse.com
First responders rush into this "nifty" setting "in a converted old South [Loop] Chicago firehouse" for "upscale"
yet "homestyle" Traditional American fare and "one of the
best patios in the city"; a few alarmists, however, feel the
"overpriced" "food doesn't live up to the decor"; P.S. it's a
"great pre-game place for Bears night games."

Chicago Pizza &　　　　　22 15 17 $21
Oven Grinder Co. ⇓
2121 N. Clark St. (bet. Dickens & Webster Aves.), 773-248-2570;
www.chicagopizzaandovengrinder.com
"There are long lines for a reason" at this Lincoln Park "landmark" and "great old family place", "a true Chicago original" to pie-sanos who praise its "awesome pizza pot pies",
"gigantic salads", "out-of-this-world grinders" and a host
who "never forgets where you are in the wait order"; even
fans, though, "wish they'd take reservations" and find the
"cash-only policy" "slightly irritating", while idealists insist the "unique" signature dish "is not pizza" and "claustrophobes" criticize its "catacombs"-like setting.

Chicago Prime Steakhouse　　25 22 23 $53
1370 Bank Dr. (Meacham Rd.), Schaumburg, 847-969-9900;
www.chicagoprimesteakhouse.com
"Wonderful [prime] steaks", "shareable sides" and a "great
bar (cigars and all)" convince carnivores that this Northwest
Suburban "favorite" "for an upscale night out" is "as good
or better" but "less pretentious than the competition";
peeved peers perceive the provender as "pricey", though,
and say a visit's "only worth it as long as they're not too
busy", as service suffers when it's crowded; N.B. there's
live music Tuesday through Saturday.

CHIC Cafe　　　　　　▽ 20 12 19 $25
Cooking & Hospitality Institute of Chicago, 361 W. Chestnut St.
(Orleans St.), 312-873-2032
It's a split decision over this student-staffed New French–
Eclectic "fine-dining" BYO in a River North culinary college:
gourmands gush that there must be "great teachers" at this
"unknown gem" with a "lovely view" and "excellent
brunch", adding it's "very cheap for what you get" (prix fixe
or à la carte lunch, prix fixe–only dinner), but stricter stan-
dardists "expected better from aspiring chefs"; N.B. its
schedule synchs with the school's season, so phone ahead.

Chief O'Neill's Pub　　　▽ 18 22 20 $22
3471 N. Elston Ave. (Addison St.), 773-583-3066;
www.chiefoneillspub.com
Neighbors of this "casual Irish pub/restaurant" on the
Northwest Side call it "cozy", "with "unique decor high-

lighting Chief O'Neill", a "nice fireplace in winter and outdoor dining in warm weather" (though the "bar atmosphere" can be "a little loud on weekends"); add the somewhat "ambitious" food, "good beer specials" and weekend entertainment and natives label it "like Ireland."

China Grill
20 | 22 | 19 | $49

Hard Rock Hotel, 230 N. Michigan Ave. (Lake St.), 312-334-6700; www.hardrockhotelchicago.com
"It's a scene" at this "splashy", "high-class chain" outpost in the Loop's Hard Rock Hotel, where the "big portions" of "trendy, tasty" Asian dishes are "meant for sharing"; still, some supporters who "love the food" think it's "overpriced" (though better bargains may be had with the pre-theater and fixed-price lunch menus), while those who fault the fare as "fake Chinese" and the servers for "up-selling" suggest you "have a drink at the bar and then take a cab to Chinatown."

Chinn's 34th St. Fishery
22 | 11 | 19 | $30

3011 W. Ogden Ave. (bet. Fender Ave. & Naper Blvd.), Lisle, 630-637-1777; www.chinns-fishery.com
"Cousin of the famous Bob Chinn's" ("but without the long waits"), this "low-key family seafood spot" in Lisle is "still serving up tasty", "incredibly fresh" fish – and displaying "documentation of today's-catch flights in the foyer" – along with notorious mai tais that "take the edge off the subpar", "cafeteria-style" ambiance.

Chinoiserie ⊘ 🕾
20 | 10 | 16 | $26

509 Fourth St. (Linden Ave.), Wilmette, 847-256-0306
"Not your typical Chinese restaurant", this "quaint" Wilmette Asian BYO features a "great blend of cultures" in its "inventive food", which helps backers "be tolerant of service foibles" and the "bizarre" "bed-and-breakfast decor" ("it would be lovely if all the fake flowers would disappear, along with the wallpaper").

Chiyo
– | – | – | M

3800 W. Lawrence Ave. (Hamlin Ave.), 773-267-1555
Owners of the former Matsumoto have simplified its off-the-beaten-path Albany Park storefront: the dining room has been redone in soothing neutrals and the kaiseki-only (chef's tasting) menu replaced by a range of less pricey Japanese fare encompassing sushi and sashimi, teriyaki and tempura and shabu-shabu (available with Kobe or prime beef), plus 30 varieties of sake; N.B. fans of the degustation menu can arrange for it with advance notice.

Cité
17 | 24 | 18 | $57

Lake Point Tower, 505 N. Lake Shore Dr., 70th fl. (Navy Pier), 312-644-4050; www.citechicago.com
After an aborted name/concept change and chef switch, this "romantic" dinner-only New American "special-occasion

spot" in Streeterville carries on with its "matchless view" from high atop Lake Point Tower and, some say unfortunately, "tired food" that's "not memorable"; meanwhile, would-be summiters who "hear they are changing the menu" and updating the decor hope "that will improve it."

Clubhouse, The   21 | 22 | 20 | $35 |
Oakbrook Center Mall, 298 Oakbrook Ctr. (Rte. 83), Oak Brook, 630-472-0600; www.theclubhouse.com
Fans figure this "hip but dignified" Traditional American clubhouse in Oak Brook's mall is "a fun place to meet for martinis" "after work", a "power lunch", a "fine Sunday brunch" or a "special meal" of "fantastic sandwiches, sizzling steaks" and desserts "bigger than your head" – but duffers dis it as an "overpriced", "noisy" "suburban" "pickup place"; P.S. there's a "large outdoor dining area."

Club Lago ⊠   17 | 11 | 20 | $24 |
331 W. Superior St. (Orleans St.), 312-951-2849
"Friendly family owners" welcome River North "locals" to this "checkered-tablecloth" "time machine" back to the 1950s, "a great place to have some simple traditional [Northern] Italian fare" with a "minimalist wine list" and "without the fuss of trendier venues"; despite this, disenchanted doubters declare it a "dumpy" "throwback to old-school red-sauce joints", adding "if only the red sauce lived up to the memories."

Club Lucky   20 | 17 | 19 | $29 |
1824 W. Wabansia Ave. (bet. Honore & Wood Sts.), 773-227-2300; www.clubluckychicago.com
Boasters for this "lively" Bucktown "local favorite" "smack dab in a residential neighborhood" swear its "large servings" of Southern Italian "comfort food", "romantic" "retro atmosphere", "all-ages clientele", "great" "hefty martinis" and "attentive service" amount to "an offer you can't refuse"; P.S. "outdoor dining is a plus in nice weather."

Coast Sushi Bar ●   23 | 21 | 20 | $28 |
2045 N. Damen Ave. (bet. Dickens & McLean Aves.), 773-235-5775; www.coastsushibar.com
Surf's up says the "hot crowd" that haunts this "hipster" Bucktown Japanese BYO for its "creative, tasty" sushi served in "recently expanded" environs that exude a "sexy, minimalist vibe"; still, cooler heads consider the experience "hit-or-miss" and note that the "no liquor license" thing "is a real bummer."

Coco Pazzo   24 | 22 | 22 | $49 |
300 W. Hubbard St. (Franklin St.), 312-836-0900; www.cocopazzochicago.com
Firmly "in the first tier of upscale Italian restaurants", this "understated", "reliable" River North "mainstay" is "innovative without being trendy", featuring "fresh, fresh, fresh"

"contemporary" Tuscan fare served by a "well-trained staff" in "a lofty, open atmosphere" with "high-beamed ceilings" – all the ingredients for "haute", some say "haughty", dining; yes, it's "pricey" – but fans find it "worth every penny" just "to get away from classic 'Chicago Italian' (aka piles of bad pasta)."

Coco Pazzo Cafe
22 | 19 | 20 | $38

Red Roof Inn, 636 N. St. Clair St. (Ontario St.),
312-664-2777

"One block off the Mag Mile" in Streeterville, this "great city neighborhood restaurant" is "ever-popular" for its "high-quality" Northern Italian output at a "better value" than its "fancier" parent in River North; there's also a "good midpriced wine list", and alfresco addicts appreciate the "nice outdoor seating for people-watching"; P.S. "who would have thought – in a Red Roof Inn?"

Cold Comfort Cafe & Deli
22 | 13 | 17 | $12

2211 W. North Ave. (Leavitt St.), 773-772-4552

Stop into this "casual" Bucktown BYO for "some of the most creative", "quality deli sandwiches" – with "the meat piled high" – amid "modern" digs decorated with "works by local artists", but be warned that the "friendly" folks "can be overwhelmed by the lunchtime rush"; P.S. it's "a fun brunch/breakfast spot" too (they close mid-afternoon).

Comida Bebida
– | – | – | M

5139 Main St. (Curtiss St.), Downers Grove, 630-434-0300;
www.comida-bebida.com

This casual, colorful south-of-the-border storefront aims to exceed the expectations of West Suburbanites with fresh, moderately priced Mexican preparations; while the ambiance is 'friends and family', tipplers can sample premium tequilas by the flight or mixed in margaritas made with just-squeezed juices; N.B. neighboring Trucchi Italian Bistro shares the same owners, chef and kitchen.

Coobah ◗
19 | 20 | 16 | $29

3423 N. Southport Ave. (bet. Newport Ave. & Roscoe St.),
773-528-2220; www.coobah.com

"Swank and exotic", this Lakeview "date spot" is considered "a full-flavored experience" by "the mid- to late-twentysomething" crowd, which frequents it for "tasty" Nuevo Latino–Filipino fusion fare, "fun drinks" and "loud music" – but more staid surveyors say "the atmosphere is better than the food" and cite "service issues"; P.S. "the outdoor seating is great for people-watching."

copperblue ⌧
– | – | – | E

Lake Point Tower, 580 E. Illinois St. (Navy Pier), 312-527-1200;
www.copperbluechicago.com

Whimsically named after a Bob Mould album, this stylish French-Med on the ground floor of Streeterville's Lake

Point Tower showcases an intriguing menu of unusual ingredients and preparations by chef Michael Tsonton (ex Tizi Melloul, Courtright's) and an affordable all-Euro wine list; the cozy, warmly lit dining room features bright murals themed 'work, rest and play' on yellow and orange walls.

Costa's   21 19 20 $30
340 S. Halsted St. (Van Buren St.), 312-263-9700
1 S. 130 Summit Ave. (Roosevelt Rd.), Oakbrook Terrace, 630-620-1100
www.costasdining.com
"Zorba would be proud" of the "great, authentic" "traditional Greek dishes", "old-world service" and "comfortable" milieu at these Greektown and West Suburban "standbys", even if they're "pricier" and "more formal" than most in the genre; N.B. Oakbrook Terrace has piano entertainment on Wednesdays and weekends, and a roaring fireplace in winter.

COURTRIGHT'S   26 25 26 $58
8989 S. Archer Ave. (Willow Springs Rd.), Willow Springs, 708-839-8000; www.courtrights.com
Excursionists to the Southwest Surburbs eagerly enthuse about this "excellent out-of-the-way" "destination restaurant" where "marvelous", "creative seasonal" New American "meals are carefully planned, expertly prepared and exquisitely presented" in a "classic atmosphere" with "beautiful gardens" ("grazing deer appear magically as if on cue outside the [nearly] floor-to-ceiling windows"); P.S. "the wine alone is worth the trip."

Cousin's Incredible Vitality   - - - I
(fka Cousin's)
2833 N. Broadway (Diversey Pkwy.), 773-880-0063
Reborn from its former Turkish incarnation, this Lakeview venue is now a moderately priced raw vegan (meat-free) mecca whose Mediterranean vittles (pistachio falafel, collard greens wraps, raw cacao desserts) are paired with smoothies, 'elixirs' and organic wines (including pomegranate) and served in a vibrant jungle-inspired setting; there's also a take-out market, as well as classes in detox, food preparation and yoga; N.B. not related to Cousin's Turkish Dining on Irving Park Road.

CROFTON ON WELLS ⊠   26 19 23 $56
535 N. Wells St. (bet. Grand Ave. & Ohio St.), 312-755-1790; www.croftononwells.com
Surveyors sweet on Suzy Crofton swoon for her "seasonal" New American fare that's "inventive without being over-intellectualized", "wonderfully matched" by a "wine list with plenty of midpriced selections" and served in a River North setting of "spare elegance"; still, some scribes are sour on the "understated decor", seeing it as "stark"

and "clinical", while others posit the experience is perhaps a pinch "pricey."

Cuatro ◗
23 | 18 | 18 | $38

2030 S. Wabash Ave. (20th St.), 312-842-8856; www.cuatro-chicago.com
"*Muy delicioso!*" maintains a majority optimistic about this "terrific addition to" the "up-and-coming" South Loop, an "outpost of coolness" cooking up "wonderful" "creative" Nuevo Latino fare "for a reasonable price" and pouring "great drinks at the bar" – even if a minority isn't raving about the room; N.B. live Latin jazz is presented nightly.

CUSTOM HOUSE
24 | 26 | 22 | $61

Hotel Blake, 500 S. Dearborn St. (Congress Pkwy.), 312-523-0200
"One of the city's best chefs", Shawn McClain (Spring, Green Zebra) "gives meat and potatoes a whole new meaning" at this Printer's Row "carnivore's delight" that's "worth a field trip to the south side" for its "tremendous menu" of "top-notch" New American fare and "extensive wine list" offered in "lush", "retro-metrochic surroundings"; most maintain it has "the makings of an instant classic" – once management addresses the chorus of "service kinks" comments; P.S. professionals are pleased "it's open for [breakfast and] lunch."

Cyrano's Bistrot & Wine Bar
20 | 19 | 19 | $38

546 N. Wells St. (Ohio St.), 312-467-0546; www.cyranosbistrot.com
"Personable" chef-owner Didier Durand "takes a great deal of pride in this restaurant and it shows" in the "fine", "authentic" bistro fare, "good wine recommendations", "romantic atmosphere" and "reasonable prices" (the "prix fixe is always a great deal") – all aspects of a "French country experience" right in River North; P.S. music mavens maintain the Café Simone Parisian Cabaret downstairs "is a bonus", with live entertainment Wednesday through Saturday, and pet people "love" the "dog-friendly" sidewalk cafe.

D & J Bistro
25 | 19 | 23 | $39

First Bank Plaza Ctr., 466 S. Rand Rd./Rte. 12 (Rte. 22), Lake Zurich, 847-438-8001; www.dj-bistro.com
A preponderance of respondents prizes this Northwest Suburban "find" that "continues to impress" with the "Gallic charm" of its "excellent" (and "fairly priced") "classic bistro cooking", its "well-chosen wine list" and the "friendly French decor" of its "lovely interior", which stands "in stark contrast to" its "strip-plaza setting."

Dave's Italian Kitchen
17 | 11 | 16 | $18

1635 Chicago Ave., downstairs (bet. Church & Davis Sts.), Evanston, 847-864-6000; www.davesik.com
Despite "long waiting times", diehards submit this is "still one of the [Evanston] area's best bargains" for "large por-

tions" of Southern "Italian just like mom used to make" and "tremendous wine bargains" in a "loud", "crowded" "basement" "zoo"; others who "don't understand why this place is so popular" opine that the "ordinary-to-bland" offerings are only for "impoverished" "NU students" or those "too lazy to boil water at home."

David Burke's Primehouse　　– | – | – | E |

The James Chicago Hotel, 616 N. Rush St. (Ontario St.), 312-660-6000; www.brguestrestaurants.com

Dry-aging their own prime beef in a salt-tiled 'cave', the B.R. Guest gang (Blue Water Grill) brings David Burke of Park Avenue Café fame back to town – at least in spirit – with this meaty new concept featuring upscale steakhouse classics (paired with interesting sauces or 'mousses') and New American fare including some former Café favorites (spicy angry lobster, crackling pork shank); the posh, modern setting in The James Hotel is an architectural feat of sleek urban chic right in River North.

David's Bistro　　▽ 24 | 20 | 22 | $36 |

Wolf Plaza, 623 N. Wolf Rd. (Central Ave.), Des Plaines, 847-803-3233; www.davidsbistro.com

The name says 'bistro' but the cuisine is more "creative" than you'd think thanks to "offbeat and interesting" seasonal New American fare (with an "excellent wine selection") at this "quaint", "quiet" Northwest Suburban "gem" situated in a "nondescript", "out-of-the-way" "strip shopping center"; P.S. chef-owner David Maish also gives "great cooking classes."

Davis Street Fishmarket　　19 | 15 | 18 | $30 |

501 Davis St. (Hinman Ave.), Evanston, 847-869-3474; www.davisstreetfishmarket.com

"There are no mysteries" at this "straightforward" and "satisfying" "fresh seafooder" in Evanston pen pragmatists pleased with its "variety of fish" dishes, "prepared without frills" ("you'll find daily choices on the wall menu"), plus some "decent Cajun" cookin' and a "raw bar" offered amid "funky" "New England-ish decor" with "fishnets hanging from the ceiling"; moderates maintain it's "always good, never great", though, and call the service simply "competent."

De Cero ⊠　　21 | 16 | 17 | $31 |

814 W. Randolph St. (bet. Green & Halsted Sts.), 312-455-8114; www.decerotaqueria.com

Muchachos meet at this "tapas-style" Market District taqueria for a "fun alternative to traditional Mexican fare", with "many inventive fillings" of "fresh ingredients" for the "tasty tacos" and "delicious drinks" served in a "hip" yet "rustic environment" with a side of "loud music"; iffier inputters indicate "indifferent service", though, adding that their "appreciation for the novelty idea wanes a little more with every visit"; N.B. DJs spin on weekends.

Dee's   19 | 17 | 18 | $29 |
1114 W. Armitage Ave. (Seminary Ave.), 773-477-1500;
www.deesrestaurant.com
Loyalists love this Lincoln Parker for its "wide selection of Asian favorites" (Mandarin, Szechuan, sushi) served in a "cozy" "neighborhood" atmosphere with a "great garden for outside dining" – not to mention "hands-on, ever-present owner Dee" Kang, who always "sees to customers' needs"; still, querulous quills question the quality and value of what they call "inconsistent" output that's "considerably more expensive" than in Chinatown.

Deleece   21 | 17 | 18 | $30 |
4004 N. Southport Ave. (Irving Park Rd.), 773-325-1710;
www.deleece.com
Regulars rank this Wrigleyville Eclectic a "neighborhood gem" for its "scrumptious", "interesting global menu", "fantastic [weekend] brunch" and a "cozy feel" abetted by "exposed brick and candles on each table", as well as touting the Monday–Tuesday prix fixe as a "great deal"; P.S. "summer on the sidewalk patio is a treat."

Del Rio ⊠   18 | 14 | 19 | $35 |
228 Green Bay Rd. (Rte. 22), Highwood, 847-432-4608
Either way, it's "déjà vu all over again" for diners at this "North Shore classic": one Del-egation finds it a "comfortable" "neighborhood" "standby" for "old-fashioned [Northern] Italian food" and the fruits of a "vast" wine cellar, whereas the other tells of a "tired" time warp where "not much has changed – although it should have."

del Toro   ∇ 20 | 25 | 19 | $36 |
1520 N. Damen Ave. (bet. LeMoyne St. & Pierce Ave.),
773-252-1500
"It's Barcelona in Bucktown" at this "young, noisy and vibrant" makeover of Mod. that "takes the bull by the horns" with "sleek, modern" Gaudí-inspired decor and "a lot of delicious bites" on its "innovative, *nuevo* tapas–style" Spanish menu – though some snubbed sharers suggest the "beautiful staff" can be a bit self-absorbed.

Devon Seafood Grill   – | – | – | M |
39 E. Chicago Ave. (Wabash Ave.), 312-440-8660;
www.devonseafood.com
Fresh seafood is flown in daily from both coasts for lunch and dinner at this casually upscale chowhouse (sibling of a Philadelphia original) with global menu accents as well as classics, a few surf 'n' turf options and a moderately priced wine list; the comfy, clubby bi-level space boasts a visible kitchen, cozy booths in the dining room and a big, convivial bar upstairs.

Dine
　　　　　　　　　　　　　–　–　–　M

*Crowne Plaza Chicago Metro Hotel, 733 W. Madison St.
(Halsted St.), 312-602-2100; www.dinerestaurant.com*
Located in the new Crowne Plaza Chicago Metro Hotel,
this retro American with a '40s feel woos West Loopers
with classic cocktails and upscale, updated comfort food
from an exposed kitchen; multiple dining areas on various
levels break up the 7,000-sq.-ft. setting done up in rich
earth tones and outfitted with comfy leather banquettes.

Dining Room at　　　23　20　21　$37
Kendall College, The ⌧

*Kendall College, 900 N. North Branch St. (Halsted St.),
312-752-2328; www.kendall.edu*
"Expect a quality meal" "with a bent toward the unusual" –
and "without shelling out big bucks" – at this "culinary
college" venue where the New French fare is "cooked by
the future stars of the Chicago restaurant scene"; ok, so
"service by the students can be spotty", but the "swish"
space with its "third-floor perch" offers "killer views of the
Loop"; N.B. it's closed during school breaks and holidays.

Dinotto Ristorante　　　20　17　19　$31

*215 W. North Ave. (Wells St.), 312-202-0302;
www.dinotto.com*
"Tasty" "everyday" eats greet goers to this "great neighborhood Italian", an Old Town "standby" with "reliably
good service"; it's a "convenient" stop "before catching a
movie across the street", and the "romantic setting" is
"nice" for a "date night" – especially the prime "courtyard" patio (with its own bar) that's "like eating in a piazza
in Italy"; a minority of *mangia*-ers, however, marks it "middle of the pack."

Di Pescara　　　　　　　–　–　–　M

*Northbrook Court Shopping Ctr., 2124 Northbrook Ct.
(Lake Cook Rd.), Northbrook, 847-498-4321; www.leye.com*
Though the name conjures images of seafood from The
Boot, the something-for-everyone menu goes much farther afield at this Lettuce Entertain You Italian-Eclectic
(named for a fishing village on the Adriatic coast) in the
former Bice space in Northbrook Court; celeb sommelier
Alpana Singh's smart wine list is also on offer in the dark,
swanky casual-contemporary setting, and a separate
take-out area provides convenient curbside parking.

Dixie Kitchen & Bait Shop　19　17　17　$19

*5225 S. Harper Ave. (53rd St.), 773-363-4943
825 Church St. (Benson Ave.), Evanston, 847-733-9030
2352 E. 172 St. (Torrence Ave.), Lansing, 708-474-1378*
"Put some south in your mouth" at this "charming", "fun-as-
cow-tipping" city and suburban trio "serving" "solid",
"stick-to-your-ribs" Southern-Cajun cooking ("staples like

fried green tomatoes, po' boys, étouffée and gumbo") to "a diverse clientele" of Dixie chicks and Dicks; the "rustic decor" is "contrived but cute", and the vittles are a "value."

Don Juan

21 | 16 | 21 | $30

6730 N. Northwest Hwy. (bet. Devon & Ozark Aves.),
773-775-6438; www.donjuanschicago.com

Gringos go for this "great mix-and-match" Mex 'cause there are "lots of options for the gourmet, and the rest can get tacos"; co-owner "Maria Concannon is the quintessential hostess with the mostess", and her staffers "make a mean margarita" – cementing this "upbeat", "family-run" Northwest Sider's status as "Number Juan in Edison Park."

Don Roth's Blackhawk

20 | 17 | 21 | $37

61 N. Milwaukee Ave. (Dundee Rd.), Wheeling, 847-537-5800;
www.donroths.com

Vintagists vouch for this Northwest Suburban surf 'n' turfer, a "quiet", "friendly", "golden oldie" that "retains its glory" with "great" fare like "to-die-for prime rib", "scrod with a ton of tartar sauce" and "the re-creation of the spinning salad bowl from the original Blackhawk", all served amid nostalgic Chicago photography – but modernists who eschew "food the way it used to be back in the '70s" title it "tired."

Dorado

▽ 23 | 15 | 22 | $29

2301 W. Foster Ave. (bet. Claremont & Oakley Aves.),
773-561-3780; www.doradorestaurant.com

Though next to "nobody knows it" yet, this "welcome addition" to Lincoln Square boasts an "innovative" kitchen "churning out some serious Mexican"-French fusion fare "at bargain prices", with "bold flavors that jump off the plate"; it's a bit of a "hole-in-the-wall", but at least it's "bright and cheerful", and the BYO policy is an "added bonus"; P.S. "have you tried those duck nachos?"

Dover Straits

18 | 16 | 19 | $34

1149 W. Golf Rd. (Gannon Dr.), Hoffman Estates, 847-884-3900
890 E. US Hwy. 45 (Butterfield Rd.), Mundelein, 847-949-1550
www.doverstraits.com

Strait-shooters swear by the "quality and variety" of fish fare (starring "great Dover sole"), "nice service" and "old-style setting" that's a "throwback to supper clubs of yesteryear" at these "reliable" suburban seafood sibs; perhaps raters "just a few years away from AARP membership" feel "young" here, but even greenhorns grade it a "righteous value" for "good food – if you don't mind the 1960s look"; P.S. "for a real deal", "catch the early-bird."

Dragonfly Mandarin

14 | 18 | 14 | $33

832 W. Randolph St. (Green St.), 312-787-7600;
www.dragonflymandarin.com

This "swanky", "upscale" "Chinese transplant from the Gold Coast" to the Market District draws defenders of its "delicious" dining amid decor that's "a delight to the senses" (including "a cool lounge" and "great outside seating"), but disenchanted diners give it demerits as "dark, dull and pricey" for the category, suggesting "the neighborhood has so many good restaurants" that you "can get better elsewhere."

Drake Bros.' Steaks Chicago   17 | 18 | 19 | $59
The Drake Hotel, 140 E. Walton St. (Michigan Ave.),
312-932-4626; www.drakebros.com
"Below the radar of most", this Traditional American meat 'n' seafooder in Streeterville's Drake Hotel has boosters who believe it's a "quiet" place for a "good", "old-fashioned" dinner; unfortunately, the "unimpressed" pronounce the food "boring for a new restaurant" and complain that the "killer view is not worth the killer price", adding "it was better when it was" the Oak Terrace; N.B. breakfast, Sunday brunch and lunch are also served.

Duke of Perth   18 | 17 | 18 | $18
2913 N. Clark St. (Oakdale Ave.), 773-477-1741
This "friendly" Lakeview "Scottish pub seems transported from the old country", with "solid" "grub" "at a good price" including burgers, shepherd's pie and "some of the city's best [all-you-can-eat] fish 'n' chips on Wednesdays and Fridays" ("this greasy food is just what the doctor ordered"); there's also a "great choice of ales on tap" and "the best scotch list around", plus it's "one of the few bars in Chicago without TVs"; P.S. the patio's "fantastic."

Eatzi's   18 | 13 | 16 | $19
Century Shopping Ctr., 2828 N. Clark St. (bet. B'way & Surf St.),
773-832-9310; www.eatzis.com
Lincoln Parker's who "love" having "so many choices under one roof" drop into this Eclectic "gourmet-to-go" "in the basement of an indoor shopping mall" "to get takeout" "when they have no time to cook", or to grab "a fast bite" in a "dining area that's like a fast-food court or cafeteria"; conversely, some contrary consumers claim "confusion reigns", everything "looks better than it tastes" and "the novelty and expense wear thin."

Ed Debevic's   14 | 19 | 16 | $18
640 N. Wells St. (Ontario St.), 312-664-1707
157 Yorktown Shopping Ctr. (bet. Butterfield Rd. & 22nd St.),
Lombard, 630-495-1700
www.eddebevics.com
If you're "feeling snarky", "trade insults" with the "smart-aleck staff" at this "campy" River North and South Suburban diner duo, "fun places" for a "'50s" "drive-in type experience" of "fair to good" burgers and milkshakes and a side of "obnoxious-by-design service"; more staid surveyors sidestep the "sass" and "so-so" sustenance, though, hint-

ing it's "had its moment" and wondering "why would anyone" "line up to be treated" "like a private in the army"?

Edelweiss
▽ 21 18 21 $31

7650 W. Irving Park Rd. (bet. Cumberland & Harlem Aves.), Norridge, 708-452-6040

If you "have a hearty appetite and low cholesterol", head to this "friendly" "neighborhood" 35-year-old in the near Suburban Northwest for the "best authentic German[-American] food left in Chicago" – not only is it "tasty" and "reasonably priced" but you also get "the real deal with the beer", plus you can "oompah" the night away to German bands (Friday–Sunday).

Edwardo's Natural Pizza
20 10 15 $17

1321 E. 57th St. (Kimbark Ave.), 773-241-7960
1212 N. Dearborn St. (Division St.), 312-337-4490
2662 N. Halsted St. (bet. Schubert & Wrightwood Aves.), 773-871-3400
521 S. Dearborn St. (bet. Congress Pkwy. & Harrison St.), 312-939-3366
6831 North Ave. (Grove Ave.), Oak Park, 708-524-2400
9300 Skokie Blvd. (Gross Point Rd.), Skokie, 847-674-0008
401 E. Dundee Rd. (Milwaukee Ave.), Wheeling, 847-520-0666
www.edwardos.com

"Man, what a great pie" moan memoirists about this widespread chain whose "natural" pizzas, "whether stuffed or thin", are topped with "fresh-tasting sauce" and ingredients such as "ambrosial spinach" and "great pesto"; the locations may "not be much in the way of decor or service" but they "still deliver the box of pizza some people dream of" (though others opine they're "good but not the best"); P.S. the lunch specials are perfect "for people on the go."

EJ's Place
19 15 18 $47

10027 Skokie Blvd. (Old Orchard Rd.), Skokie, 847-933-9800

Earning enthusiasm for its "expensive, quality [prime] meat" and other more "reasonably priced" Northern Italian dishes, this North Suburban steakhouse "relative of Gene and Georgetti" features "uniformly above average" food in a "faux Wisconsin lodge" locale that's "great if you like real wood-burning fireplaces"; knockers note the "knowledgeable service" can "seem stretched", though, adding that for the cost you "might as well make the trek" Downtown.

Eleven City Diner
– – – I

1112 S. Wabash Ave. (11th St.), 312-212-1112;
www.elevencitydiner.com

Filling a niche in the South Loop, this retro-inspired revisit of Jewish diner/delicatessens from decades past purveys comforting classics amid cozy dark-wood-and-leather-booth environs with a vintage soda fountain and a lunch counter manned by old-school countermen; modern touches include a barista, the use of local/sustainable produce and phone-ahead curbside takeout; N.B. breakfast is served all day, and late-nighters can nosh till 3 AM on weekends.

El Nandu
▽ | 21 | 15 | 20 | $22 |

2731 W. Fullerton Ave. (California Ave.), 773-278-0900

This "hidden treasure" in Logan Square is a "fun" find for "wonderful Argentinean fare" including "huge steaks", a "great selection" of "empanadas that burst with flavor" and "tasty sangria" served in "authentic, cozy" environs with "live entertainment on weekends"; N.B. the Decor score may not reflect a recent renovation and expansion.

El Presidente ●
▽ | 14 | 9 | 12 | $16 |

2558 N. Ashland Ave. (Wrightwood Ave.), 773-525-7938

Seems there's always "at least one cop present" at this Far West Lincoln Park "late-night must" serving "a good, hot, greasy meal" of "basic Mexican" "anti-hangover food" around the clock; true, there's "no fuss, no fancy" in the "shabby", "dive" setting, but most still find it "fun"; N.B. be sure to BYO.

Emilio's Sunflower Bistro
– | – | – | M |

30 S. La Grange Rd. (Harris Ave.), La Grange, 708-588-9890; www.sunflowerbistro.com

Named both for partner and local tapas legend Emilio Gervilla and for its decorative motif (many examples of which were painted by Christopher Spagnola, co-chef with wife Mary), this "cozy" West Suburban offers "well-put-together plates" of "fresh, organic" New American fare, "a clever wine list" and an "eclectic" "bistro feel"; P.S. there's a "tiny martini bar in back with an alley entrance."

Emilio's Tapas
21 | 17 | 19 | $31 |

444 W. Fullerton Pkwy. (Clark St.), 773-327-5100
4100 W. Roosevelt Rd. (Mannheim Rd.), Hillside, 708-547-7177

Emilio's Tapas La Rioja
230 W. Front St. (Wheaton Ave.), Wheaton, 630-653-7177

Emilio's Tapas Sol y Nieve
215 E. Ohio St. (St. Clair St.), 312-467-7177
www.emiliostapas.com

"True tapas fans" tout Emilio Gervilla's "tapalicious" tribe for an "elegant experience", "whether you are looking for a bite", "a full dinner" or just to "share some sangria with friends"; its Spanish small plates feature "interesting combinations and flavors" – "three words: bacon, wrapped, dates; three more: garlic, potato, salad" – though a few feel it all adds up to an evening that's "pricey for what you get."

Emperor's Choice ●
23 | 12 | 18 | $23 |

2238 S. Wentworth Ave. (Cermak Rd.), 312-225-8800

The "excellent Chinese food" is "fit for royalty" and can be "authentic if desired" – including some "dishes that can be frightening for the casual newcomer" – or "cooked more for the American taste" at this "seafood heaven" that serves until midnight six nights a week, 11 PM on Sundays; it's not every emperor's choice, though, with some despots decrying the "indifferent service" and "ho-hum decor" (though the saltwater tank of "live fish is cool").

Enoteca Piattini 21 | 20 | 21 | $31 |
934 W. Webster Ave. (bet. Bissell St. & Sheffield Ave.), 773-281-3898; www.enotecapiattini.net
"For groups or an intimate date", surveyors savor "a satisfying menu" of "quality" Southern "Italian small plates" and a "huge wine list" with "great" "reasonably priced flights" at this "romantic" Lincoln Parker where the "generous portions" are "truly a bargain"; the outdoor dining "is pleasant if you don't mind the noise from the el train", and if you "get a table by the fireplace in winter you'll never want to leave."

Entourage on American Lane – | – | – | E |
1301 American Ln. (bet. Meacham Rd. & National Pkwy.), Schaumburg, 847-995-9400; www.entourageventures.com
Whether you're a VIP or just a wannabe, check out this sprawling spot for upscale indulgence in the Northwest Suburbs, where Traditional American fare (prime steaks, chops, seafood, salads) is served amid 22,000 sq. ft. of swank; a 48-ft.-tall illuminated martini shaker stands sentry outside, while inside there's a winding staircase, 40-ft.-tall waterfalls, fireplaces, plasma TVs, a baby grand piano, a cigar humidor and a 2,000-bottle wine cellar (plus a private wine locker program).

Erie Cafe 23 | 19 | 22 | $48 |
536 W. Erie St. (Kingsbury St.), 312-266-2300; www.eriecafe.com
"Take the boys for a power lunch" or dinner at this "real Italian steakhouse", a Gene & Georgetti descendent in River North, where "meat and fish in the best Chicago tradition" (including "elephantine prime rib") is delivered with "no-nonsense service" amid "good old-fashioned-joint" atmo complete with a "great river location" (the terrace seating is a "hidden treasure"); still, some offput outsiders opine that the output is "overpriced."

erwin, an american cafe & bar 23 | 19 | 22 | $37 |
2925 N. Halsted St. (Oakdale Ave.), 773-528-7200; www.erwincafe.com
Aficionados of Erwin Drechsler's "homey" yet "urban" Lakeview "neighborhood standby" affirm it's "always a good choice" for a monthly changing menu of New American dishes ("some unusual, some standard, all well prepared"), an "out-of-the-ordinary brunch menu" and an

"extensive, excellent wine list"; the "relaxed", "intimate" room is "conversation-friendly" and decorated with a "whimsical mural that makes great Chicago references"; P.S. wallet-watchers appreciate that it's a "good value."

Essence of India   21 | 15 | 18 | $24

4601 N. Lincoln Ave. (Wilson Ave.), 773-506-0002; www.essenceofindiachicago.com

Gourmands 'goa' to this "good place to experiment with Indian cuisine" that's "convenient to all that Lincoln Square has to offer" and harbors "helpful servers" (and a liquor license); a portion of Punjab proponents purports that "portions tend to be small for the price", though, and opts for the "drive to Devon" instead; N.B. lunch buffet is served on Fridays and Saturdays.

Ethiopian Diamond   24 | 11 | 15 | $19

6120 N. Broadway (Glenlake Ave.), 773-338-6100

An "excellent variety for vegetarians and carnivores alike" keeps 'em coming back to this Edgewater Ethiopian, a "fun place to go with a group" and eat "non-greasy, healthy, yummy food" "with your fingers" – so yummy, in fact, that it makes it "worth missing out on the other fronts", namely decor and service; N.B. a one-man band performs on Friday nights.

EVEREST ⊠   27 | 26 | 27 | $91

One Financial Pl., 440 S. LaSalle St. (Congress Pkwy.), 312-663-8920; www.everestrestaurant.com

Financiers feel an affinity for this "romantic", "formal" "expense-account haven", "still at its peak" thanks to Jean Joho's "delectable" New French–Alsatian cuisine, an "exemplary wine list", "totally professional service" and "a breathtaking view" from "the top of the [Loop] Financial District"; even fans feel the "nouveau riche" "decor is stuck in the '80s", though, and a regiment of revolutionaries reports the "attitude is loftier than the location."

Evergreen ◗   22 | 12 | 17 | $23

2411 S. Wentworth Ave. (24th St.), 312-225-8898

The "interesting", "authentic" Cantonese-Mandarin cooking is "always good" at this "comfort-food" classic "at a quiet end of Chinatown", so most munchers overlook that it boasts some of the area's "worst ambiance"; P.S. owls love that it's "open late" (midnight nightly).

Extra Virgin   ▽ 19 | 20 | 18 | $32

741 W. Randolph St. (Halsted St.), 312-474-0700; www.restaurants-america.com

Find your way to this "friendly addition" to the Market District, a good "fit in the area" with "interesting and tasty" Italian-Mediterranean small plates and "great drinks" offered in a "lovely space" with an "open feel" – plus patio dining in season.

Fattoush   ▽ 23 8 21 $19
2652 N. Halsted St. (bet. Deversey Pkwy. & Wrightwood Ave.),
773-327-2652; www.fattoushrestaurant.com
"Very authentic" Lebanese food made "with fresh ingredients" ("just like homemade") and offered at a "friendly
price point" lures Lincoln Parkers to this "small, family-
run" BYO – so "don't let the" "simple", "cafeterialike decor
scare you away" declare "delighted" diners; N.B. bargains
include prix fixe deals for lunch and dinner.

FAT WILLY'S   23 12 18 $21
2416 W. Schubert Ave. (Western Ave.), 773-782-1800;
www.fatwillysribshack.com
"Everything is homemade and tasty" at this "family-
friendly" Logan Square Southern setup serving "sweet
and smoky" "BBQ the way it should be", with "lots of meat
choices", including "tender ribs" with "tangy sauce", plus
"heart attack–worthy macaroni and cheese", "more
soups and salads than you'd think" and "awesome
desserts" – all at "reasonable prices"; true, its decor
is merely "decent", but at least it's "comfortable (and
convenient for takeout)."

Feast   18 17 16 $28
1616 N. Damen Ave. (North Ave.), 773-772-7100;
www.feastrestaurant.com
Debbie Sharpe's "dependable" Bucktown New American
pairs a "tasty, varied menu" of "good comfort food" incorporating "a dash of contemporary" with a "very nice wine
selection" – and "romantics" rave about the "beautiful
alfresco dining"; some surveyors see the service as
"spotty", though, and those who deem dinner "hit-or-miss"
write the weekend "brunch is the best meal they offer."

Filippo's   20 14 19 $30
2211 N. Clybourn Ave. (Webster Ave.), 773-528-2211;
www.filipporistorante.com
"Not flashy" "but consistently good", this Lincoln Park
Italian "neighborhood standby" serves "big plates" of
"unique pastas that never miss" and a "wide variety of
seafood dishes" – all of which "make up for the sometimes
spotty service and average ambiance"; N.B. the Deerfield
location has closed.

Finley's Grill Room ◗   – – – M
3131 Finley Rd. (Branding Ln.), Downers Grove, 630-964-3131;
www.finleysgrillroom.com
This spacious West Suburban crowd-pleaser serves
substantial American vittles such as a one-pound
meatloaf – as well as lighter-weight alternatives – in an
exposed-brick-and-hardwood-floor setting; there's also a
lounge outfitted with big-screen TVs and a fireplace, befit-
ting a spot from nightclub veterans the Gatziolis brothers.

Fixture ◗ | – | – | – | M |

2706 N. Ashland Ave. (Diversey Pkwy.), 773-248-3331;
www.fixturechicago.com

The Meritage folks have expanded their horizons with this
New American small-plates spot in a made-over version of
the old Burgundy Inn space on the fringe of Lincoln Park;
the hot and cold dishes are creative enough to require a
chef's glossary, and the cozy, updated space in warm
browns and cool blue is also home to a moderately priced
wine list with flights and a couple dozen glass pours.

Flat Top Grill | 19 | 14 | 16 | $20 |

3200 N. Southport Ave. (Belmont Ave.), 773-665-8100
319 W. North Ave. (Orleans St.), 312-787-7676
1000 W. Washington Blvd. (Carpenter St.), 312-829-4800
707 Church St. (bet. Orrington & Sherman Aves.), Evanston,
847-570-0100
726 Lake St. (Oak Park Ave.), Oak Park, 708-358-8200
www.flattopgrill.com

"If you're not full and happy when you leave it's your own
fault" say fans of this "young, fun" chain of "do-it-yourself"
all-you-can-eat Asian stir-fries, "solid cheap eateries"
where "you choose your own ingredients" from a "great
variety of fresh" provender; then again, those lacking
"culinary can-do" may end up with "not the best out-
come", and certain staffers who "tend to overcook" leave
weary wokkers wondering "is the 15 minutes over for
these types of restaurants?"

Fleming's Prime Steakhouse & Wine Bar | – | – | – | E |

Lincolnshire Commons, 930 Milwaukee Ave. (Rte. 33),
Lincolnshire, 847-793-0333;
www.flemingssteakhouse.com

North Suburban Lincolnshire now has an outpost of
the upscale national chophouse chain popular for its
prime beef cuts ranging from eight to 40 ounces and 100
wines by the glass; purists will be pleased by the traditional preparations as well as the clubby steakhouse
decor of the swanky, 8,000-sq.-ft. space, which includes
an open kitchen; N.B. be sure to take advantage of the
seasonal outdoor seating.

Flight ◗ | 19 | 20 | 18 | $36 |

1820 Tower Dr. (Patriot Blvd.), Glenview, 847-729-9463;
www.flightwinebar.com

Frequent fliers land at this "hip", "friendly" North Suburban
"quickie" for a "fun place to nosh and drink with friends"
on Eclectic "Asian-influenced" small-plate eats in a "sophisticated wine bar" setting that also features an "interesting selection of wines and presentation of flights";
grumps ground it as a "noisy" "mall stop", though, adding
that the "concept fails more than it succeeds."

Flo
22　17　18　$19

1434 W. Chicago Ave. (bet. Bishop & Noble Sts.), 312-243-0477; www.eatatflo.com

A flo-tilla of fans favors this "arty", "off-the-beaten-track" West Towner that "caters to the twentysomething pierced crowd" with American "cheap eats", including "great Southwestern" fare (the "Frito pie is a must"), and a "standing-room-only" weekend brunch – "go midweek to avoid the crowds."

FOGO DE CHÃO
24　20　24　$55

661 N. LaSalle St. (Erie St.), 312-932-9330; www.fogodechao.com

"Come hungry" to this River North Brazilian-style "never-ending" "orgy" of "spit-roasted" flesh, an outpost of an "all-you-can-eat South American" steakhouse chain, for a milieu of "meat, men and macho gauchos" bringing "a beef ballet" to your table "on traveling swords" ("food on a weapon always rocks!"), "boosted by a bountiful hot and cold buffet"; dainty eaters demur it's only "for the real meatasaurus", though, and belt-tighteners who eschew an "expensive night out" advise you to "go for lunch instead of dinner."

Follia
22　19　19　$46

953 W. Fulton St. (Morgan St.), 312-243-2888

Though "you wouldn't expect to find" it "amongst the 18-wheelers" and warehouses, this "hip" "jewel" makes its home in the Market District, where its "very tasty" Northern Italian cooking includes "marvelous" "little pizzas" from a "wood-fired oven"; you can also choose from a "good selection of wines", and a "beautiful staff" enhances the "minimalist" "Milano decor" – even if opponents peg it as "pricey."

Fonda del Mar
–　–　–　M

3749 W. Fullerton Ave. (Ridgeway Ave.), 773-489-3748

At this affordable Logan Square Mexican 'marisqueria' created by veterans of Frontera Grill and Mia Francesca, coastal artwork adorns a sunny yellow dining room where finatics tuck into authentic seviche, soups, shellfish cocktails and seafood entries from the open kitchen; landlubbers can also choose from a limited selection of meat options.

foodlife
16　13　12　$16

Water Tower Pl., 835 N. Michigan Ave. (bet. Chestnut & Pearson Sts.), 312-335-3663; www.leye.com

Sixteen kitchens issue an Eclectic mix of eats that includes "every kind of ethnic and comfort food" "for the health nut to the trencherman" at this food court in Streeterville's Water Tower Place that's a "notch above" the norm; it's "fast" for when you need to "drop while you shop" (especially "for families of picky eaters"), though snarky shoppers say this "glorified cafeteria" is "overpriced" for a "self-serve concept" and can be as "frenetic as *MTV News*."

Fornetto Mei ▽ 19 17 20 $39

107 E. Delaware Pl. (bet. Michigan Ave. & Rush St.), 312-573-6300

Named for its "wood-burning pizza oven", this "friendly", "intimate" Gold Coast "boutique hotel" restaurant delivers a hybrid of Northern Italian and Chinese chow with a "generous selection of wines by the glass" in "an elegant but not stuffy dining room" – plus "a glassed-in porch with views of a pretty street scene"; adventurers affirm the "fusion" fare is a "neat surprise" but confused contributors complain the "strange menu makes it difficult to decide what to eat"; N.B. low-key live musicians entertain on weekend nights.

1492 Tapas Bar 19 18 17 $30

42 E. Superior St. (Wabash Ave.), 312-867-1492; www.1492tapasbar.com

Some explorers find this Spanish small-plate purveyor "tucked" away in a "quaint" River North "brownstone" with "lots of levels" to be a "sophisticated", "romantic" destination for "quality" tapas and "yummy sangria" – minus the "loud post-college crowd" of some competitors; still, others chart a course elsewhere, citing "slow service" and an "unimaginative", "overpriced" menu; N.B. the occasional Flamenco dancers on weekend nights are "a lot of fun."

FRANCESCA'S AMICI 23 19 20 $32

174 N. York Rd. (2nd St.), Elmhurst, 630-279-7970
FRANCESCA'S BRYN MAWR
1039 W. Bryn Mawr Ave. (Kenmore Ave.), 773-506-9261
FRANCESCA'S BY THE RIVER
200 S. Second St. (Illinois St.), St. Charles, 630-587-8221
FRANCESCA'S CAMPAGNA
127 W. Main St. (2nd St.), West Dundee, 847-844-7099
FRANCESCA'S FIORE
7407 Madison St. (Harlem Ave.), Forest Park, 708-771-3063
FRANCESCA'S FORNO
1576 N. Milwaukee Ave. (North Ave.), 773-770-0184
FRANCESCA'S INTIMO
293 E. Illinois Rd. (Western Ave.), Lake Forest, 847-735-9235
FRANCESCA'S ON TAYLOR
1400 W. Taylor St. (Loomis St.), 312-829-2828
LA SORELLA DI FRANCESCA
18 W. Jefferson Ave. (bet. Main & Washington Sts.), Naperville, 630-961-2706
www.miafrancesca.com

"Consistently" "scrumptious" Italian "with an upscale touch", and "at reasonable prices", is the hallmark of this ever-extending family of "rustic, homey" city and suburban eateries, where the frequently "changing menu" makes "everything a special"; peripatetic patrons purport "service can vary" "across locations", however, and ambiance ranges from "romantic" to "ear-splitting", as some branches make "great use of space" whereas others have "tables on top of each other."

Francesco's Hole in the Wall ⊘ | 24 | 13 | 20 | $33 |

254 Skokie Blvd. (bet. Dundee & Lake Cook Rds.), Northbrook, 847-272-0155

"If you can get into" this "quaint", "tiny" North Suburban 25-year-old "with a huge following", you'll find "outstanding" "old-world [Southern] Italian" fare; "regulars" who rave about the "handwritten menu filled with delectable offerings" − including "fresh fish and" "great pastas" − resolutely "put up with long waits, crowded tables, lots of noise" and a "cash-only" policy.

Froggy's French Cafe ☒ | 22 | 18 | 23 | $42 |

306 Green Bay Rd. (Highwood Ave.), Highwood, 847-433-7080; www.froggyscatering.com

A "casual" classic for "high-quality" Classic "French country food" with a seafood focus, this "North Shore standby" with a "personable staff" is a "popular" "gathering spot for the older group" and also "welcomes families, including kids"; that said, revivalists report that "redecorating and revamping the menu wouldn't hurt"; P.S. "the prix fixe meal has to be one of the best deals out there."

FRONTERA GRILL ☒ | 26 | 21 | 22 | $39 |

445 N. Clark St. (bet. Hubbard & Illinois Sts.), 312-661-1434; www.fronterakitchens.com

"Top-of-the-line Mexican with a focus on fresh ingredients" comes courtesy of "culinary hero Rick Bayless" at this River North "treasure" with a "national reputation"; "bold, bright" and "somewhat raucous", it's "less expensive and more casual" than its "refined big brother", Topolobampo, with the same "superb wine selections" and "great margarita-tequila menu", but some say "service can be spotty when it's busy − which is always"; P.S. reservations are accepted for dinner (parties of five or more) and lunch.

Fulton's on the River | 20 | 21 | 19 | $51 |

315 N. LaSalle St. (Wacker Dr.), 312-822-0100; www.fultonsontheriver.com

Cousin to Fulton's Crab House at Florida's Disney World, this "huge", "contemporary" "expense-account seafooder" and steakhouse is a "great new find for on-the-river dining" in River North; hooked honchos hail the "big", "diverse menu" of "fresh fish" and "prime steaks" and the "magnificent view", while holdouts who hint at early "kinks" hope "in time it might be a great restaurant."

Fundajo Grill ⊠　　　　　　　－　－　－　M
3140 N. Lincoln Ave. (bet. Barry & Belmont Aves.), 773-404-4500;
www.fundajo.com

Though the name hints at Latin cuisine, there's little evidence
of it at this romantic Lakeview haunt offering Eclectic fare
by chef Carlos Contreras (ex Boca, Spiaggia), who laces
his menu with delicacies such as white truffle polenta and
ginger aïoli; the candlelit space featuring silky russet-hued
velvet seating is romantic enough to secure a second date.

GABRIEL'S ⊠　　　　　　　26　22　26　$62
310 Green Bay Rd. (Highwood Ave.), Highwood, 847-433-0031;
www.egabriels.com

It's "heaven in Highwood" say habitués of Gabe Viti's
French-Italian, a "favorite" for "fantastic", "timeless food"
that's "expensive but worth it", plus a "complete, com-
manding and comforting wine list", "effortless service
with impeccable timing" and "elegant" environs; a few
who feel it's getting "stale" object that the owner seems
less in evidence at "his first creation" now that he has
"opened more restaurants" (Miramar, Pancho Viti's).

Gale Street Inn　　　　　　　20　15　19　$28
4914 N. Milwaukee Ave. (Lawrence Ave.), 773-725-1300;
www.galestreet.com
935 Diamond Lake Rd. (Rte. 45), Mundelein, 847-566-1090;
www.galest.com

"The supper clubs of old" live on in these "comfy" "neighborhood institutions" – a "perennial Northwest Side establishment across from the Jefferson Park el stop" and a
younger Mundelein location – that are separately owned
but serving a similar, "fairly priced" Traditional American
menu of "rocking ribs" and other "plain, simple" offerings;
the "uninspired", though, report "uneventful meals", advising "do not go out of your way."

Gaylord Fine Indian Cuisine　　22　14　19　$28
678 N. Clark St. (Huron St.), 312-664-1700
555 Mall Dr. (Higgins Rd.), Schaumburg, 847-619-3300
www.gaylordindia.net

A "pleasant" pair of city and Northwest Suburban sites,
these "Indian comfort-food" stations "consistently" serve
sustenance "that isn't too spicy" as well as "authentic options"; lauders who "love the tandoor dishes, wonderful
naan" and "terrific" lunch buffets write "who goes for the
ambiance?" – though the Decor score may not reflect that
the River North original "finally received a makeover."

Geja's Cafe　　　　　　　　　21　21　21　$45
340 W. Armitage Ave. (bet. Clark St. & Lincoln Ave.),
773-281-9101; www.gejascafe.com

"Classic fondue done right" is the calling card of this "can't-
miss date location" in Lincoln Park, where the "kitschy"

"'70s" "fun" "will leave you feeling warm and satisfied" – with help from the "excellent wine selection"; cuddlers coo that the "flamenco guitarist" nightly "adds a touch of mystery" to the "catacomblike underground environment" ("secure a booth"), but "splattered" surveyors say it's only "romantic" "if you like sterno with your sweet nothings", warning "don't wear anything you care about."

Gene & Georgetti ☒   23 | 14 | 19 | $54
500 N. Franklin St. (Illinois St.), 312-527-3718;
www.geneandgeorgetti.com
A "local landmark" "under the el tracks" in River North, this "classic Chicago beefatorium" and "boys' club" provides a "complete cholesterol transplant" via "decadent" "Fred Flintstone–sized portions" of prime steaks with "good Italian thrown in", all served by "old-fashioned waiters"; fed-up feeders feel that "regulars get preferred treatment" from the otherwise "grumpy" staffers, though, and say the "tired interior" (like something "from a movie set") is "badly in need of an update."

GIBSONS STEAKHOUSE ●   25 | 19 | 23 | $56
1028 N. Rush St. (Bellevue Pl.), 312-266-8999
Doubletree Hotel, 5464 N. River Rd. (bet. Balmoral &
Bryn Mawr Aves.), Rosemont, 847-928-9900
www.gibsonssteakhouse.com
"Aggressive carnivores" take an "authentic Chicago power trip" at this Gold Coast "high-roller" haven "where everything is big", including the "excellent cuts of [prime] meat cooked to perfection", "lampshade-sized martinis", the personalities of the "outgoing staff" – and "big check"; there's a "fantastic" "cigar-friendly" bar scene for those "long, crowded waits", so "make a reservation, arrive early and hope for your table before the seasons change"; P.S. "the Rosemont location is as good – and easier" to navigate.

Gio   19 | 19 | 20 | $29
1631 Chicago Ave. (bet. Church & Davis Sts.), Evanston,
847-869-3900; www.giorestaurant.com
"Excellent wood-fired pizza" from the brick oven behind the bar plus "good salads" (even a "salad pizza" that's "a winner"), "daily risotto and fish specials", and an "above-average, affordable wine selection" lure Evanston locals to this "unpretentious" Northern Italian charmer "where you can actually talk" most times – though it "can get loud when near capacity"; P.S. it's also "priced very well."

Gioco   21 | 20 | 18 | $39
1312 S. Wabash Ave. (13th St.), 312-939-3870;
www.gioco-chicago.com
"Always hip and always reliable" for "fresh, well-made" "up-scale [Northern] Italian" in the "hot new South Loop" neighborhood, this "warm and inviting" "former speakeasy" also

serves up "lots of character", along with "loud", "clubby music" and – unfortunately – sometimes "spotty service"; P.S. "romantics" request "the private vault room in back."

GIORDANO'S
21　12　15　$19

135 E. Lake St. (Upper Michigan Ave.), 312-616-1200
2855 N. Milwaukee Ave. (Wolfram St.), 773-862-4200
730 N. Rush St. (Superior St.), 312-951-0747 ◗
6314 S. Cicero Ave. (63rd St.), 773-585-6100
5159 S. Pulaski Rd. (Archer Ave.), 773-582-7676 ◗
1040 W. Belmont Ave. (Kenmore Ave.), 773-327-1200
5927 W. Irving Park Rd. (Austin Ave.), 773-736-5553
223 W. Jackson Blvd. (Franklin St.), 312-583-9400
310 W. Randolph St. (Franklin St.), 312-201-1441
815 W. Van Buren St. (Halsted St.), 312-421-1221
www.giordanos.com
Additional locations throughout the Chicago area

A passel of pie-faces prefers the signature "knife-and-fork" stuffed 'za, "thick, juicy and cheesy" with "sinful" "pastry-like crust", though there are those who "particularly love the thin-crust" at this "chain" contender; fans feel the "slow, unfriendly service" and "lacking decor" "don't even matter" since "the focus is on the pie", but a faction of foes finds the "famous" pizza "pedestrian" and reckons "the rest of the menu needs work"; N.B. the "homey" River North flagship does not accept reservations.

Glunz Bavarian Haus
19　15　19　$30

4128 N. Lincoln Ave. (bet. Belle Plaine & Warner Aves.), 773-472-4287

Lately a "favorite among the Teutonic taverns", this "updated" German-Austrian venue in Lincoln Square offers Bavarian renditions that are "more modern" than most, but still "hearty" (and "not everything is brown"), along with a "fantastic beer selection on tap" and a location that "looks like a movie set for *The Sound of Music*"; add in garden seating and seasonal entertainment and you get an experience that's "nothing to schnitzel at."

Gold Coast Dogs
19　6　13　$8

Midway Int'l Airport, 5700 S. Cicero Ave. (55th St.), 773-735-6789 ◗
159 N. Wabash Ave. (bet. Lake & Randolph Sts.), 312-917-1677
O'Hare Int'l Airport, Terminal 3, 773-462-9942
O'Hare Int'l Airport, Terminal 5, 773-462-0125 ◗ ⇛
17 S. Wabash Ave. (Monroe St.), 312-578-1133 ⇛
Union Station, 225 S. Canal St. (Jackson Blvd.), 312-258-8585 ⇛
2349 W. Howard St. (Western Ave.), 773-338-0900 ⇛
1429 W. Montrose Ave. (Clark St.), 773-472-3600 ⇛
www.goldcoastdogs.net
Additional locations throughout the Chicago area

"Drunk or sober", supporters say "arf!" to this litter of hot dog stands supplying "one helluva" "quintessential

Chicago dog" ("tell 'em to 'drag it through the garden!'")
plus "awesome cheese fries"; naysayers neuter this pack,
though, vaunting "better versions" of these vittles elsewhere, and suggest some of these doghouses could use a
visit from a housekeeper.

Golden Budha Chinese Steakhouse
∇ 18 15 16 $23

*312 W. Randolph St. (bet. Franklin St. & Wacker Dr.),
312-609-0000; www.goldenbudhachicago.com*

"Undiscovered" because it's "hidden in the basement of a
[Loop] office building", this Szechuan setup is a "treasure"
to supporters of its "extensive menu" of "solid if not spectacular" Chinese-American eats and "killer mai tais"; still,
wafflers worry about decor that's "a bit gaudy" and service that's "uneven"; N.B. a prix fixe is offered at both
lunch and dinner.

Goose Island Brewing Co.
16 16 17 $20

*3535 N. Clark St. (Addison St.), 773-832-9040
1800 N. Clybourn Ave. (Sheffield Ave.), 312-915-0071
www.gooseisland.com*

"You won't find better microbreweries in Chicago" than this
"fun", "family-friendly" Lincoln Park–Wrigleyville pair pouring "delicious beers", available in "flights" and "growlers to
go"; the "upscale" Traditional American "pub food" ("with
some beer in it") comes in second to the suds, though the
"Stilton burger is an awesome choice", but "let's be
honest – you didn't really come here for the food, did you?"

Grace O'Malley's
17 16 17 $23

*1416 S. Michigan Ave. (14th St.), 312-588-1800;
www.graceomalleychicago.com*

A "casual", "comfortable destination in the area" of the
South Loop, this sophomore Irish-American pub is "a great
addition to the neighborhood" for the "young, professional
crowd", and a "Bears hot spot during football season",
with "friendly service"; while a majority vindicates the
"good", "varied" offerings, which include a "great" "buffet brunch" and "wine and beer specials", a collection of
critics considers it of "inconsistent quality."

Grand Lux Cafe
20 21 19 $26

*600 N. Michigan Ave. (Ontario St.), 312-276-2500;
www.grandluxcafe.com*

"Basically an upscale Cheesecake Factory" "with many of
the same items" – and "just as crammed as its sister"
spot – this "boisterous" River North pack-'em-in purveyor
proffers an "insanely diverse" Eclectic menu ("fabulous
Asian nachos") with an emphasis on "oversized everything" amid "opulent", "over-the-top" surroundings
(the "rotunda" "room" provides a "sensational view" of
Boul Mich); bashers, though, brand it as "big hype on

Michigan Avenue" that's "not bad if you don't mind" "formula" feeding, "crowds with lots of children and strollers", and "medium lux service."

Great Lakes Fish House   – – – M
275 Parkway Dr. (Aptakisic Rd.), Lincolnshire, 847-808-9463
The Great Lakes theme is carried throughout this redo of the North Suburban Bin 36 via cedar-centric natural-nautical decor, hundreds of fishing-and-tackle photos and an all-Midwestern/Canadian microbrewery list (plus a downsized roster of 20 wines by the glass), but the daily changing, moderately priced seafood menu casts a wider net, including offerings from the pre-existing Kamehachi sushi bar, fresh and saltwater selections paired with a variety of sauces and a juicy raw bar – plus you get saltwater taffy when you leave.

Greek Islands   21 18 20 $27
200 S. Halsted St. (Adams St.), 312-782-9855 ☽
300 E. 22nd St. (Highland Ave.), Lombard, 630-932-4545
www.greekislands.net
Though it probably "hasn't changed since the last time you were there", this "huge, busy" Greektown "standby" is "beyond criticism" to fans of its "lively", "family-style" "comfort-food" "classics", "fun staff" ("love the '*opa*' cries") and "homey", "Mediterranean-decorated" setting – plus "you can't beat the price"; Trojans take issue, though, saying its "steam-table" sustenance is "for the masses", not the "adventurous"; P.S. to Lombard locals it's "great to have good" Greek cuisine "in the [Western] 'burbs."

Green Dolphin Street   19 20 18 $46
2200 N. Ashland Ave. (Webster Ave.), 773-395-0066;
www.jazzitup.com
"Dinner comes with free entrance to the adjoining jazz club/bar" at this fringe-dwelling Lincoln Park "date place" "on the riverfront" (with the "perfect patio" and boat docking in summer); "you could drive by this place a million times and never realize" what a "cool environment" is inside, though opinions on the New American cuisine range from "solid" and "creative" to "overpriced" and "somewhat forgettable."

Green Door Tavern   14 18 18 $21
678 N. Orleans St. (Huron St.), 312-664-5496;
www.greendoorchicago.com
"You'll be walking crooked before your first drink" at this River North "haunt", a "landmark" with "leaning walls", "local charisma" and a circa-1921 speakeasy in the basement; it represents a "fast-disappearing Chicago-type bar/restaurant" (it's "now surrounded by million-dollar condos"), with "fun decor" that will "keep your eyes busy for hours" and help you overlook the "simple" – some say "so-so" – Traditional American "grub."

GREEN ZEBRA
25 | 23 | 23 | $51

1460 W. Chicago Ave. (Greenview Ave.), 312-243-7100;
www.greenzebrachicago.com

"You don't have to be a tree-hugger to love" this West Town "winner" where Shawn McClain (Spring, Custom House) "makes you want to eat your vegetables" with his "phe-nomenal", "complex" "seasonal" "small plates" ("con-verts" crow "you'll never miss the meat" – though a few "chicken and fish dishes" are also offered); add "knowl-edgeable service" and "smart" "Zen" surroundings and you have a "haute" "heaven" – though catty carnivores contend "nothing impresses as much as the prices."

Grill on the Alley, The
18 | 18 | 18 | $42

Westin Hotel, 909 N. Michigan Ave. (Delaware Pl.),
312-255-9009; www.thegrill.com

A "varied menu" of "very good" Traditional American vit-tles in an "old-fashioned", "formal bar-and-grill" setting satisfies Streeterville steakhouse seekers, especially given that it's "superior for a hotel" venue and "always a safe bet for getting a table"; still, critical correspondents "who have been to the real Grill on the Alley in Beverly Hills" are "not thrilled" by what they consider "average" meals at "Michigan Avenue prices."

Grillroom, The
17 | 18 | 18 | $35

33 W. Monroe St. (bet. Dearborn & State Sts.), 312-960-0000;
www.restaurants-america.com

"When you're looking to take lunch up a notch", or for a "pre-show, pre-symphony spot", supporters suggest this "well-located" Loop venue where the "reliable" if "nothing-fancy" "steakhouse fare" comes with an "excel-lent variety of salads" and "specials showing more of a seasonal flair", all in a "classic wood-finish" locale; de-spite this, diners who deem it "decidedly average" yawn "you sit in a room, and apparently the food is grilled, and there's not much more to it than that."

Grotto ⊠
18 | 17 | 17 | $40

1030 N. State St. (Rush St.), 312-280-1005; www.grottoonstate.com

Gold Coasters who go for "good dining just off Rush Street" (including "great chicken Vesuvio") frequent this Italian steakhouse for its "romantic setting" with an "awe-some bar" and "great tables overlooking the atrium"; wor-riers "wonder if it can compete with the heavyweights", though, believing it's best suited to "a slightly older crowd looking for drinks."

Gulliver's Pizzeria & Restaurant
17 | 22 | 18 | $19

2727 W. Howard St. (California Ave.), 773-338-2166;
www.gulliverspizza.com

A Rogers Park "staple" "for a zillion years" (since 1965), this "extremely kid-friendly" Eclectic eatery serves up "not just pizza but a whole experience" amid "wonderful, weird decor" with a "huge collection of collections", including "antiques", "statuary and chandeliers", plus a "great outdoor beer garden"; still, some Lilliputians who lament the "huge menu" of "bland" fare "wish the food was as interesting" as the interior, adding "stay away from the Mexican and Asian entrees."

Hachi's Kitchen   – | – | – | M

2521 N. California Ave. (Altgeld St.), 773-276-8080;
www.hachiskitchen.com
The name sounds quaint, but this sexy Logan Square spot – with its sunken lounge area, curving sushi bar and clubby music – is anything but; an omakase offering (chef's choice) and a dozen premium sakes add spark to the Japanese menu featuring all the moderately priced standards you'd expect from a Sai Café sister.

Hacienda Tecalitlan   ▽ 20 | 22 | 21 | $21

820 N. Ashland Ave. (Chicago Ave.), 312-243-6667
Supporters say the eats at this "two-story" Ukrainian Villlage "Mexican colonial fantasy palace" are "a bit more authentic than the more trendy spots", plus the "cozy adjoining bar serves big margaritas" – and if that isn't enough to "love", the "festive" mood comes "complete with mariachis on weekends."

Hackney's   18 | 13 | 17 | $20

733 S. Dearborn St. (bet. Harrison & Polk Sts.), 312-461-1116
1514 E. Lake Ave. (bet. Sunset Ridge & Waukegan Rds.),
Glenview, 847-724-7171
1241 Harms Rd. (Lake Ave.), Glenview, 847-724-5577
880 N. Old Rand Rd. (Rand Rd.), Lake Zurich, 847-438-2103
9550 W. 123rd St. (La Grange Rd.), Palos Park, 708-448-8300
241 S. Milwaukee Ave. (Dundee Rd.), Wheeling, 847-537-2100
www.hackneys.net
For "a great big heaping helping of nostalgia", surveyors say these suburban American "time warps" (or the newer Printer's Row location) are "still the place to go" thanks to "great greasy burgers" on "black bread soaked by the juice" plus "that onion loaf thing" that's "to die for – probably literally"; unsentimental sorts surmise the "service can be iffy", though, and hint these "hackneyed" hamburger haunts are "living on past laurels."

Hai Yen   22 | 13 | 17 | $17

1055 W. Argyle St. (bet. Kenmore & Winthrop Aves.),
773-561-4077; www.haiyenrestaurant.com
Though "the entire Asian restaurant scene on Argyle is getting more competitive", this "fancier" find "still stands out" as "one of the best of its class" to savorers of its "lovely" "fresh" Mandarin-"Vietnamese" victuals ("their seven courses of beef make life complete"), which "don't

intimidate neophytes" and are accompanied by "great bubble tea"; a few faultfinders, however, feel it doesn't deliver overall "authenticity."

Half Shell ◑⌂ 22 | 9 | 12 | $29
676 W. Diversey Pkwy. (bet. Clark & Orchard Sts.), 773-549-1773
"Lovers" of "outstanding, fresh seafood" insist you "can't go wrong" at this longtime Lakeview lair, even though it "holds the infamous reputation" of being a "seedy" "hole-in-the-wall" with "crotchety" "personnel", a "cash-only" collection policy and sometimes "killer waits" that can make some claw-craving customers "crabby" (they don't take reservations).

Happy Chef Dim Sum House ◑ 23 | 9 | 14 | $16
2164 S. Archer Ave. (Cermak Rd.), 312-808-3689
"Highly recommended" dim sum is served "à la carte" – but with "no carts" – from 9 AM to 4 PM, while "authentic" and "crazy-cheap" Cantonese fare is offered throughout the day and into the "late night" (2 AM) at this Chinatown chowhouse; "don't expect great service", though, and do expect "minimal decor" that really "needs a kick in the pants."

Harbour House — | — | — | E
Laundry Mall, 566 Chestnut St. (Spruce St.), Winnetka, 847-441-4600
Set in the former Fio space in Winnetka's Laundry Mall, this "sophisticated, yet unpretentious" spot fills a niche with "truly delicious", "innovative seafood dishes" offered along with "outstanding air and land selections", making for one of "the best combined food and atmosphere" experiences in the Northern Suburbs; P.S. other assets include "live music" on Fridays, summer patio seating and weekend brunch.

Hard Rock Cafe ◑ 13 | 20 | 13 | $25
63 W. Ontario St. (bet. Clark & Dearborn Sts.), 312-943-2252; www.hardrock.com
The "awesome" "memorabilia on the walls" is "why you go" to this 20-year-old "chain" member that's "full of spirit" (and "loud music") and serves up "average" American eats that appeal to "kids" and "tourists"; rock critics call it a "T-shirt factory" where the "bland food" is "a sideline" and the "service is always close to bad", quipping that they'll "just drop off the out-of-town relatives next time."

Haro ⌦ — | — | — | M
2436 S. Oakley Ave. (24th Pl.), 773-847-2400; www.harotapas.com
This budget-friendly Basque specialist brings tapas, *pintxos* (open-face sandwiches) and entrees to the Heart of Italy, as well as regional wines and three types of sangria served in *porrons*, ceramic pitchers from which you pour

the drink directly into your mouth; it's housed in a former antiques shop with ochre walls, warm wood and exposed brick, where live bands and flamenco guitarists perform.

Harry Caray's　　　　　　19　20　19　$37
33 W. Kinzie St. (Dearborn St.), 312-828-0966
Holiday Inn Select, 10233 W. Higgins Rd. (Mannheim Rd.),
Rosemont, 847-699-1200
Harry Caray's Seventh Inning Stretch
Midway Int'l Airport, 5700 S. Cicero Ave. (55th St.), 773-948-6300
www.harrycarays.com
"Named after the beloved former Cubs announcer", these slices of "baseball junkie heaven" where "you could spend hours looking at all the memorabilia on the walls" serve "plentiful plates of flavorful" Italian steakhouse food ("they don't serve steaks here – they serve cows") in an "upscale sports bar" setting; unimpressed umpires, though, flag them as "average" "for the money"; P.S. "fans must come" to the River North original to "grieve over the 'Bartman ball.'"

Harvest　　　　　　　　　–　–　–　E
Pheasant Run Resort, 4051 E. Main St. (Pheasant Run),
St. Charles, 630-524-5080; www.pheasantrun.com
A West Suburban getaway in the historic dairy barn of the Pheasant Run Resort, this New American showcases Midwestern ingredients – including pan-roasted Wisconsin pheasant, fresh produce in season and artisanal cheeses – along with hearty steak, seafood and game classics paired with California and regional wines, microbrews and fruit-infused martinis in a warm, retro lodge setting.

Hashalom ⊄　　　　　　　–　–　–　I
2905 W. Devon Ave. (Francisco Ave.), 773-465-5675
"Known mostly by regulars", this Northwest Side "store-front" BYO is noteworthy for its Moroccan-"Israeli fusion cuisine", including what some say are the "best falafel" and lamb shish kebab going; the "staff tries to please", and partialists "wish the place were open more hours" (it serves from noon to 9 PM, Wednesday through Sunday).

HB　　　　　　　　　　　22　18　19　$32
3404 N. Halsted St. (Roscoe St.), 773-661-0299;
www.heartyboys.com
"Creative, cheeky [New] American eats" courtesy of Lakeview caterers and "Food Network celebrities" Dan Smith and Steve McDonagh and their executive chef, JonCarl Lachman, beckon a "beautiful straight/gay crowd" to this "quaint" "keeper" in a "petite" "store-front", where "BYO helps keep the tab down"; holdouts hedge, though, saying "when service catches up to the food quality, we may have a Boys Town hit"; P.S. the "tasty" weekend brunch boasts "amazing beignets."

Heartland Cafe   16 | 15 | 16 | $17

The Heartland Building, 7000 N. Glenwood Ave. (Lunt Ave.),
773-465-8005; www.heartlandcafe.com

For 30 years, this "earthy-crunchy" Rogers Park "health-food" "haven" has been "where the hippies go" for "great beer", "live bands" and poetry, and "good, hearty" Eclectic and vegetarian eats served with "optimism" (plus some of "the best outdoor seating" in town) – but eaters with images of "everyone wearing tye-dye and putting daisies in soldiers' gun barrels" say the "slacker" staff is too "laid-back" and "wish the food were better"; P.S. there's a "fabulous general store" on-site.

Heat ⊠   25 | 21 | 23 | $85

1507 N. Sedgwick St. (North Ave.), 312-397-9818;
www.heatsushi.com

Sushi is a life and death matter at this "unique" Old Town Japanese omakase-only outpost offering the "most amazing selections of imported seafoods and sake"; the "live-kill" candidates "swim by your feet at the bar", making for plates of "food so fresh it's still moving" – in other words, it's "not for the faint of heart", or the light of wallet, given that it's "very expensive"; N.B. bringing children is discouraged.

HEAVEN ON SEVEN   21 | 16 | 18 | $24

Garland Bldg., 111 N. Wabash Ave., 7th fl. (Washington Blvd.),
312-263-6443 ⊠ ⊟
600 N. Michigan Ave., 2nd fl. (bet. Ohio & Ontario Sts.),
312-280-7774
224 S. Main St. (bet. Jackson & Jefferson Aves.), Naperville,
630-717-0777
www.heavenonseven.com

"Tourists" and regulars relish the "reliable" "rajun Cajun" and Creole food served "in good portions" at this "Mardi Gras-ish" trio, home of "spicy" "done right", "more hot sauces than Imelda Marcos had shoes" and a "nonstop party"; some suggest it's "the best you can get in Chicago", though purists purport it "can't compete with real New Orleans food", say "service can be hit-or-miss" and contend it's "coasting on its rep"; N.B. the Loop location still doesn't take credit cards.

Hecky's Barbecue   21 | 5 | 13 | $17

1902 Green Bay Rd. (Emerson St.), Evanston, 847-492-1182;
www.heckys.com
Hecky's of Chicago
1234 N. Halsted St. (Division St.), 312-377-7427;
www.heckysofchicago.com

"Leave the fancy duds at home" and head for this Evanston "institution" earning "thumbs-up" for "cheap eats" with "true BBQ flavor", including "some of the best ribs" around, with "tangy, tasty sauce" – not to mention "authentic, mouthwatering Southern-style fried chicken"; tipsters tell us "takeout is better", though, due to "nonexistent ambiance", and traditionalists tout the original as "better than the [Near West] Chicago" sequel.

Hema's Kitchen　　　20 | 10 | 13 | $20 |
2411 N. Clark St. (Fullerton Pkwy.), 773-529-1705
6406 N. Oakley Ave. (W. Devon Ave.), 773-338-1627
"Wonderful", "offbeat dishes" of "succulent" Indian cuisine made from "fresh ingredients" and "available at all spice levels" appeal to allegiants of this "favorite" "Devon-area choice", who sometimes "miss seeing Mama Hema around since she now divides her time between two restaurants" (and is planning a third); Lincoln Park locals sense their spin-off is "not as cheap or as good as its sister" spot – but "very little ambiance" and "crazy-slow" service seem to be constants; N.B. both are BYO and "good for vegetarians."

Hemmingway's Bistro　　　▽ 21 | 21 | 21 | $33 |
The Write Inn, 211 N. Oak Park Ave. (Ontario St.), Oak Park, 708-524-0806; www.hemmingwaysbistro.com
"Left Bank dining" from a "really nice" menu of "creative" French "bistro fare" and Traditional American classics – all fashioned from predominantly organic ingredients and accompanied by a "great wine list" – make this "very relaxed" and "beautiful" "undiscovered jewel" in the "quaint" Write Inn a "great couples' night out" in Oak Park.

Hot Chocolate　　　23 | 22 | 21 | $33 |
1747 N. Damen Ave. (Wabansia Ave.), 773-489-1747;
www.hotchocolatechicago.com
"Chocoholics" will "go here in a heartbeat" for the "scrumptious" sweets from dessert diva Mindy Segal (ex mk), "definitely the high point" of this "trendy", "crowded" Bucktowner ("the pastry work station front and center is proof"); that said, "the savory side" of its "limited but interesting" Traditional American "comfort-food" menu "is no slouch either", and even the "chocolaty decor" is rich – but wallet-watchers warn so are the comestibles' "high prices."

HOT DOUG'S ⊠⊅　　　25 | 13 | 19 | $9 |
3324 N. California Ave. (Roscoe St.), 773-279-9550;
www.hotdougs.com
Though its new location is bigger, you still might "wait in line" at Doug Sohn's "legendary encased-meats emporium", as there's "more seating" and better parking but the same "lousy hours" (the kitchen closes at 4 PM); rest assured, though, that "it's worth" it for his "outrageously decadent sausage sandwiches", including more than a dozen "gourmet hot dogs" – no, it's "not an oxymoron" – ranging from "rabbit" to "rattlesnake"; P.S. he "puts the fry in Friday with his duck-fat fries" (available on Saturday too).

Hot Tamales　　　　　　　　21　12　18　$21
493 Central Ave. (St. John Ave.), Highland Park, 847-433-4070;
www.hottamales4u.com
"The atmosphere is loud but the cuisine is louder" at this
"crowded" North Shore family "favorite" for "delicious",
"creative" (some say "inauthentic") "made-to-order"
Mexican such as "duck tacos from heaven" and a "wonderful salmon burrito"; the "non-romantic atmosphere" – and
sometimes the staff – "will hurry your meal along", especially "if there's a wait" (no reservations); P.S. "the summer outdoor dining is the hottest seat in town."

House of Blues Back Porch　　16　23　17　$29
329 N. Dearborn St. (Kinzie St.), 312-923-2007; www.hob.com
"Known more for fun" and for "strong drinks" than for its
"chainlike" American food "with a Southern slant", this
River North haunt harbors "cool" "theme" decor, "especially
for music fans"; it's "a little pricey for casual dining", but
"eating here lets you skip the line for that night's show" – and
the "Sunday gospel brunch" will "cleanse your sins away."

HUGO'S FROG BAR &　　　　24　19　22　$48
FISH HOUSE
1024 N. Rush St. (bet. Bellevue Pl. & Oak St.), 312-640-0999 ◗
Main Street Promenade Bldg., 55 S. Main St. (bet. Benton &
Van Buren Aves.), Naperville, 630-548-3764
www.hugosfrogbar.com
"Always a hoppin' scene", this "Gold Coast favorite" for
"fresh fish" ("unreal crab cakes") shares a kitchen and has
some menu crossover with its sib, Gibsons Steakhouse, as
well as a "similarly authentic Chicago power trip", "Rush
Street prices" and "noise" level; still, waverers "wish the
service was as consistent as the food", and penny-wise
patrons posit the "portions and prices could both be reduced"; P.S. the Naperville outpost makes locals "feel as if
[they're] in on all the action."

Il Mulino New York　　　　　–　–　–　E
1150 N. Dearborn St. (bet. Division & Elm Sts.), 312-440-8888;
www.ilmulinonewyork.com
New York's old-guard Italian has settled into the Gold
Coast mansion once home to Biggs; a showy antipasto display graces the foyer, which leads to multiple posh dining
rooms (all with fireplaces) where tuxedoed servers
present well-heeled diners with high-tariff traditional
fare – including many dishes prepared tableside – and a
list of 200 Italian wines.

Improv Kitchen ◗🗷　　　　　–　–　–　M
3419 N. Clark St. (bet. Newport Ave. & Roscoe St.),
773-868-6423; www.improvkitchen.com
A "cool idea for a restaurant", this "unique" Wrigleyviller
makes for a "great date or special-event place" "for groups

who want to laugh" since "you watch live improv on a TV and interact through cameras and microphones" that make you part of the "lowbrow humor"; no one's raving about the New American eats, but tickled funny-bones still think it "should be packed."

Ina's
| 19 | 15 | 19 | $22 |

1235 W. Randolph St. (Elizabeth St.), 312-226-8227; www.breakfastqueen.com

"Innovative and delicious" New American "home cooking" "is made from scratch with care" at this "cozy" West Loop "winner" where owner Ina Pinkney is the "great hostess" and diners "delight in" a "funky" feel, "friendly staff", "free parking" and "charming salt and pepper sets"; some surveyors say "stick to breakfast" (if you don't mind a "long wait"), but boosters brag "everything is good here, including dinner."

INDIA HOUSE
| 23 | 17 | 19 | $25 |

59 W. Grand Ave. (bet. Clark & Dearborn Sts.), 312-645-9500
Buffalo Grove Town Ctr., 228-230 McHenry Rd. (Lake Cook Rd.), Buffalo Grove, 847-520-5569
1521 W. Schaumburg Rd. (Springinsguth Rd.), Schaumburg, 847-895-5501; www.indiahouseschaumburg.com

Chicago's "best Indian" fare can be found at this threesome that thrives thanks to "generous portions" of "fantastic", "fresh, authentic" "standards" for both "those who like spicy" and "novices" too; even contributors who consider it "a bit pricey" think the "extensive" lunch buffets are "an affordable delight", and raters out of River North range are grateful for the "convenient suburban locations."

Indian Garden, The
| 22 | 13 | 17 | $25 |

247 E. Ontario St., 2nd fl. (Fairbanks Ct.), 312-280-4910
2546 W. Devon Ave. (Rockwell St.), 773-338-2929
855 E. Schaumburg Rd. (Plum Grove Rd.), Schaumburg, 847-524-3007
6020 S. Cass Ave. (60th St.), Westmont, 630-769-9662

"Excellent" curries, tikka dishes and vegetarian choices are on the "large" menu at this quartet of Indian installations favored as places "for the entire family to have a great meal" "at a sensible price" (especially via the "bargain lunch buffets"); few mind that they're "not much to look at", though some say "service varies from cordial and attentive to brusque" and slow.

Indie Cafe
| ▽ 19 | 13 | 18 | $22 |

5951 N. Broadway (bet. Elmdale & Thorndale Aves.), 773-561-5577; www.indiecafe.us

"Creative sushi" meets "spice-authentic" Siamese at this "microscopic" BYO "hipster" in Edgewater with "a large, innovative menu" that's "perfect for the bipolar eater" – or for anyone "squeamish" about raw Japanese fare "since their Thai food is equally delicious" (and "the plate presentation is even better"); P.S. when the "cramped" space is "crowded", one can "wait at the bar across the street" and they'll "call you via your cell when your table's ready."

Irazu 🖾⇆   22 | 8 | 17 | $13
1865 N. Milwaukee Ave. (Western Ave.), 773-252-5687
"Nice", "earnest" people run this "still-relatively hidden gem", a "small" BYO "with big food" in the form of "consistently fresh", "genuine" Costa Rican cuisine (and some Mex) with "lots of vegetarian choices" – and "don't miss the tropical-fruit-and-oatmeal shakes"; it's "a hole-in-the-wall for sure" ("so basic it's hip"), but there's a "busy, Latin vibe", and "bargain"-hunters bask in "prices that make you think they don't know Bucktown has gentrified."

Irish Oak Restaurant & Pub   ▽ 19 | 19 | 20 | $18
3511 N. Clark St. (Addison St.), 773-935-6669;
www.irishoak.com
"More than just a cheap imitation", this Wrigleyville watering hole with "true Irish character" is like "a visit to the Emerald Isle without leaving the city", delighting denizens with "pub-style" "comfort food" including "great burgers" and "fantastic fish 'n' chips" paired with "a perfect pour of Guinness" "at the correct temperature"; P.S. the "decor was actually imported from Erin" in crates.

ISABELLA'S ESTIATORIO   26 | 23 | 25 | $45
330 W. State St. (4th St.), Geneva, 630-845-8624;
www.isabellasgeneva.com
"Excellent, innovative Mediterranean" fare that's "full of flavor" (and mostly organic ingredients), accompanied by a "limited" but "very nice wine list" and served by a "staff committed to delivering an exceptional meal" will "make you feel like you're at the best restaurant Downtown" – "without the attitude" – at this "elegant" new favorite in the Western Suburbs; N.B. there's pleasant patio seating.

Itto Sushi ❶🖾   22 | 12 | 20 | $31
2616 N. Halsted St. (Wrightwood Ave.), 773-871-1800;
www.ittosushi.com
"Basic" "no-frills sushi" and other "authentic Japanese fare" bring loyalists to this longtime Lincoln Park neighborhood "favorite"; it's "friendly" and "family-owned", with "attentive service", making it "great for the price – even if the decor won't win any awards."

Izumi Sushi Bar & Restaurant ❶   ▽ 23 | 18 | 19 | $33
731 W. Randolph St. (Halsted St.), 312-207-5299;
www.izumisushi.com
A "hidden" contemporary Japanese "jewel" and sake bar in the Market District, this "quiet alternative" to some of its noisier neighbors harbors "terrific" "innovative sushi" in a "fun" setting with "great background music"; raters reckon

it's "worth a return visit" and owls hoot that it's "open late" (2 AM on Fridays and Saturdays, midnight otherwise).

Jack's on Halsted   21 | 17 | 19 | $36 |
3201 N. Halsted St. (Belmont Ave.), 773-244-9191;
www.jackjonesrestaurants.com
The menu is "daring", the setting "denlike" and most of the "dates are of the same sex" at this seasonal New American "on the edge of Boys Town", where the "casual" "fine dining" has its constituents, as does the "nice brunch" and "perfectly twinkly" "upscale atmosphere" afforded by the "great attached wine bar, outdoor patio and fireplaces"; doubters have decided it's "dependable but not extraordinary", though theatergoers think it might be the "best of the pre–Briar Street options."

Jacky's Bistro   23 | 20 | 23 | $44 |
2545 Prairie Ave. (Central St.), Evanston, 847-733-0899;
www.jackysbistro.com
New American meets "hearty French" in the near North Suburbs at this "cozy place to linger over a good meal" "in a bistro setting" with an "impressive wine list" and "excellent service"; those who judge that "Jacky's departure hasn't hurt" call it "a sure bet", but other jurists are jaded by his "absence from the kitchen" – not to mention the "city prices."

J. Alexander's   20 | 19 | 20 | $31 |
1832 N. Clybourn Ave. (bet. Willow & Wisconsin Sts.),
773-435-1018
4077 Lake Cook Rd. (bet. I-294 & Sanders Rd.), Northbrook,
847-564-3093
1410 16th St. (bet. Castle Dr. & Spring Rd.), Oak Brook,
630-573-8180
www.jalexanders.com
Chums of this Traditional American chain champion its "hearty" "grown-up" "comfort food" offered in a "spacious", "conversation-friendly" "steakhouse atmosphere" with "solid service", "comfortable seating" and "no hype", cheering "your dollar is well spent" for a "date" or a "family meal – without going over the top"; still, some chowhounds are "unimpressed" with what they find to be "formula" fare, especially "in a city of excellent independent dining" options.

Jane's   21 | 19 | 21 | $30 |
1655 W. Cortland St. (Paulina St.), 773-862-5263;
www.janesrestaurant.com
It's "cozy but alive" "with good vibes" at this "adorable", "crowded" "place for a date", "for girls to catch up or for a family brunch" that's "tucked away" on a Bucktown "residential street"; the New American–Eclectic edibles include "some unique takes on comfort food" and "plenty

of grazing for vegetarians", and "now that they've expanded, the waits aren't so bad" – and, as always, it's "nice to enjoy dining outside in warm weather."

JAPONAIS   24 | 26 | 20 | $58

600 W. Chicago Ave. (Larrabee St.), 312-822-9600;
www.japonaischicago.com
"Toward the top of the list for sushi", this Near West "up-market [Japanese] fusion" "hot" spot dishes out a "re-markable menu" of "innovative cuisine" and "dazzling decor" enhanced by a "very attractive crowd of twenty- to fiftysomething" "eye candy"; ok, it's a "budget buster", "but you're paying for" the "chic, happening ambiance" (and folks "love" the "hoppin' lounge" "on the river"), though classicists who call it "too trendy for its own good" also aren't savoring the "serious attitude."

Jay's Amore Ristorante 🗷   – | – | – | M

(fka Amore)
1330 W. Madison St. (bet. Ashland & Racine Aves.),
312-829-3333; www.amorechicago.com
Habitués of the West Loop's former Amore who "hope the new owners kept the cooks" will be happy to hear they've been retained, as well as the extensive menu of "solid", "predictable" Northern Italian classics "at reasonable prices", though the cozy exposed-brick-and-wood interior has been dressed up with tablecloths, mirrors and art-work, art deco light fixtures and plasma TVs playing sports in the bar; P.S. it's a "great place to go before a Bulls or Blackhawks game."

Jilly's Cafe   23 | 17 | 23 | $40

2614 Green Bay Rd. (Central St.), Evanston, 847-869-7636;
www.jillyscafe.com
"Romantics" frequent this "tiny" New American–New French "treasure" in the near North Suburbs for "consis-tently high-quality food and service" amid "charming" country inn surroundings that feel "cozy and familiar, even if it's your first visit"; claustrophobes caution "go on a slow night", though, or you'll find yourself "listening to three conversations at once" in the "crowded" setting; P.S. "Sunday brunch is a great buy."

Jin Ju   22 | 20 | 20 | $31

5203 N. Clark St. (Foster Ave.), 773-334-6377
The "fresh and creative" "upscale Korean food with a twist" at this Andersonville spot may be "a bit pricey" for the genre, but it comes with "great style" and "hip, dark" ambiance that "makes even a bad date tolerable"; even those who generally "eschew trendy ethnic-tini drinks" swear that "their soju concoctions hit the spot" – which is part of why it's "noisy" and "packed on week-ends" with "pretty people."

JOE'S SEAFOOD, PRIME STEAK & STONE CRAB
26 21 25 $57

60 E. Grand Ave. (Rush St.), 312-379-5637;
www.joesstonecrabchicago.com
Some sated surveyors swear this River Norther, a "great Midwestern version of Joe's Stone Crab" in Florida, is "better than the Miami original" thanks to "wonderful seafood feasting", "terrific" prime steaks and "to-die-for sides and Key lime pie", all "professionally served" in a "classic", "clubby", sometimes "raucous" setting; still, waverers who wither during the "long waits (even with reservations)" figure "for this kind of money" you could "head south to SoBe for the real thing."

Joey's Brickhouse
18 17 16 $25

1258 W. Belmont Ave. (Racine Ave.), 773-296-1300;
www.joeysbrickhouse.com
Lakeview locals are glad to have this "interesting take on" Traditional American "home cooking" – including a "great [jazz] brunch" – in the neighborhood, especially since it's "very kid-friendly" and "fits any budget"; supporters say it "should be more popular", but critics call out "sporadic service" and "hit-or-miss" cooking as hindrances.

John's Place
18 13 17 $20

1200 W. Webster Ave. (Racine Ave.), 773-525-6670
"Homey-hip" and "family-friendly", this Lincoln Park "neighborhood haunt" is regarded as "reliable" for "solid, basic American food" with an "excellent kids' menu"; some commenters cavil it "could use some menu updates", while others veto it as a "veritable babypalooza", but moderates maintain it's "much more enjoyable now that one room is for adults" and the other for families with kids – except at "crowded weekend brunch."

Joy Yee's Noodle Shop
21 11 15 $16

2159 S. China Pl. (Archer Ave.), 312-328-0001
521 Davis St. (Chicago Ave.), Evanston, 847-733-1900
1163 E. Ogden Ave. (Iroquois Ave.), Naperville, 630-579-6800
www.joyyee.com
"Gargantuan portions" at "modest prices" draw "noisy" "crowds" to this Asian noodle network wielding "a wide variety of unusual dishes" – "the menu has a picture of every" item – and about "a billion choices" of "awesome bubble teas" and "excellent fruit drinks" ("with blenders whirring above the din"); though they're "extremely popular", a faction feels the meals "lack authentic taste."

Julius Meinl Café
21 21 19 $14

3601 N. Southport Ave. (Addison St.), 773-868-1857;
www.meinl.com
"Attention is paid to every last detail" at this "civilized" Lakeview coffeehouse, a "truly Austrian cafe experience"

where patrons polish off "pastries to die for", "crave"-worthy salads and soups, "the best coffee in this country" and a "ridiculous selection of teas" "served on silver platters" in a "fancy European dining room" with occasional "live classical music" – small wonder "it's become a favorite spot (if you can get a seat)."

Kabul House　　　　20 | 13 | 20 | $18
3320 Dempster St. (McCormick Blvd.), Skokie, 847-763-9930;
www.kabulhouse.com
For "an excellent intro to an unusual cuisine", try this North Suburban "gem" where "authentic" Afghani fare (including "mouthwatering vegetarian entrees") is "humbly prepared and served" in "modest surroundings" by a staff that "values your business"; it's also a "good place to take kids with an adventurous palate", even if the "limited menu" "never changes", and though there's "no alcohol", you can BYO; N.B. the city sequel is no more.

Kamehachi　　　　22 | 18 | 19 | $32
240 E. Ontario St. (bet. Fairbanks Ct. & St. Clair St.), 312-587-0600
1400 N. Wells St. (Schiller St.), 312-664-3663 ◗
Westin River North, 320 N. Dearborn St. (Kinzie St.), 312-744-1900
City Park Complex @ BIN 36, 275 Parkway Dr. (Aptakisic Rd.), Lincolnshire, 847-541-8800
Village Green Shopping Ctr., 1320 Shermer Rd. (Waukegan Rd.), Northbrook, 847-562-0064
www.kamehachi.com
Raters rely on this "traditional Japanese" clan for "fresh sushi", as well as "really good non-sushi" sustenance, in settings that vary by venue (the Old Town location has a "nice garden in the summer"); perhaps it's "not innovative", but it's certainly dependable – though hedgers who hint it "has not kept up" in the raw-fish race bemoan "bite-sized portions" and "hit-or-miss" help.

Kan Zaman　　　　▽ 21 | 16 | 18 | $25
617 N. Wells St. (Ontario St.), 312-751-9600
"Yummy", "interesting" Lebanese food (including a "great veggie platter"), as well as comfortable "booths" and "coveted pillow couches" – plus "the sounds and sights of belly dancing [on weekends] while you smoke" hookahs – combine to make this River North BYO an exotic "good time."

Karma　　　　▽ 24 | 28 | 20 | $42
Crowne Plaza Hotel, 510 E. Rte. 83 (Rte. 45), Mundelein, 847-970-6900; www.karmachicago.com
With a "room that feels more like a trendy Downtown hot spot than a [North] Suburban hotel restaurant", this "beautiful" "surprise" "in an unexpected location" – Mundelein's Crowne Plaza Hotel – serves "elegant", "genuinely good" Asian fusion fare amid "cool" decor that

reminds some of a "postmodern rice paddy" (careful: "don't step into the reflecting pool").

Karyn's Cooked ▽ 19 | 17 | 19 | $22 |
738 N. Wells St. (Superior St.), 312-587-1050; www.karynraw.com
"For those who like to eat healthy or vegan, but still want good, tasty food", this "small", "*très* chic" River North "gem" with a "copper-accented" interior fills the bill with "vegetarian gourmet" fare (including Sunday brunch), "high levels of comfort and class", and organic beers and wines; still, some carnivores call it a "weird trip", yawping "you gotta wanna eat this stuff before you come."

Karyn's Fresh Corner ▽ 17 | 14 | 15 | $27 |
1901 N. Halsted St. (Armitage Ave.), 312-255-1590; www.karynraw.com
If you like it raw, consider this casual cafe/market and fine-dining BYO combo in Lincoln Park offering all-day dining (including Sunday brunch) on 'raw vegan living foods'; the casual side, affiliated with a holistic health center, offers an all-you-can-eat buffet plus ice cream and sandwich bars, while the restaurant has a serene spa-like setting with outdoor seating.

Katsu Japanese ▽ 26 | 18 | 21 | $45 |
2651 W. Peterson Ave. (California Ave.), 773-784-3383
Seekers of "sublime sushi" say it's "well worth the detour" to this "off-the-beaten-path" Northwest Sider filleting the "freshest fish around", including "noteworthy items from the market in Tokyo", and serving "some Japanese dishes not commonly found in other restaurants"; "Katsu and his wife make every guest feel like longtime friends" – or "like royalty" if you opt for "the omakase meal, ordered in advance and not on weekends" for larger parties.

Kaze Sushi 24 | 20 | 19 | $45 |
2032 W. Roscoe St. (Seeley Ave.), 773-327-4860; www.kazesushi.com
Disciples of this "elegant", "upscale" Roscoe Village Japanese "standout" devour its "inspired", "innovative sushi" "with amazing seasonal toppings", urging others to "just do the chef's choice menu – you won't regret it" ("you pick from a price range"); passers perceive the personnel as "pretentious", though, and the eats "too experimental" ("I don't like my sushi oiled and 'shroomed") and "overpriced for the serving size"; P.S. "excellent outdoor seating" entices in warm weather.

Keefer's ☒ 23 | 22 | 22 | $51 |
20 W. Kinzie St. (Dearborn St.), 312-467-9525; www.keefersrestaurant.com
"Known for its excellent steaks but offering great food in all categories", including "wonderful seafood", "Keefer's is a keeper" to coveters of its "contemporary American"

"urban"-"chic" setting ("more stylish" "than the typical steakhouse"), "attentive staff" and "great happy-hour grown-up bar scene" with "fish bowl–sized martinis"; challengers who lack "expense accounts" complain about the "steep prices", though, suggesting you "try it for lunch", as the tariff is "easier to handle."

KEVIN ⊠　　　　　　　26　22　23　$58
9 W. Hubbard St. (State St.), 312-595-0055;
www.kevinrestaurant.com
Kevin Shikami's "passion for food shows" in his "excellent" and "visually stunning" "haute" New French–Asian fusion fare at this "refined" River Norther with "beautiful, calming decor" that's "equally good for business or romance"; still, contributors concerned about "uneven" experiences cite an "elitist attitude", saying they'd more easily tolerate the price tag "if only the service lived up to the food"; N.B. a new Loop location is planned.

KiKi's Bistro ⊠　　　　　23　19　22　$44
900 N. Franklin St. (Locust St.), 312-335-5454;
www.kikisbistro.com
"There's a reason the classics are classic" crow confreres of this "real bistro" that "looks like it belongs in the French countryside", despite its River North setting; the "mature crowd" that calls it a "cozy" and "affordable" "delight" with "consistent preparations" of "traditional fare" says it "never changes, thank goodness", though some "underwhelmed" upstarts find "nothing memorable" about this "old-fashioned" offering.

Kinzie Chophouse　　　　20　17　20　$45
400 N. Wells St. (Kinzie St.), 312-822-0191;
www.kinziechophouse.com
"Under the radar" in River North, this "red-blooded steakhouse" is a "cozy little corner place with lots of regulars" who tout is as "tried-and-true", with "very tasty" steaks and chops served in a "friendly" setting that's not as "glitzy" or "plastic" as some competitors' (and "a good choice for lunch if you're near the Mart"); still, walletwatchers might consider it more often if they "cut the portions and prices in half."

Kit Kat Lounge & Supper Club ◗　15　19　19　$33
3700 N. Halsted St. (Waveland Ave.), 773-525-1111;
www.kitkatchicago.com
"Nothing like being serenaded with torch songs by a drag queen while you're eating a steak" say supporters who go for the "amazingly fun" entertainment and "expansive list" of "cleverly named cocktails" – not the "merely average food" – at this Eclectic Boys Town eatery that's "popular for bachelorette parties"; P.S. there's also "great outdoor seating."

Kitsch'n on Roscoe
17 | 19 | 18 | $18

2005 W. Roscoe St. (Damen Ave.), 773-248-7372
Kitsch'n River North
600 W. Chicago Ave. (Larrabee St.), 312-644-1500
www.kitschn.com
"Kitschy, kooky" and "kid-friendly", this "groovy" couple of "retro" "trips" are "just plain fun" "for fans of '60s/'70s TV and memorabilia", with a "surprisingly creative menu" of Eclectic "comfort food" at "reasonable prices"; still, bummed buzzkills bag the "weird concoctions" and "seriously cheesy" concept, and some raters regard the River North branch as "much less cozy than the Roscoe Village" original (which is "even better when the back garden is open"); N.B. hours vary by location and season.

Kizoku Sushi & K Lounge
▽ 25 | 22 | 21 | $47

358 W. Ontario St. (Orleans St.), 312-335-9888;
www.kizokusushi.com
"Inventive presentations" of "stellar sushi" and "innovative drinks" impress indulgers in the "enjoyable" (if "pricey") experience at this "lovely, tranquil" River North Japanese "beautifully done up in a lounge style" – plus "people are talking about" its "bold", "buzz-generating" 'body sushi' offering, wherein raw-fish fare is served atop a scantily clad woman (starting at $500 for a party of four); N.B. the ratings may not reflect the post-*Survey* arrival of new owners and the addition of French-Vietnamese dishes.

Klay Oven
20 | 15 | 17 | $33

414 N. Orleans St. (Hubbard St.), 312-527-3999;
www.klayovenrestaurant.com
"Good, basic Indian" fare that's "fresh" and "beautifully served" makes this "serene" River Norther a "solid" choice for city dwellers; it may not be "as authentic as the places on Devon", and the decidedly "typical" decor adds up to rather "bland ambiance", but its "buffet lunch is a deal" – and it's "great for pickup" too.

Kohan Japanese
– | – | – | M

University Village Mktpl., 730 W. Maxwell St. (Halsted St.),
312-421-6254
The South Loop's down-and-dirty Maxwell St. Market now boasts a string of spiffy storefronts, including this Japanese steak-and-sushi setup where the dining-room grilling lacks the circus factor typical of the old-guard chains; the clean, casual space – done up in wood and slate, ceramic tiles and backlit paper panels – is similarly gimmick-free.

Koi
19 | 22 | 18 | $30

624 Davis St. (bet. Chicago & Orrington Aves.), Evanston,
847-866-6969; www.koievanston.com
To gourmands who get this "upscale Chinese-sushi" hybrid as "a great addition to the Evanston dining scene",

there's gold in the "delicious Pan-Asian fare", "excellent drink list including rare and delicious teas" and "hip" "yet elegant" environs with a "welcoming fireplace"; on the flip side, disheartened diners "wish" the "expensive", "inconsistent food" and sometimes "inattentive staff" "lived up to the style."

Koryo
▽ 19 | 16 | 20 | $23

2936 N. Broadway St. (bet. Oakdale & Wellington Aves.), 773-477-8510

Surveyors split over whether this "trendy" "upscale" Lakeview Korean is "authentic" and "interesting" (with "real kimchi" that "would make a statue sweat") or overly "Americanized" and "bland", with some moderates maintaining the "menu offers a variety of choices for both the timid and adventurous"; eaters agree, however, on the "helpful" nature of the staff.

Kroll's
– | – | – | M

1736 S. Michigan Ave. (18th St.), 312-235-1400; www.krolls-chicago.com

Green Bay's Lambeau Field neighbor and butterburger stalwart (the patties arrive on buttered, toasted buns, hence the name) encroaches into Bears territory – the South Loop near Soldier Field, no less – with this American oupost whose menu features items both traditional (deep-fried cheese curds, chili with spaghetti, milkshakes) and contemporary (salads, wraps); the casual, upscale space, with upholstered booths, high-top tables, sports memorabilia and a vast bar/lounge, though, bears little resemblance to the retro diner-style original.

Kuma's Corner ◐
– | – | – | I

2900 W. Belmont Ave. (Francisco Ave.), 773-604-8769; www.kumascorner.com

"Gaining in popularity", this "wonderful addition" to Logan Square is a "cozy" spot with "great service" and "excellent" American "bistro food", "from crab cakes and Kobe [beef] to the world's best macaroni and cheese"; "don't let the tattoos and piercings fool you": the "nice staff" is "extremely knowledgeable about food, wine and beer pairings" – and "the patio is terrific."

Kuni's
25 | 14 | 19 | $31

511-A Main St. (bet. Chicago & Hinman Aves.), Evanston, 847-328-2004

For 20 years, faithful fish fans have flocked to this "consistently excellent" North Suburban, the "best in a wide, wide radius" for sushi and sashimi that "can't be beat for flavor or freshness", "beautifully carved by Kuni-san", "a traditional sushi master", as well as "a full range of other Japanese dishes"; N.B. impatient sorts are advised to go early, as they don't take reservations.

Kyoto ▽ 22 | 16 | 20 | $28

*2534 N. Lincoln Ave. (Altgeld St.), 773-477-2788;
www.kyotochicago.com*
*Best Buy Shopping Ctr., 1408 Butterfield Rd. (bet. Finley Rd. &
Highland Ave.), Downers Grove, 630-627-8588 ⍉*
1062 Gage St. (Green Bay Rd.), Winnetka, 847-784-9388
Raters who regard the raw fish at this "friendly" trio of
Japanese outposts in the town and country as "excellent"
also recommend the "combination plate that fills you up for
a very reasonable price"; still, some diners who deem the experience merely "decent" recommend takeout; N.B. the
ratings may not reflect recent menu and decor changes.

La Bocca della Verità 18 | 15 | 19 | $30

*4618 N. Lincoln Ave. (bet. Lawrence & Wilson Aves.),
773-784-6222; www.laboccachicago.com*
A "quaint" "neighborhood Italian" with "family character", this Lincoln Square spot has adherents who admire
its "simple, delicious" fare and "homey atmosphere", saying it "will bring you back to that last Roman holiday"; a
chorus of antis, though, claims that it's "nothing special"
and the output is "overpriced for what it is" – though the
"outdoor dining is comfortable."

La Bonita Ixcapuzalco Recipes 21 | 15 | 18 | $32

(fka Ixcapuzalco)
*2165 N. Western Ave. (bet. Armitage & Fullerton Aves.),
773-486-7340*
"Authentic Mexican food" from the recipes of the former
Ixcapuzalco (the last Bahena bastion in town, as the brothers are no longer involved here – or in Chicago) makes
amigos at this "out-of-the-way" Bucktown cantina with
"superior moles", "unreal tamales" and "great
margaritas" – all "without the pretense"; still, some
mournful Mex lovers rue the "cavernous" new digs with
an "odd layout", saying the "original location had more
character", while others just wonder "what happened?"

La Cantina ⍉ 19 | 18 | 22 | $32

*71 W. Monroe St. (bet. Clark & Dearborn Sts.), 312-332-7005;
www.italianvillage-chicago.com*
"Part of the Italian Village" complex (and of "Chicago history"), this Northern "Italian seafood" "classic" has been
serving it up in a "straightforward" manner for 50 years in a
"quaint, dark basement" setting that regulars find "comfortable and familiar" – "get a booth near the fish tanks"
"for romance or privacy" – and "excellent for pre-theater
or Symphony Center dining" due to its central Loop locale.

La Cazuela Mariscos – | – | – | I

6922 N. Clark St. (bet. Farwell & Morse Aves.), 773-338-5425
"Amazing", "inexpensive" "fresh fish served Mex-style" is
the draw at this "fun", "friendly" Rogers Park BYO taqueria

where the "brightly lit" "coffee-shop ambiance" comes complete with "Formica tables" and outdoor seating in season; P.S. "it helps to know Spanish."

La Crêperie 20 17 16 $22
2845 N. Clark St. (bet. Diversey Pkwy. & Surf St.), 773-528-9050; www.lacreperieusa.com
Devotees declaim "don't mess with anything" at this Lakeview lair that "seems like it should be located off a cobblestone side street" – from the "wonderful", "huge" "crêpes and other traditional French [bistro] dishes" to the "well-worn", "old-world" "dive" digs that may make you "want to smoke long, thin cigarettes and feverishly scribble manifestos"; demi-mondaines also dig the "easy-on-the-wallet" prices, "excellent brunch" and "romantic, bohemian garden area."

La Cucina di Donatella ▽ 22 15 16 $31
2221 W. Howard St. (Ridge Blvd.), 773-262-6533
The namesake owner's "personal touch" and "European zest for life" are evident at this Rogers Park "favorite", where "everything is cooked to order" from a menu of "sophisticated, super-fresh" seasonal Italian cuisine ("diners can stuff themselves and never touch a tomato"); expect "genuine trattoria atmosphere" with an "open kitchen" and "small outdoor dining area", and remember "to bring your own wine."

La Donna 19 16 19 $29
5146 N. Clark St. (Foster Ave.), 773-561-9400; www.ladonnaitaly.com
Amici announce it's "always crowded and for good reason" at this Andersonville "neighborhood" ristorante cooking a "combination of authentic Italian dishes" and some "with creative touches" ("oh, the pumpkin ravioli!") in a "casual-romantic" setting "with floor-to-ceiling windows"; conflicted consumers mark it "middle of the pack", though, and note that it's "not comfortable."

La Fette – – – E
163 W. North Ave. (bet. LaSalle & Wells Sts.), 312-397-6300; www.lafette.net
Its "balanced" New American–French "bistro cooking" appeals to champions of this "small" and "friendly" "undiscovered gem" in Old Town, home to an "unassuming, ever-changing menu" served with "personal attention" in a "quaint", "romantic" room; N.B. the global grape list spotlights Illinois wines.

La Fonda Latino 19 15 17 $26
5350 N. Broadway St. (Balmoral Ave.), 773-271-3935
"Authentic Colombian", including "awesome arepas" and "great empanadas", plus other South American table treats are the call at this "cozy" "plantain paradise", a

"great little place to try something different" set behind an "unassuming facade" in Andersonville; well-wishers also write about the "wonderful lunch buffet" and "tropical fruit juices", and there are those who "would kill for the sangria recipe."

La Gondola   – | – | – | I |

Wellington Plaza, 2914 N. Ashland Ave. (Wellington Ave.), 773-248-4433; www.lagondolachicago.com

"Extremely reliable old-school" "bargain Italian" such as "homemade pastas", "terrific pizza" and "kick-ass eggplant Parmesan" is still being served in this "small" Lincoln Park longtimer in a "strip mall" with a lot of "parking spots"; fans who feel it's "better for takeout" or delivery may be pleased by a post-*Survey* renovation.

Lake Side Café   – | – | – | I |

1418 W. Howard St. (Sheridan Rd.), 773-262-9503; www.lake-side-cafe.com

Value-conscious vegetarian specialists have set up shop in this smart, casual Rogers Park storefront with about a dozen bamboo tables and a 95 percent organic menu offering lots of vegan options and ever-changing specials; place your order with the cooks at the counter and they'll bring it to you (the same multitaskers also make a broad range of beverages, including smoothies, juices, tea and coffee drinks).

Lalo's   16 | 16 | 17 | $23 |

Midway Int'l Airport, 5757 S. Cicero Ave. (55th St.), 773-838-1604
1960 N. Clybourn Ave. (bet. Clifton Ave. & Cortland St.), 773-880-5256
500 N. LaSalle St. (Illinois St.), 312-329-0030
3515 W. 26th St. (bet. Drake & St. Louis Aves.), 773-522-0345
4126 W. 26th St. (Kedvale Ave.), 773-762-1505
3011 S. Harlem Ave. (31st St.), Berwyn, 708-484-9311
1432 Waukegan Rd. (Lake Ave.), Glenview, 847-832-1388
804 S. Oak Park Ave. (Rte. 290), Oak Park, 708-386-3386
425 S. Roselle Rd. (bet. Schaumburg Rd. & Weathersfield Way), Schaumburg, 847-891-0911
www.lalos.com

A "good variety" of "solid", "Americanized Mexican food served in a fun party atmosphere" with "powerful" "fishbowl" "margaritas" and "mariachi" music (at some sites) is enough for frequenters of this family of "kid-friendly" cantinas; still, some say "skip it" due to "subpar" sustenance without "much flair or flavor", while other "disappointed" diners deem them "not authentic."

Landmark ●   21 | 22 | 22 | $43 |

1633 N. Halsted St. (North Ave.), 312-587-1600

"The BOKA boys [Kevin Boehm and Rob Katz] did it again" at this Lincoln Park "see-and-be-seen" "hit in the making", where a "trendy, thirtysomething crowd" indulges in "quality" New American offerings from an exhibition kitchen presented in a "chic" setting whose "various levels and nooks" – including a "noisy", "funky lounge" – feature "different feels"; P.S. it's "convenient to the theaters" nearby.

L'anne ⊠   ▽ 20 19 15 $48
221 W. Front St. (bet. Hale St. & Wheaton Ave.), Wheaton, 630-260-1234; www.lannerestaurant.com
A "unique", "inventive menu" of Vietnamese-focused French-Asian fusion fans the flames for followers of this "quaint" West Suburban supplier of a "city dining experience", which for critical contributors can include "portions" that "are very small in comparison to the prices" and "spotty service"; N.B. a piano player tickles the ivories on weekend nights.

LAO SZE CHUAN HOUSE   24 10 16 $19
1331 West Ogden Ave (Main St.), Westmont, 630-663-0303
LAO SZE CHUAN SPICY CITY ●
2172 S. Archer Ave. (Princeton Ave.), 312-326-5040
SZECHUAN HOUSE
321 E. Northwest Hwy. (Hicks Rd.), Palatine, 847-991-0888
www.laoszechuan.com
Those who "like it spicy" say "chef Tony" Hu delivers "the real thing" with his "fresh, well-seasoned, authentic dishes" at these Szechuan-Mandarin mainstays; of the service surveyors say "some days it's good, some days it's not", but they still swear the "Chinatown establishment sets the standard" (it's "worth the occasional line-out-the-door wait") and the suburban sites are the "best around" of their kind; N.B. the Decor rating may not reflect the Taylor Street branch's closing or the Westmont's relocation.

La Peña   ▽ 20 13 16 $24
4212 N. Milwaukee Ave. (Montrose Ave.), 773-545-7022; www.lapenachicago.com
Expect a "great evening" at this "fun", "bustling" Northwest Sider serving "good portions" of "innovative Ecuadorian preparations", including "lots of fish and seafood dishes", plus "some of the best cocktails" such as its signature tropical-fruit margarita; this place "pumps with energy" (i.e. "can be noisy") since there's nightly live music or DJ entertainment and a dance floor – perhaps the sidewalk seating is quieter.

la petite folie   24 19 19 $44
Hyde Park Shopping Ctr., 1504 E. 55th St. (Lake Park Blvd.), 773-493-1394
"Hyde Park's sole claim to fine dining" rests with this "fancy" Classic French "surprise" "hidden" "in a strip mall", serving "top-notch traditional" cuisine with a "criminally cheap wine collection" in its "lush Parisian rooms"; even surveyors who sense the "service is not as profes-

sional as the food" and find the whole affair "behind the times" agree it's of "generally high quality", and the "early-bird prix fixe" dinner and "lunches are a fantastic value."

La Piazza ⌦   ∇ 25 | 21 | 24 | $35

410 Circle Ave. (Madison St.), Forest Park, 708-366-4010;
www.piazzacafe.com

Effusive eaters enthuse about this "excellent find" in the Western suburbs for "simply outstanding" regional Italian that's "authentic, freshly prepared" and "elegantly presented" with "attentive service", "usually with a visit from chef-owner" Gaetano di Benedetto, "a real charmer"; look for "lots of" "strong" choices among the "fresh, creative daily specials and traditional favorites on the menu", as well as a "great wine list" and "unique decor"; N.B. no relation to the Naperville spot of the same name.

La Piazza ⌦   – | – | – | M

Naperville Plaza, 192 W. Gartner Rd. (Catalpa Ln.),
Naperville, 630-305-9280

This "great little" independent Naperville Italian-Eclectic is "better than it looks from the outside", with an "interesting menu" of "imaginative cuisine" and a "cozy", "understated" "cafe feel" that "adds to its appeal" – plus free weekly wine tastings are offered on Wednesdays; N.B. no relation to the Forest Park spot of the same name.

La Sardine ⌦   23 | 20 | 22 | $41

111 N. Carpenter St. (bet. Randolph St. & Washington Blvd.),
312-421-2800; www.lasardine.com

"Well-executed *classique* French" bistro fare packs 'em into this "delightful" West Looper that's "perfect for a Paris-style lunch or dinner" but with "better service" – plus it's "not as frenetic as" its tiny sister, Le Bouchon (though it can be just as "noisy when busy"); P.S. the penny-wise praise the "half-price wine nights on Mondays" and "Tuesday night prix fixe (a steal)."

La Scarola   23 | 12 | 17 | $32

721 W. Grand Ave. (bet. Halsted St. & Milwaukee Ave.),
312-243-1740; www.lascarola.com

"Consistently one of the best medium-range" Italian *ristoranti* around, this "crowded", "bustling" "Near Wester" features "excellent", "no-nonsense" "comfort food" (kudos for the heaps of "fresh pastas"); enthusiasts insist that if you "eat there more than once they treat you like family", even if some critics don't dig being "crushed into the little storefront" space.

Las Tablas   21 | 13 | 16 | $24

2965 N. Lincoln Ave. (Wellington Ave.), 773-871-2414
4920 W. Irving Park Rd. (Cicero Ave.), 773-202-0999

It's "always hopping" at these "warm and friendly" Colombian steakhouses serving "different and tasty" "meat, meat and more meat" "on wooden tablas" – with, some say, "uncomfortable benches" – that add up to "great value for the money" (plus "BYO helps you save" even more); locationwise, the Lincoln Park branch is "more authentic" while the Northwest Side spot is more "family-friendly", but both are "especially busy on weekends."

La Strada Ristorante 🗷   19 | 17 | 19 | $38
155 N. Michigan Ave. (Randolph St.), 312-565-2200; www.lastradaristorante.com
Raters who rely on this quarter-centarian for "consistently good", "real Italian" fare also like its "lively bar", "windows overlooking Michigan Avenue" and setting "near Millennium Park and the Art Institute"; "other than its convenient location" in the Loop, though, "nothing sets it apart" according to detractors who decry the decor as "dark" and "dated", bemoan the food as "bland" and condemn the service as "cavalier."

La Taberna Tapatia ●   ▽ 21 | 10 | 15 | $21
3358 N. Ashland Ave. (Roscoe St.), 773-248-5475
"Interesting selections" of "not-the-basic Mexican" served in small-plate format make friends for this "hip" haunt in Roscoe Village, where "yummy margaritas, a nice outdoor area" and DJ entertainment Wednesday–Sunday augment the appeal; it's "small" and popular with "celebrating groups", though, so be warned that a "shortage of tables" can "lead to lines."

La Tache   21 | 20 | 19 | $39
1475 W. Balmoral Ave. (bet. Clark St. & Glenwood Ave.), 773-334-7168
Andersonville has adopted this "popular hideout" for "solid" "traditional French" bistro plates – as well as some featuring "creative twists"; it's "a great deal for Sunday brunch", especially "outside when summer finally finds Chicago", but a few gourmets grade it "good but not spectacular", while motivational experts maintain that the "service could be better."

La Tasca   23 | 21 | 21 | $32
25 W. Davis St. (Vail Ave.), Arlington Heights, 847-398-2400
27 S. Northwest Hwy. (Touhy Ave.), Park Ridge, 847-698-4500
www.latascatapas.com
Respondents pick this pair of Spanish purveyors in the Northwest Suburbs for "a great variety of options" in the small-plate department (though "full entrees are available" as well), plus "killer sangrias"; their "fun", "friendly" settings make them "great places to go with friends" or "kids" – or even "to have a romantic evening" with that special someone.

La Vita

∇ 20 21 23 $34

1359 W. Taylor St. (Loomis St.), 312-491-1414;
www.lavitarestaurant.com

For surveyors who flag this "real [Northern] Italian" as a
Little Italy "favorite", the cuisine is "a cut above the average", as are the "excellent service and wine list"; it's "not
one of the most famous", but partialists praise the "pretty"
place with "great atmosphere" as "well worth a visit";
N.B. you can catch rays on the rooftop in warm weather.

Lawry's The Prime Rib

24 21 23 $49

100 E. Ontario St. (Rush St.), 312-787-5000; www.lawrysonline.com

"There's still something exciting about seeing them roll a
cart up and carve off a caveman-size piece of prime rib"
"with all the trimmings" ("love the spinning salad bowl"
and the "good Yorkshire pudding") for fans of this "old-
school" Traditional American "meatery" in River North's
"historic", "ornate" McCormick mansion, it's "getting long
in the tooth but is still a classic", and while not everyone
agrees it's "worth the price", the "delicious sandwiches"
at lunch are certainly "a value."

Le Bouchon ☒

22 17 19 $39

1958 N. Damen Ave. (Armitage Ave.), 773-862-6600;
www.lebouchonofchicago.com

Bistro junkies "just can't get enough of" this "lively, authentic" Bucktown "institution" that "attracts well-
mannered diners" looking for "solid" "country French"
"favorites" – "some of the best" around – courtesy of
Jean-Claude Poilevey's kitchen; no wonder many are willing to put up with "interminable waits for a table" in
"noisy", "closetlike" confines, and service that swings
from "wonderful" to "grumpy."

LE COLONIAL

23 24 21 $46

937 N. Rush St. (bet. Oak & Walton Sts.), 312-255-0088;
www.lecolonialchicago.com

"Beautiful people" consume "beautiful food" – "high-
quality", "traditional" "French-influenced Vietnamese"
preparations "you long for later" – at this Gold Coast "semi-
chain" outpost "blending romantic and trendy" within an
"ethereal" environment that fairly "oozes Saigon" (plus a
"sexy, sultry" "world-class bar upstairs"); there's nothing
like "a private balcony table overlooking Rush Street for a
romantic evening", but even so, quibblers question "sky-
high prices" for "sparse portions."

LE FRANÇAIS ☒

28 25 28 $93

269 S. Milwaukee Ave. (Dundee Rd.), Wheeling, 847-541-7470;
www.lefrancaisrestaurant.com

"Thank you for coming back to us" say surveyors about the
return of "masterful" chef Roland Liccioni, who has "re-
created the magic" at this "delightful, upscale special-

occasion" North Suburban spot after "many ownership changes" with his New French cooking featuring "bold, delicious flavors" and "incredible sauces"; serving the "select clientele" are "helpful" staffers who are "professional" but "not afraid to be human", and the wine list is similarly "outstanding", so few fault it for being "fully priced" – especially given the "reasonable prix fixe lunch"; N.B. jackets are suggested.

LE LAN ⊠   26 | 22 | 24 | $56
749 N. Clark St. (Chicago Ave.), 312-280-9100;
www.lelanrestaurant.com
"Elegant" New French–Vietnamese fusion fare featuring a "quiet innovation in flavors" and "outstanding presentations" lures a "lively" crowd to this "dark, stylish" den in River North that sports "spare", "tasteful decor", a "service-oriented" staff and "some gems" on its "terrific wine list"; conversely, a coterie of critics "expected more" "given its lineage" – executive chef Roland Liccioni (Le Français) collaborated with Arun Sampanthavivat (Arun's) in conceiving the menu.

Lem's BBQ ●𝄒   ▽ 24 | 4 | 13 | $16
311 E. 75th St. (bet. Calumet & Prairie Aves.), 773-994-2428
It's all about "great" "BBQ at an unbeatable price" at this "takeout-only" spot that's "worth the journey" to the Far South Side for what cohorts crow "could be the best ribs" in Chicago ("get extra sauce" for the "lean, tender smoky meat"); N.B. they're open till 2 AM nightly, closed Tuesdays.

Leonardo's Ristorante   ▽ 23 | 19 | 25 | $37
5657 N. Clark St. (Hollywood Ave.), 773-561-5028
Discoverers of this Northern Italian, an "unexpected gem in an upcoming area of town", salute its "great food and value" that's "definitely worth checking out"; "really nice waiters", "widely spaced tables" and "modest wine prices" also help to make it a "nice" (if sometimes "noisy") addition to Andersonville.

Le P'tit Paris   ▽ 22 | 18 | 23 | $51
260 E. Chestnut St. (Dewitt Pl.), 312-787-8260
Camarades of candlelit Continental-Gallic dining appreciate this "gem" in the Streeterville site of the former Zaven's, where "retro selections" of "very good, rich food" are "professionally" served in an atmosphere "friendly" enough to call "a French version of *Cheers* after your first visit"; N.B. the Food rating may not reflect the post-*Survey* appointment of Michael Foley (ex Printer's Row) as consulting chef.

Les Deux Autres   ▽ 27 | 21 | 23 | $57
462 N. Park Blvd. (bet. Crescent Blvd. & Duane St.), Glen Ellyn, 630-469-4002
"Surprisingly sophisticated" yet "less stuffy than its [unaffiliated] predecessor, Les Deux Gros", this West Suburban

"secret" in an upscale "strip-mall location" renders "out-standing", "refreshing" New French "taste combinations" from chef Greg Lutes (owner Louisa Lima is pastry chef); still, some peg it as "pricey for suburbia", while others report "erratic service."

LES NOMADES ☒   28 | 26 | 28 | $90

222 E. Ontario St. (bet. Fairbanks Ct. & St. Clair St.), 312-649-9010; www.lesnomades.net

"Despite a change in chef", this "refined" former private club in Streeterville "still satisfies": newcomer Chris Nugent "uses generous quantities of luxury ingredients" in his "excellent" New French cuisine, which is backed by a "fine" wine list, "superb service" and a "formal" (some say "stuffy") setting whose "understated", "hushed" tone befits "a romantic rendezvous" or "an important business dinner" for a "cut-above" clientele that can afford "top-of-the-line prices."

LE TITI DE PARIS   26 | 24 | 25 | $63

1015 W. Dundee Rd. (Kennicott Ave.), Arlington Heights, 847-506-0222; www.letitideparis.com

"Still a superb spot" under longtime chef and now owner Michael Maddox, this "island of culinary excellence among the strip malls and highways" of the Northwest Suburbs issues "essential modern French cuisine" along with an "encyclopedic wine list"; a "fresh service perspective" contributes to a "fine-dining value" "without the pretense" – though some conservatives consider the style too "friendly" "for a fancy restaurant."

Le Vichyssois   ▽ 24 | 21 | 22 | $53

220 W. Rte. 120 (2 mi. west of Rte. 12), Lakemoor, 815-385-8221; www.levichyssois.com

Traditionalists who "miss real French cuisine the way it was meant to be done" "wish they lived closer" to Bernard Cretier's "out-of-the-way" Northwest Suburban "bastion" of "authentic", "old-school" Franco fare that's been "very consistent over" the past 30 years; stalwarts suggest you "get the prix fixe menu and relax in the gracious atmosphere", even if "the service is sometimes not up to the cuisine."

LOBBY, THE   23 | 26 | 23 | $49

Peninsula Hotel, 108 E. Superior St., 5th fl. (bet. Michigan Ave. & Rush St.), 312-573-6760; www.peninsula.com

Lobby loiterers revel in the rarefied air of this "understated but extremely elegant" River North hotel retreat with "gorgeous floor-to-ceiling windows" (that "high ceiling matches the prices") and an "excellent", "light" seafood-centric Continental menu supplemented by "wonderful afternoon tea", a "decadent" "chocolate buffet" and jazz band on Friday and Saturday evenings, and a "fabulous

Sunday brunch"; the jury is still out, though, on whether the service is up to "the standards of the Peninsula."

LOU MALNATI'S PIZZERIA   24 13 17 $18
439 N. Wells St. (Hubbard St.), 312-828-9800
3859 W. Ogden Ave. (Cermak Rd.), 773-762-0800
958 W. Wrightwood Ave. (Lincoln Ave.), 773-832-4030
85 S. Buffalo Grove Rd. (Lake Cook Rd.), Buffalo Grove, 847-215-7100
1050 E. Higgins Rd. (bet. Arlington Heights & Busse Rds.), Elk Grove Village, 847-439-2000
1850 Sherman Ave. (University Pl.), Evanston, 847-328-5400
6649 N. Lincoln Ave. (bet. Devon & Pratt Aves.), Lincolnwood, 847-673-0800
131 W. Jefferson Ave. (Washington St.), Naperville, 630-717-0700
1 S. Roselle Rd. (Schaumburg Rd.), Schaumburg, 847-985-1525
www.loumalnatis.com
Standing "supreme", this "local chain" boasts a "cult following" of "addicts" who relish its "ridiculously good", "real Chicago pizza" – both the "decadent deep-dish" and the "even-better thin-crust" version – and "love the butter crust", "pure, simple sauce" with "chunks of tomato" and "thick cheese"; still, its reign at the top of the pie charts "of the known world" (and the local competition) is "not undisputed", with some citing "inconsistent service" and "cookie-cutter decor" as drawbacks.

Lou Mitchell's   22 11 19 $15
565 W. Jackson Blvd. (Jefferson St.), 312-939-3111 🕀
O'Hare Int'l Airport, Terminal 5, 773-601-8989 ◑
"Welcome to the City of Big Shoulders" at this "landmark" West Loop coffee shop, a "piece of old Chicago" serving a "great" American breakfast still "in the skillet" as well as other "honest diner food" from the crack of dawn to mid-afternoon; the retro setting's "kitschy", the "veteran servers can be insulting" and the "cash-only [policy] is a pain" – and "prepare to wait in line" (with free "doughnut holes and Milk Duds to nosh on"); N.B. the airport outpost is a quick take-out station.

Lovell's of Lake Forest   20 23 22 $53
915 S. Waukegan Rd. (Everett Rd.), Lake Forest, 847-234-8013; www.lovellsoflakeforest.com
Boosters believe this "classy" capsule "belongs in the top flight of Chicago suburban choices" thanks to its "lovely" "North Shore decor" done up with "NASA mementos" and "Apollo 13 artifacts", chef-owner Jay Lovell's "imaginative-without-being-cute" "gourmet" New American cooking and the chance to meet his father, "real hero and astronaut" Jim Lovell – though others fault the "pseudo-formality", "uneven service" and food that "fails to please for the price"; P.S. "check out the basement bar and grill for a less expensive visit."

Lucca's   19 22 20 $35

2834 N. Southport Ave. (Wolfram St.), 773-477-2565;
www.iloveluccas.com

This "lovely little corner restaurant" in Lakeview is a "neighborhood favorite" to locals who like its "quaint atmosphere" ("love to see the latest artwork for sale on the walls") and "surprisingly private" "alfresco dining in the summer", as well as its "carefully crafted plates" featuring "a delicious blend" of Mediterranean and Traditional American flavors; still, some who "wouldn't rush back" submit "if only they put more effort into execution, this would be a terrific spot."

Lucia Ristorante   ▽ 22 14 19 $22

1825 W. North Ave. (Honore St.), 773-292-9700

An "interesting combination of deli and eatery", this Wicker Park BYO is a "fun place to go with friends" for "delicious" Italian fare; the "friendly" service includes attention from the "hands-on owner", and it's "great for a quick lunch" as the counter "up front makes the best sandwiches in the neighborhood."

Lula   25 17 19 $29

2537-41 N. Kedzie Blvd. (bet. Fullerton Ave. & Logan Blvd.),
773-489-9554; www.lulacafe.com

"The official cool spot of Logan Square", Jason Hammel and Amalea Tshilds' "arty" "cafe" with "high (organic) ideals and reasonable prices" "stakes out a territory midway between trendy and comfort food" with an "Eclectic" "vegetarian- and vegan-friendly" menu "marrying complex flavors"; the "funky" setting with "rotating art" is home to a "hip crowd and servers" – in fact, the only "bad news" is that "the no-reservations policy leads to long waits every night of the week."

LuLu's Dim Sum & Then Sum   19 14 17 $20

804 Davis St. (Sherman Ave.), Evanston, 847-869-4343;
www.lulusdimsum.com

For a fix of "very good Americanized" Pan-Asian small plates, "soups and noodle dishes that never disappoint", "Northwestern students" and others "who don't want a big bill" descend upon this Evanston "hangout" offering a "fantastic array" of foods amid "fun decor using everything from wild colors to funky art to Godzilla figurines"; purists, however, pan the provender as a "pale imitation" of the original cuisine.

Luna Caprese   ▽ 25 15 20 $34

2239 N. Clybourn Ave. (Greenview Ave.), 773-281-4825

A "sweet, cozy, date spot" in Lincoln Park, this "undiscovered gem" serves a "diverse menu" of "wonderful" Southern Italian sustenance, including "housemade pastas", along with "well-priced wines"; adding to the warm "welcome" of its "hospitable chef-owner" is the "wonderful aroma" of its "quaint" setting, which just might make "you feel like you're in an Italian home."

Lupita's   21 | 15 | 19 | $20
700 Main St. (Custer Ave.), Evanston, 847-328-2255;
www.lupitasmexicanrestaurant.com
Regulars rate this "pleasant and bright" North Suburban "neighborhood place" as "better than a typical Mexican restaurant has to be" thanks to "very good food" featuring "homemade sauces" and "extra-special menu specials"; of course, "dynamite margaritas" also add to the festivities, as does the "daily entertainment of people-watching" and "live guitar music on weekends."

Lutnia   – | – | – | E
5532 W. Belmont Ave. (Central Ave.), 773-282-5335
"People wanting to explore the world via their meals" promote this "elegant Polish venue" on the Northwest Side that makes you "feel you have gone to Warsaw", "with true old style you don't find often anymore" – including "some things cooked at your intimate and carefully decorated table" by "people [who] try very hard to give you a pleasant, satisfying experience"; N.B. live piano music is offered Thursday–Sunday.

Lux Bar ☻   17 | 19 | 18 | $30
18 E. Bellevue Pl. (State St.), 312-642-3400; www.luxbar.com
"For the young, successful" "super-tight jeans" and "busy power-lunch crowds", this casual Gold Coaster (a spin-off of Gibsons, "without the wallet-breaking cost") is a "swanky little cocktail" "hot spot" where "tasty staffers" serve "pretty decent", even "upscale" Traditional American "bar food" in a "fun, noisy", "upbeat city atmosphere"; conversely, some contributors criticize it as conceptually confused, i.e. "trying to be down-home, trendy and a neighborhood spot all in one."

L. Woods Tap & Pine Lodge   19 | 18 | 19 | $29
7110 N. Lincoln Ave. (Kostner Ave.), Lincolnwood, 847-677-3350;
www.leye.com
"Consistently good, standard" Traditional "Americana fare" feeds fans of this "comfy" "rib, steak, burger and bar joint" with a "woodsy" "Wisconsin"-esque "cabin look" located "halfway between the North 'burbs and the city"; unhappy campers, however, size it up as "spectacularly ordinary"; P.S. when faced with the "sometimes long wait", regulars report "the take-out [store] is a viable alternative."

MAGGIANO'S LITTLE ITALY   20 | 19 | 20 | $31
516 N. Clark St. (Grand Ave.), 312-644-7700
Oakbrook Center Mall, 240 Oakbrook Ctr. (Rte. 83), Oak Brook,
630-368-0300

(continued)

(continued)
MAGGIANO'S LITTLE ITALY
1901 E. Woodfield Rd. (Rte. 53), Schaumburg, 847-240-5600
Westfield Shoppingtown, 175 Old Orchard Ctr. (bet. Golf &
Old Orchard Rds.), Skokie, 847-933-9555
www.maggianos.com
Regulars "rely" on these "red-sauce" "Italiano" chain joints for their "can't-lose formula" of "affordable", "hearty" "standards" served "family-style" in a "boisterous" "retro" atmosphere where "everyone always seems to be having a great time" – but some dissenters who knock what they call a "faux" vibe and "obscenely large portions" of "blah", "cookie-cutter" cuisine believe it's better to "bring the kids [than] the Italian food lovers."

Magnolia Cafe   25   21   22 $36
1224 W. Wilson Ave. (Magnolia Ave.), 773-728-8785
"Uptown needs a place like this" "sophisticated yet approachable" New American "neighborhood gem" serving "succulent" "gourmet" fare, "with regular changes to the [seasonal] menu" and "without the pretentious surroundings"; in fact, this "petite" place is "warm and inviting" enough to make you "feel like you're dining at your best friend's house" – even if "the seating is a bit tight."

Magnum's Prime Steakhouse   23   19   20 $50
777 E. Butterfield Rd. (bet. Highland Ave. & Meyers Rd.),
Lombard, 630-573-1010
1701 W. Golf Rd. (New Wilke Rd.), Rolling Meadows,
847-952-8555 ⌂
www.aceplaces.com
"Consistently good" prime "steaks as they should be" continue to please patrons ("more of a business crowd") of these suburban beeferies boasting "intimate" settings that smack of "city sophistication", with live piano music nightly and "nice people" on staff; skeptics, however, submit that "service varies widely" and the "enormous portions" are "pricey" but "not exceptional."

Maiz ⊄   ▽ 25   19   23 $24
1041 N. California Ave. (Cortez St.), 773-276-3149
"Absolutely delicious Mexican street treats" "based on corn products" and "made by hand" using "authentic everything" "speak of the culture of Mexico City" at this "unassuming" "Humboldt Park" "winner" (now in its third location) from chef-owner–head waiter Carlos Reyna; it's a "foodies' haven" "when you consider the quality", "unusual menu items" and "low prices"; N.B. it's cash only, and no reservations.

Mama Desta's Red Sea   ▽ 18   9   13 $19
3216 N. Clark St. (Belmont Ave.), 773-935-7561
"A solid choice" for "really tasty, filling, Ethiopian finger food" with a "good amount of spice and flavor" ("vegetar-

ians can't go wrong here"), this Lakeview longtimer remains a "fun" "place to share" an "inexpensive" "meal" and some "honey wine" "with a group of people" – as long as you don't mind the "ugly room" and "disappointing service."

Mambo Grill ☒ 19 15 16 $30

412 N. Clark St. (bet. Hubbard & Kinzie Sts.), 312-467-9797; www.mambogrill.com

Fans fandango to this "loud, upbeat" River North "nightspot" for "flavorful" Nuevo Latino cuisine and "bargain" drink specials; picky eaters "prefer the interesting" cocktails to what they consider to be "forgettable food" – and some even prefer "the people-watching to the cocktails"; P.S. it's also "good for lunch", with sidewalk seating in summer.

MANNY'S 23 8 15 $15

1141 S. Jefferson St. (Roosevelt Rd.), 312-939-2855 ☒
Midway Int'l Airport, 5700 S. Cicero Ave. (55th St.), 773-948-6300
www.mannysdeli.com

"The local color is laid on as thick as the corned beef" at this beloved South Loop breakfast-and-lunch "institution", an "anachronistic" "steam-table cafeteria, with sandwiches made to order", peopled "by old-timers, new wavers, tourists and politicians" enjoying a taste of "true Chicago" – so go ahead and "just yell out what you want" to the "countermen, who are caricatures of themselves" (and now you can pay by credit card); N.B. the airport site serves dinner and alcohol.

Marché 20 22 19 $44

833 W. Randolph St. (Green St.), 312-226-8399; www.marche-chicago.com

"Still going strong" as a "be-seen" boîte, this onetime Market District "pioneer" has evolved to "standby" status for its "boisterous" brasserie setting with "bizarre", "dramatic decor", "solid, classic [French] bistro fare" and "hipster staff"; ok, so it's "not as wild as it once was, but it still knocks the socks off out-of-towners, and it's fun even for locals", though its legacy of "lots of turnover" in the kitchen has some saying that "inconsistency is the downfall."

Margie's Candies 23 16 17 $11

1960 N. Western Ave. (Armitage Ave.), 773-384-1035 ◐
1813 W. Montrose Ave. (Ravenswood Ave.), 773-348-0400

Though "you can eat lunch or dinner" here, "it's really about the ice cream" at this Bucktown American "classic" "with an old-fashioned parlor feel", "disabled table jukeboxes" and "staffers in bow ties and vests", where "sundaes as big as your head" topped "with homemade caramel and fudge sauce" are served in "giant seashell bowls" (and don't forget to take home some "hand-dipped chocolates"); P.S. "they haven't updated it in years", but they have added a second scoop in Ravenswood.

Mas   22 | 19 | 20 | $37 |
1670 W. Division St. (Paulina St.), 773-276-8700;
www.masrestaurant.com
Still "trendy" and "entertaining", this Wicker Park "date-night place" issues "inventive" and "delicious" Nuevo Latino food, along with "wonderful cocktail choices", "attentive service" and a "great vibe" that have raters requesting "*mas, por favor*" – though budgeters balk, saying prices are "high" "for what you get"; N.B. sidewalk seating adds to the summer scene.

Matsuya ⏺   21 | 12 | 17 | $23 |
3469 N. Clark St. (Sheffield Ave.), 773-248-2677
Before the raw-fish frenzy, this "traditional" Wrigleyville Japanese "with a long history" was serving "solid and simple sushi" – along with "excellent chicken and steak teriyaki" and "really good udon" – in a "casual, family-friendly atmosphere" staffed by "competent" servers; devotees have decided it "deserves a spot on anyone's midweek list", but some saddened veterans swear it's gone "downhill."

Matsu Yama   ▽ 22 | 13 | 19 | $27 |
1059 W. Belmont Ave. (bet. Kenmore & Seminary Aves.),
773-327-8838; www.matsuyamasushi.com
"Tasty, inventive rolls" and "numerous traditional" Japanese selections, all "at a fair price", rack up a roster of regulars for this "unsnooty" Lakeview "sushi joint"; some say the "cooked dishes are not as good", and most agree there's "no atmosphere to speak of", but "BYO is a huge plus" and the "lunch specials are a buy."

Max & Benny's   – | – | – | I |
332 E. Illinois St. (bet. New St. & Park Dr.), 312-321-9490
461 Waukegan Rd. (bet. Dundee & Lake Cook Rds.),
Northbrook, 847-272-9490; www.maxandbennys.com
Streeterville supports this modern spin-off of a longtime North Shore deli classic, bringing big sandwiches, brisket, smoked fish, breakfast and soda fountain faves to the table along with updated options like tortilla wraps, veggie burgers and lots of salads; the decidedly untraditional loftlike space with booths and cafe tables, modern art and mosaic tile has a separate bar with flat-screen TVs and a carry-out counter offering house treats to go.

May Street Market ⊠   – | – | – | M |
1132 W. Grand Ave. (May St.), 312-421-5547
New American fare with German-Austrian and other global influences comes to the Near West neighborhood via this chic, moderately priced eatery; the neutral dining room is accented with open ductwork and a flowing vine mural while a separate lounge with plush aqua furniture is anchored by a massive flagstone wall with a candle-filled

alcove; N.B. the value-oriented wine list was created in conjunction with a retailer to reduce the usual markup.

Maza 23 16 19 $28
2748 N. Lincoln Ave. (Diversey Pkwy.), 773-929-9600
This "dreamy" Lincoln Park place for Middle Eastern mezze ("a million little plates" of "excellent appetizers", including lots of veggie options) is "family-owned and -operated with Lebanese graciousness" and is blessed with a "homey", "old-world feel" and an "eager-to-please staff"; in short, it's "just what you want in a neighborhood restaurant" – no wonder regulars "would eat here every night."

McCormick & Schmick's 21 19 20 $43
41 E. Chestnut St. (Rush St.), 312-397-9500;
www.mccormickandschmicks.com
Teeming with a "tremendous variety of" "good, fresh fish, simply prepared", this "clubby", "masculine" Gold Coast seafooder cheers chums with "a constantly changing menu", "private booths", a "nice summer patio" and a "happy hour that couldn't be happier", considering the "great specials"; raters who don't take the bait, however, rank the repasts as "run-of-the-mill, high-end chain food" "for expense-accounters" and say service swims between "delightful" and "uninterested."

Medici on 57th ● 18 16 13 $15
1327 E. 57th St. (bet. Kenwood & Kimbark Aves.),
773-667-7394
A sentimental "favorite" of South-Siders, this "classic Hyde Park" "college hangout" and BYO comforts colleagues with "consistent" Traditional American fare, including "juicy burgers", "very good pizza" and "nice" "breads baked next door", all dished up in a "dark", "traditional grunge" "coffee-house atmosphere" where it's "fun to read the writing on the walls" and "famous carvable wood tables"; P.S. "the patio garden is an oasis."

Meiji 24 23 21 $42
623 W. Randolph St. (bet. Desplaines & Jefferson Sts.),
312-887-9999; www.meijirestaurant.com
"Impress your date" at this West Loop "entrant in a crowded field" where the "upscale sushi" is "creative and novel" and the "other authentic Japanese dishes" include some "not found elsewhere"; the "attentive staff", "specialty martinis with Asian and American influences", and the "dark", "minimalist" ambiance also "shine."

Melting Pot, The 21 18 20 $41
Millennium Center Towers, 609 N. Dearborn St. (bet. Ohio & Ontario Sts.), 312-573-0011 ●
1205 W. Dundee Rd. (Arlington Heights Rd.), Buffalo Grove, 847-342-6022

(continued)

(continued)
Melting Pot, The
17 W. 633 Roosevelt Rd. (Summit Rd.), Oakbrook Terrace, 630-495-5778
255 W. Golf Rd. (bet. Higgins & Roselle Rds.), Schaumburg, 847-843-8970
www.meltingpot.com
If you relish a "long, leisurely" "interactive dining experience", this "enjoyable" city and suburban fondue family makes for a "unique night" of "dunkin' fun" – whether on "business", with "the whole family" or for a "romantic date"; still, authenticists assess the execution as "Americanized" and "too expensive" considering you're "cooking your own meal"; P.S. decor varies by location, but the River North branch has "one of the coolest bars in Chicago, where you can play chess, backgammon or shuffleboard."

Meritage Cafe & Wine Bar　　22　20　20　$43
2118 N. Damen Ave. (bet. Armitage & Webster Aves.), 773-235-6434; www.meritagecafe.com
With a focus on "delicious" Pacific Northwest preparations and a "special affinity for fish and game", an "always-innovative" seasonal New American menu is paired with an "extensive list" of regional wines at this "trendy, romantic" Bucktown "date spot" that also offers "upscale brunch"; there are those who find the service "uneven", though, and the fare "overpriced for what you get"; P.S. "the patio offers amazing calm and charm in an otherwise bustling neighborhood."

Merle's Smokehouse　　21　17　19　$24
1727 Benson Ave. (Church St.), Evanston, 847-475-7766; www.merlesbbq.com
Gluttons go for a "great meaty gnaw" at this "funky" North Suburban "palace of BBQ" that "delivers" "very good" "saliva-inducing" eats "with lots of options on the ribs preparation, sauces and sides", all served by a "friendly staff" in a "relaxed" "barnlike" atmosphere "that the college students love and adults enjoy" (or you can opt for delivery or carryout); a rack of "unimpressed" raters, though, judges it "just an average experience."

Merlo　　23　20　21　$44
2638 N. Lincoln Ave. (Wrightwood Ave.), 773-529-0747
16 W. Maple St. (bet. Dearborn & State Sts.), 312-335-8200
www.merlochicago.com
An "ever-changing menu" showcasing "sophisticated preparations" of "totally authentic" Bolognese fare – including some of the "best pasta in the city" ("you can tell it was just handmade") – with "authentic sauces" and "a quality wine list" are served in "charming, staid" settings to the tune of "opera music", making for "a special evening out" at this Northern Italian twosome (a Lincoln Park orig-

inal and a Gold Coast offshoot); "disappointed" diners who "were expecting more", however, point out that "prices have increased" and the "vibe is a little pretentious."

MESÓN SABIKA
23 | 21 | 19 | $35

1025 Aurora Ave. (east of West St.), Naperville, 630-983-3000

TAPAS GITANA
(fka Mesón Sabika)

Northfield Village Ctr., 310 Happ Rd. (bet. Willow Rd. & Winnetka Ave.), Northfield, 847-784-9300
www.mesonsabika.com

TAPAS VALENCIA
241 E. Lake St. (Lakeview Dr.), Bloomingdale, 630-582-1500; www.tapasvalencia.com

"Good choices for suburban tapas", this Spanish trio under the Mesón Sabika roof serves similar "strong" slates of "delicious" small plates plus "especially good desserts", "refreshing sangria" and "excellent Sunday brunch" – though those who nag it as "not all that inspired" also snark about "slow service"; "set in an old mansion", the Naperville original "makes you feel like a guest at a millionaire's estate" with a "most inviting patio"; N.B. the Northfield location has a new name, and the jury's still out on the recently added Bloomingdale bastion.

M. Henry
24 | 18 | 19 | $18

5707 N. Clark St. (Hollywood Ave.), 773-561-1600

"You can't get naughtier pancakes anywhere" than at this "imaginative, upscale" Andersonville BYO hosting New American breakfasts, brunches and lunches that are "always packed – and for good reason"; the "egg dishes hold surprise hot/sweet/tart tastes", the "vegetarian dishes are the bomb", the service is "friendly" and the "charming", "cozy" confines include "old windows suspended between tables to act as dividers"; sensitive sorts can't stand the "extreme noise level" and "lengthy waits", but hank-erers "wish they were open for dinner."

Mia Cucina
21 | 17 | 18 | $32

56 W. Wilson St. (Brockway St.), Palatine, 847-358-4900; www.miacucina.com

They "don't drown everything in garlic" at this "converted" Northwest Suburban "grocery store", where the "authentic [Northern] Italian cuisine" is served "at a reasonable price" by a "friendly" staff; P.S. "live [piano] music on weekends" makes the "cute" and "energetic" (some say "noisy") interior a "celebratory place."

Mia Francesca
23 | 17 | 19 | $32

3311 N. Clark St. (School St.), 773-281-3310; www.miafrancesca.com

"For a reasonably priced meal" from a "daily changing menu" of "high-quality and creative but approachable Italian food", "you "can't go wrong" at this "elbow-to-elbow" Lakeview "staple", progenitor of the prolific Francesca famiglia (live wires like "all the energy on the first floor" while refuge-seekers who "can't stand the noise" "ask for a table upstairs or in the carriage house"); meanwhile, weary wags wonder why there's "always a wait even with reservations", and a quorum of quibblers query "why is this place so busy?"

Michael ⚫ 25 | 18 | 17 | $50
64 Green Bay Rd. (Winnetka Ave.), Winnetka, 847-441-3100
Winnetkans "welcome" this "upscale" addition from chef-owner Michael Lachowicz (ex Le Français, Les Deux Gros), whose "well-crafted" New French fare with "brilliantly reduced sauces" is consumed in a "comfortable", "conversation-friendly" space; still, some fence-sitters feel its "food is better than the overall experience", saying it "needs time to perfect" the "somewhat bland" setting and "questionable service", while trenchermen suggest the "smallish" servings are "overpriced."

Mike Ditka's 20 | 19 | 19 | $43
Tremont Hotel, 100 E. Chestnut St. (Rush St.), 312-587-8989
"If you like big leather chairs, cigars and giant beers", you may want to intercept this "relaxed", "upscale Chicago-style" American steakhouse "adorned with sports memorabilia" and "testosterone", where you can dine on "succulent" meat ("gotta try 'da pork chop'"), "watch sporting events" with other "party animals" and perhaps even "shake hands with da coach"; fair-weather fans take a "pass", though, postulating the "food is not the important thing here" and designating it primarily for "dedicated Bears fans, dedicated smokers and dedicated tourists."

Milk & Honey 21 | 16 | 15 | $14
1920 W. Division St. (bet. Damen & Wolcott Aves.), 773-395-9434; www.milkandhoneycafe.com
The New American "food is particularly fresh" at this "cutie" of a Wicker Parker, where the morning meal is "better than breakfast in bed" (they mix "amazing" "granola you might dream about") and the "fantastic sandwiches" and "interesting salads" make for a "lovely lunch" – "whether you sit indoors or out"; "only counter orders are taken", and the "lines on weekends are out the door", but boosters who believe it's "worth it" ("if you can stand the cell phone and stroller" crowd) lament that "they're not open late enough."

Miller's Pub ⚫ 17 | 15 | 18 | $23
134 S. Wabash Ave. (bet. Adams & Monroe Sts.), 312-263-4988; www.millerspub.com
A "time-tested" Loop "landmark", this "true Old Chicago" "holdout" is a "classic watering hole" "with celebrity pic-

tures on the walls" and customers representing "a cross-section of humanity"; the "old-fashioned" American eats are "not haute cuisine", but they're "plain, good food" at a "bargain" price, and the "rough-around-the-edges but real" space is "bustling with activity at all hours" (the bar only closes between 4 and 10 AM); still, sterner surveyors deem it "dreary" and think "the menu, staff and decor all need an upgrade."

Millrose Restaurant & Brewing Co.   18 | 23 | 17 | $32
45 S. Barrington Rd. (Central Rd.), Barrington, 847-382-7673;
www.millroserestaurant.com
Northwest Suburbanites who "love" the "cheery", "kitschy suburban hunting-lodge" atmosphere at this compound of "old barns" with "many fireplaces" enthuse it's "easy to feel comfortable" here "for an after-work beverage or a nice dinner out" noshing on "decent American fare" with a "variety" of "good" "microbrewery" "beers that change with the seasons" (and some "stay for shopping at the country store"); still, critics contest it "could use better food."

Mimosa   23 | 17 | 22 | $39
1849 Second St. (bet. Central Ave. & Elm Pl.), Highland Park,
847-432-9770; www.mimosacafe.com
"Nice to have in Highland Park", this "pleasant" "hide-away" cooks up "carefully prepared" New French–Italian cuisine (including "seasonal specials") along with "interesting wine pairings", all "reliably served" by a "very good staff"; compatriots are also "comfortable" with the "quiet", candlelit confines, calling them more than "adequate for an in-town storefront restaurant."

Mirabell ⌧   ▽ 20 | 18 | 22 | $26
3454 W. Addison St. (bet. Kimball & St. Louis Aves.), 773-463-1962
For a schnitzel "fix", Bavaria-boosters bear toward the Northwest Side for "good, hearty" "old-style" "German food and beverages in one of the few such places left" – one where the "rustic" setting rife with steins, figurines, murals and staff in traditional costume is as heartwarming as the "reasonable prices"; N.B. there's outdoor garden seating.

MIRAI SUSHI ⌧   26 | 20 | 20 | $46
2020 W. Division St. (Damen Ave.), 773-862-8500
"In the face of a Chicago sushi explosion", this "hip" Wicker Park Japanese "remains the best" per raters who prefer its "pricey" but "pristine fish" – the "unusual" "maki don't disappoint but the quality of the straight-up sashimi sets this place apart" – or "put themselves in the chef's hands for a sublime omakase dinner"; add the "divine sake" (over 30 varieties) and the "scene", especially "upstairs", where it's "definitely darker and more swank", and it's no surprise satisfied surveyors make this their "go-to" raw fin-fare purveyor.

Miramar   19 19 20 $39
301 Waukegan Ave. (Highwood Ave.), Highwood, 847-433-1078;
www.miramarbistro.com
Fans of Gabriel Viti (Gabriel's, Pancho Viti's) say "Highwood
is hotter than ever" thanks to this "hopping" French-ster
"with a Cuban accent" and its "very good" "take on bistro
fare", "nice wine list (for a casual restaurant)", "well-
made mojitos" and "great people-watching" amid ambiance that's "quiet midweek" and a "hectic" "meet/meat
market scene" on the weekends (when DJ entertainment
adds to the "ridiculous noise level"); some say they "expected more" and hint that "service can be a little over-
bearing", but all agree the "outdoor seating is wonderful."

Mitchell's Fish Market   – – – E
Glenview Town Ctr., 2601 Navy Blvd. (bet. Eastlake Ave. &
Willow Rd.), Glenview, 847-729-3663;
www.mitchellsfishmarket.com
It's no fish tale: this upscale-casual Michigan-based chain
member in North Suburban Glenview's booming shopping-
dining enclave specializes in a vast variety of fresh-daily
seafood (from simple to internationally influenced) and a few
landlubber items as well, amid nautical decor with model
boats, an exhibition display room and oyster-bar accents;
N.B. there's outdoor dining and a literal fish market too.

Mity Nice Grill   18 15 18 $27
Water Tower Pl., 835 N. Michigan Ave., Mezzanine Level
(bet. Chestnut & Pearson Sts.), 312-335-4745; www.leye.com
"Nicer than a diner but still affordable", this "oasis" "in the
hubbub of Water Tower Place" dishes out "dependable"
Traditional American "comfort food" and "tiny desserts"
that "just hit the spot" "for only one dollar"; the "welcoming staff" and "cozy" "supper-club atmosphere" make it a
"great place to relax" (if you can "find" it "hidden away"
"in back of [the] food court"), though a share of shoppers
takes its measure as "mighty average."

Mizu Yakitori & Sushi Lounge   – – – M
315 W. North Ave. (Park Ave.), 312-951-8880
Yakitori is the specialty of this chic Old Town Japanese offering a menu of 20-plus skewered items charcoal-flamed
on an open grill, as well as traditional dishes such as tempura or tonkatsu, and the usual raw-fish suspects; you can
dine at the granite-topped sushi bar or in the adjacent dining room, where warm lighting and monochrome paintings
soften the stark black-and-white decor.

Mj2 Bistro ⊠   – – – M
800 W. Devon Ave. (Brophy Ave.), Park Ridge, 847-698-7020;
www.mj2bistro.com
"Nicely executed" Eclectic "cooking with Asian and South
American flair" has visitors to this Park Ridge bistro saying

"finally – creative food in the [Northwest] Suburbs"; "friendly service", a global wine list and "ok prices" are other reasons it's a "great find in an unexpected locale."

MK
26 24 25 $62
868 N. Franklin St. (bet. Chestnut & Locust Sts.), 312-482-9179; www.mkchicago.com
Owner Michael "Kornick has turned the toque over to Todd Stein" at this "suave" River North New American, a still-"humming" "hot spot" that's managed to "endure and re-invent itself", where the cooking is "outstanding without being fussy or pretentious", the "bi-level" "loft" interior is "sleek" and the "attentive, accommodating" staffers know the "masterful wine list" and cheeses "like it's their business"; some raters report "rushed service" and "dreadfully noisy" digs, but more maintain it's a "favorite."

MON AMI GABI
22 22 21 $41
Belden-Stratford Hotel, 2300 N. Lincoln Park W. (Belden Ave.), 773-348-8886
Oakbrook Center Mall, 260 Oakbrook Ctr. (Rte. 83), Oak Brook, 630-472-1900
www.monamigabi.com
There's "always a happy hubbub" at these "fun Frenchie bistros", "solid Lettuce" Entertain You city-and-suburban "standbys" serving "great, reasonably priced French standards", including "unbeatable onion soup" and "classic steak frites" with *magnifique sauces* (plus *loyalistes* "love the wines on the cart offered for tasting"); some purists purport that "the proliferation of locations makes even the original seem a little bit plastic", but friends insist "if you have to eat at a chain restaurant, this is the one."

Montarra
▽ 22 25 21 $45
1491 Randall Rd. (County Line Rd.), Algonquin, 847-458-0505; www.montarra.com
A "Chicago-like experience" "for the Northwest Suburbs", this "up-and-coming" New American's "excellent" if "expensive" entrees – including steakhouse favorites and "creative salads" – are served amid the "special ambiance" of an "extraordinary" space "dressed up" with genuine Dale "Chihuly glass sculptures"; some surveyors suggest it's "less unusual" than it was "when it opened", but many graders gauge it a "good choice for a celebration meal."

Moon Palace
▽ 21 13 20 $21
216 W. Cermak Rd. (Wentworth Ave.), 312-225-4081
"Surprisingly good Shanghainese dishes" – some "not really available elsewhere" in the area – join a roster of "reliable", "popular Chinese classics" and "a full bar" at this "cheap" Chinatown "standby" with "friendly service" and, sadly, some "shabby decor"; N.B. they offer validated parking.

MORTON'S, THE STEAKHOUSE   26 21 24 $59
65 E. Wacker Pl. (bet. Michigan & Wabash Aves.), 312-201-0410
Newberry Plaza, 1050 N. State St. (Maple St.), 312-266-4820
9525 W. Bryn Mawr Ave. (River Rd.), Rosemont, 847-678-5155
1470 McConnor Pkwy. (Meacham Rd.), Schaumburg,
847-413-8771
1 Westbrook Corporate Ctr. (22nd St.), Westchester, 708-562-7000
www.mortons.com
"Still the standard" for "scrumptious slabs of the best [prime] beef known to man", this "granddaddy" (tops among Chicago steakhouses) is a "candy store for carnivores" complete with the "show-and-tell" presentation cart, "huge sides" and "soufflés meant to be shared", a "great wine list" and a "professional staff"; decor at various locations may stray from the "quintessential", "manly" Gold Coast "mother ship", and some raters reckon it's "resting on its laurels", but a well-fed majority insists this "class act" is "worth" its "break-the-bank prices."

MOTO ⊠   25 23 26 $116
945 W. Fulton Mkt. (Sangamon St.), 312-491-0058;
www.motorestaurant.com
"Sophisticated palates who appreciate playfulness in cuisine" say "be prepared to be shocked and awed" at this "minimalist" Market District "marriage of science and food", where Homaro Cantu "does deconstructing wonders" with his five- to 18-course Eclectic tasting menus delivered by "knowledgeable" "staffers in lab coats"; to some "food geeks" its "amazing techniques" amount to "theatrical" postmodern "alchemy" that actually "tastes amazing", but some obdurate observers are "over the chef–mad scientist" thing.

Mr. Beef ⊠⇄   23 6 14 $9
666 N. Orleans St. (bet. Erie & Huron Sts.), 312-337-8500
"Digging in" to the "hot, delicious Italian beef" at this cash-only River North sandwich "dive" is "a Chicago tradition" for a big slice of stalwarts, as are the "surly guys behind the counter" and the "picnic tables" peopled by "cops, workers and execs"; as for "decor – who needs it?" ask insiders, considering you can just "close [your] eyes and feel the juice dripping down [your] arm"; P.S. rumor has it it's "Jay Leno's must-stop when in" town.

Mrs. Murphy & Sons Irish Bistro   ▽ 21 25 19 $29
3905 N. Lincoln Ave. (Byron St.), 773-248-3905;
www.irishbistro.com
Set "in a converted funeral home" in Lakeview, this surprisingly "lovely" contemporary Irish eatery boasts a "beautiful" interior with bars handmade in Ireland and three fireplaces; lauders love the "great" menu featuring upscale "twists on pub fare", which is paired with tap pours of Gaelic and Belgian brews plus a big native whiskey

selection, though voting vacillates on the service; N.B. live
piano music adds to the charm on weekends.

Mrs. Park's Tavern ●   17 | 15 | 17 | $33

Doubletree Guest Suites Hotel, 198 E. Delaware Pl.
(Michigan Ave.), 312-280-8882
A "good Streeterville option" for "comforting" Traditional
American eats (as well as offerings that are more "creative,
but not bizarre"), this "hotel eatery [in the Doubletree Guest
Suites] is actually popular with locals as well as convention-
eers" and a "pleasant" "spot to eat outside in the summer",
though faultfinders feel the "fair food" "fails to wow."

Mt. Everest Restaurant   21 | 14 | 18 | $22

630 Church St. (bet. Chicago & Orrington Aves.), Evanston,
847-491-1069; www.mteverestrestaurant.com
"Excellent" "Indian standards and some interesting
Nepalese homestyle dishes" "at reasonable prices" (including a "bargain" of a daily lunch buffet) please patrons
of this "popular", "comfortable" North Suburbanite with
"warm service"; holdouts, however, hedge by hinting that
the "Himalayan fare" is "great for Evanston" but "not as
good as on Devon Avenue."

My Pie Pizza   21 | 12 | 17 | $15

2417 N. Clark St. (Fullerton Pkwy.), 773-929-3380
2010 N. Damen Ave. (Armitage Ave.), 773-394-6900
"Classic, crispy, gooey thin-crust" and "great deep-dish"
"pizza is served in the pan so it stays hot at the table" at
this pair of "old-school" parlors where you can indulge in
"different pastas", "little sandwiches" and a "very good"
salad bar; the "dark", "kitschy, comfy '70s decor" at the
Bucktown original "hasn't changed in [almost] 30 years"
(though "the fireplace is a grand thing on a cold night"),
while the Lincoln Parker is BYO with limited seating.

Myron & Phil's Steakhouse   21 | 13 | 21 | $37

3900 W. Devon Ave. (bet. Crawford & Lincoln Aves.),
Lincolnwood, 847-677-6663; www.myronandphils.com
A "venerable North Side steakhouse", this "traditional"
Lincolnwood spot is a "reliable" "relic", "delivering a great
meal" – from "fish to steaks, with everything else in
between" – amid a "Rat Pack" "supper-club" setting for 35
years; "if you're under 75, you immediately drop the average age, but where else can you get a [complimentary] relish tray anymore?" ("chopped liver . . . mmm"); N.B. there's
piano music Thursday–Saturday nights and, in a nod to the
mod, the remodeled bar now sports plasma TVs.

Mysore Woodland   ▽ 17 | 9 | 13 | $18

2548 W. Devon Ave. (Rockwell St.), 773-338-8160
6020 S. Cass Ave. (60th St.), Westmont, 630-769-9663
Followers of this West Rogers Park BYO and its alcohol-
serving Westmont sibling say both are "hard to beat" for

"meatless dining" from an all-"vegetarian" menu of subcontinental standards; perhaps it's "not the Indian cuisine
most folks are used to", but supporters swear "you'll leave
very full, but be craving more very soon."

Nacional 27 ⌷   22 │ 24 │ 20 │ $42 │
325 W. Huron St. (Orleans St.), 312-664-2727;
www.leye.com
It's "a carnival for the palate" at this River North "hot spot"
with "breathtaking decor" that serves "Latin libations" and
a Nuevo Latino "smorgasbord" of chef Randy Zweiban's
"inventive", "well-prepared" fare, including "creative
tapas", "from every country south of the Rio Grande";
P.S. sedate sorts "beware": its usually "quiet", "cool vibe"
gives way "later in the evening" Thursdays–Saturdays "as
the main floor turns into a dance floor", with "salsa that
doesn't come in a bowl."

NAHA ⌷   26 │ 23 │ 24 │ $59 │
500 N. Clark St. (Illinois St.), 312-321-6242;
www.naha-chicago.com
Expect "unfussy", "innovative fine dining" at this River
North "favorite" that's considered "consistently among
the best"; Carrie Nahabedian's "exciting menu" of "fresh"
New American fare with "Mediterranean" flair is paired
with a "thoughtful wine list", "seductively served" by a
"cool staff" and "shown off" in a "clean-lined", "minimalist" space that "feels like a spa" – in fact, the "excellent"
experience is "only marred by the high decibel level"
"when it's crowded"; P.S. don't miss "one of the city's best
burgers (lunch only)."

Nancy's Original Stuffed Pizza   21 │ 10 │ 16 │ $18 │
2930 N. Broadway (Wellington Ave.), 773-883-1977 ●
3970 N. Elston Ave. (Irving Park Rd.), 773-267-8182 ⇅
940 N. York Rd. (Grand Ave.), Elmhurst, 630-834-4374
8706 W. Golf Rd. (Milwaukee Ave.), Niles, 847-824-8183
www.nancyspizza.com
"Zesty sauce is slathered on top of gooey cheese and
loads of toppings" to create the "delicious" stuffed pizza
at this pie panoply, which also garners zealots for its "filling pasta entrees" and "good antipasto salad" – plus you
can "feed your late-night cravings" at the Lakeview location; of course, since this is Chicago 'za we're talkin' about,
not everyone agrees "you can't beat it."

Narcisse ●   ▽ 20 │ 25 │ 22 │ $46 │
710 N. Clark St. (bet. Huron & Superior Sts.), 312-787-2675;
www.narcisse.us
Hungry "hip"-sters feel it's "fun to eat" at this "dark, swanky,
romantic and Euro" River North "champagne bar", a
"trendy", "unique" place to "nosh on [Eclectic] vittles
while nibbling your significant other" amid "velvety decor"

and lots of "eye candy" – though some lounge lizards insist it's "more for the bubbles than the food" ("a secondary issue"); N.B. there's DJ entertainment most nights.

Narra   18 22 17 $49
Hotel Orrington, 1710 Orrington Ave. (Church St.), Evanston, 847-556-2772; www.narrarestaurant.com
Set "in the gracious Hotel Orrington", this "cosmopolitan" steakhouse is blessed both with "minimalist", "Euro decor" that's "elegant for Evanston" and "a clever idea", cuisine-wise – namely, "the whole pick three sauces thing with the meat" (plus a choice from the "well-conceived wine selection"); for every optimist who believes it's "off to a good start", however, there's a holdout who harps it's "having growing pains", and self-styled consultants advise "keep the beautiful space but start over with" the "disappointing food", "spotty service" and "over-the-top prices."

New Three Happiness   19 11 17 $21
2130 S. Wentworth Ave. (Cermak Rd.), 312-791-1228
"The carts move fast and the staff talks faster" at this "busy" Chinatown mainstay serving "great dim sum" daily, as well as traditional Cantonese cooking; it's a "good place to bring large groups and families with kids or elderly relatives", even if "the atmosphere is lacking and the service is spotty"; N.B. no relation to the similarly named Three Happiness nearby.

Next Door Bistro ⌐   21 13 19 $34
250 Skokie Blvd. (bet. Dundee & Lake Cook Rds.), Northbrook, 847-272-1491
An "interesting mixture" of "very good" American (including "great" roast chicken) and Italian favorites "for a remarkably low price" is the draw at this "fun but always crowded" North Shore "neighborhood" eatery that's "still good after all these years" – but patrons who "prefer [Francesco's] Hole in the Wall", its co-owned next-door neighbor, mark this as merely its "waiting room", while hurt habitués heckle that "the host is only nice to his friends"; P.S. "it's about time to start taking credit cards – we're in a new millennium!"

Nick's Fishmarket   24 21 23 $56
Bank One Plaza, 51 S. Clark St. (Monroe St.), 312-621-0200 ☒
O'Hare Int'l Ctr., 10275 W. Higgins Rd. (Mannheim Rd.), Rosemont, 847-298-8200
www.nicksfishmarketchicago.com
One school of surveyors sees these "somewhat formal", "upscale" Loop and O'Hare area fisheries as "solid" choices for an "extensive selection" of "fine seafood" served by a "tuxedoed staff" in a "quiet" "supper-club setting" that's "good for business dinners" or a "date"; op-

posing forces feel these "stodgy" "throwbacks" with "unremarkable" underwater fare and "hit-or-miss service" "need to be revamped from decor to menu", and wallet-watchers wager "for these prices, you could buy oceanfront somewhere."

NINE ⊠ | 22 | 24 | 20 | $55 |
440 W. Randolph St. (Canal St.), 312-575-9900; www.n9ne.com

"To see or be seen, that is the question" at this "chic", "sleek", "slick" and "sexy" West Loop surf 'n' turfer where even those not into the "trendoid bar scene" admit the "inventive and beautifully served food" and "dramatic, architecturally stunning facility" (with a central champagne and caviar bar on weekends) make the "pageantry", "glitz factor" and "high prices" "worth the trip"; it's also a "great power-lunch spot" and "convenient to the Civic Opera House", though grudging graders say it doesn't quite "live up to the hype."

NOMI | 26 | 27 | 26 | $71 |
Park Hyatt Chicago, 800 N. Michigan Ave. (Chicago Ave.), 312-239-4030; www.nomirestaurant.com

"Ethereal" "zen" environs including "Chihuly chandeliers" and an "unbeatable view" of Water Tower earn our No. 1 Chicagoland Decor score for this Gold Coast "lap-of-luxury" lair where the "intriguing flavor combinations" of chef Christophe David's "exquisite" New French cuisine pair with "quality sushi" and an "excellent wine list" to warrant the "special-occasion" "splurge"; additional assets are the "discreet service", "killer Sunday brunch", "lovely outdoor terrace" and "very swishy bar", though you still have a segment that finds the service "stuffy" and doesn't relish "paying for the view."

Nookies ⌀ | 19 | 11 | 19 | $15 |
1746 N. Wells St. (bet. Lincoln & North Aves.), 312-337-2454

Nookies Too
2114 N. Halsted St. (bet. Dickens & Webster Aves.), 773-327-1400

Nookies Tree ◑⌀
3334 N. Halsted St. (Buckingham Pl.), 773-248-9888

"Tried-and-true", this trio of Traditional American BYOs slings "simply great breakfasts" ("wonderful pancakes", "large omelets") "any time of the day", and "diner" lunches and dinners, all at a "good value"; despite "mixed service", they're a "favorite" "for families", and "you can always find the boys out" at the Boys Town "gayborhood staple", "especially during the late night" (Too and Tree are open 24 hours on Friday and Saturday) – after which "the 'hangover helper' does not disappoint"; P.S. "get up early because the lines get long."

Noon-O-Kabab   ▽ 20 | 11 | 14 | $21

4661 N. Kedzie Ave. (Leland Ave.), 773-279-8899;
www.noonokabab.com
"Noon or night", this Northwest Side seller of sustenance
on a stick and "excellent baba ghanoush" is a safe bet for
people with a penchant for Persian, who prate that "the
food's so good you can't resist – and since it's so inexpensive, you won't need to"; some locals laud it as "something
good in the 'hood", while others who see it as "not the best
Middle Eastern" suggest you "stick with the kebabs."

NORTH POND   25 | 27 | 23 | $59

2610 N. Cannon Dr. (bet. Diversey & Fullerton Pkwys.),
773-477-5845; www.northpondrestaurant.com
The "uncommon combination" of Bruce Sherman's "wonderfully crafted" "seasonal" cuisine, a "tranquil", "idyllic
setting" of "lovely Arts and Crafts rooms" with "great skyline views" and an "excellent wine list" make this New
American "on the pond in [Lincoln] Park" "one of
Chicago's finest and most unique" places for a "romantic
meal or special occasion"; most surveyors "feel transported a million miles away", but others are earthbound by
"inconsistent food and service" and "prices that have
crept up"; P.S. they serve summer lunch and "delightful
Sunday brunch" year-round.

Oak Tree   17 | 15 | 15 | $21

Bloomingdale's Bldg., 900 N. Michigan Ave., 6th fl.
(bet. Delaware Pl. & Walton St.), 312-751-1988
"Standard" Traditional American fare "at ok prices" has its
place, such as when you're looking for a "good" breakfast
with "fresh-squeezed OJ", "a quick bite" "before a hard
day of shopping" or an early "pre-movie" dinner, and that's
what you'll find at this "diner" "oasis" in the Bloomie's
building, a "hangout for [Gold Coast] locals"; there's also a
"nice view if you are near the windows", though some
power-shoppers predict "inconsistent" service and "lots
of waiting"; N.B. alcohol is not served.

OCEANIQUE ⌀   27 | 21 | 24 | $52

505 Main St. (bet. Chicago & Hinman Aves.), Evanston,
847-864-3435; www.oceanique.com
"Unpretentious" "fine dining" is the house special at this
North Suburban New French "treasure" where chef-
owner Mark Grosz creates "a flawless assortment of
beautifully prepared dishes" featuring the "best seafood
in the Chicago area" according to our *Survey,* plus "plenty
of alternate choices for meat people"; expect an "excellent wine list" and "well-educated staff" in a "pleasant"
setting where you can "enjoy the food and your compan-
ions without being dressed to the nines" (though luxe-
lovers would "upgrade" the atmosphere); P.S. try "the $35
three-course dinner Monday–Friday."

O'Famé　　　　　　　　　　17　12　16　$22
750 W. Webster Ave. (Halsted St.), 773-929-5111;
www.ofame.com
"Both the thick and thin pizza", as well as "their signature salad", are "great" at this "friendly" and "unpretentious" Lincoln Park parlor with "fair prices" and "efficient service"; "everything else is pretty average", though, including the "unassuming decor", but at least the staff knows how to handle "groups and kids", making it a "good-in-'hood choice" – and "delivery is a plus."

Old Jerusalem　　　　　　　19　8　14　$14
1411 N. Wells St. (bet. North Ave. & Schiller St.), 312-944-0459;
www.oldjerusalemrestaurant.com
Some of "the best cheap food" in town is the "great Middle Eastern grub" – such as "yummy falafel" and "melt-in-your-mouth schwarma" – at this "laid-back" Old Town Israeli BYO that's been in business for three decades; the "simple" "small storefront" space is "friendly" and "family-run", but it's "not a date place, dude" (possibly why many consider it "great for delivery").

Olé Olé Ⓢ　　　　　　　　　–　–　–　M
5413 N. Clark St. (Balmoral Ave.), 773-293-2222
An upbeat mood prevails at this Andersonville addition with vibrant, modern decor (a spicy red color scheme, glass doors that open to the street) and a Nuevo Latino menu that updates everything from seviche to salads; N.B. there's no reserving, but the kitchen serves till 2 AM on weekends.

One North Ⓢ　　　　　　　　18　19　17　$34
UBS Building, 1 N. Wacker Dr. (Madison St.), 312-750-9700;
www.rdgchicago.com
"Cozy yet sophisticated decor", a "nice outdoor eating area" and a "convenient" Loop locale make this "bustling" New American a "great location for an after-work" "or pre-theater dinner" (plus there's a happenin' lunch scene); to some, the "consistent" eats are "very good", but badgerers believe that "unimaginative" fare, "spotty service" and "horrible acoustics" make this "much more of a watering hole than a dining destination."

ONE SIXTYBLUE Ⓢ　　　　　25　24　23　$56
1400 W. Randolph St. (Ogden Ave.), 312-850-0303;
www.onesixtyblue.com
"Exciting and adventurous meals" await at this "stylish" New French establishment co-owned by basketball icon Michael Jordan that's "worth the detour" to the fringe of the Market District for "terrific" cuisine "balancing creativity and simplicity" from Martial Noguier, "a chef who cares", plus "a good selection of reasonably priced wines" and a "beautifully designed" room by Adam Tihany;

it's a package that leads satisfied respondents to describe it as a "perfect place" "for a romantic dinner" or "before a concert at the United Center."

OPA Estiatorio   ▽ 19 | 19 | 19 | $30 |
950 Lakeview Pkwy. (Hawthorn Pkwy.), Vernon Hills, 847-968-4300; www.oparestaurant.com
"Very good Greek cuisine" "at a value", including plentiful seafood, with "wine prices" reminiscent of "what Greektown charged decades ago", lures Hellen-ophiles to this "pleasant" room in North Suburban Vernon Hills boasting "a nice patio overlooking" Bear Lake; P.S. it "can be noisy and crowded, especially on the weekends – lunch is much more sedate and comfortable."

Opera   23 | 23 | 20 | $42 |
1301 S. Wabash Ave. (13th St.), 312-461-0161; www.opera-chicago.com
Chef Paul Wildermuth "reinvents Chinese food" with his "brilliant, modern Pan-Asian cuisine" – including "gourmet vegan" options – at this "funky", "showy" South Looper with an "open", "exotic" atmosphere filled with a "bizarre mix of people"; it's "expensive", the "main room is noisy" at times and "the service could be more attentive", but the staff's "colorful", the "private" "little vault rooms" are "romantic" and the "huge sharing portions help control costs", as do the "great tasting menus" at various price points.

Orange   23 | 16 | 17 | $17 |
3231 N. Clark St. (Belmont Ave.), 773-549-4400
75 W. Harrison St. (bet. Clark & Federal Sts.), 312-447-1000
The Eclectic eats for breakfast, lunch and brunch (no dinner) are "totally tasty" at this "quirky" Lakeview and South Loop duo where the "creative spins on Traditional [American] reliables" include "inventive pancake recipes", "green eggs and ham" and "fantastic coffee" and "your own combinations" of "fresh-squeezed juices"; the "kicky" orange-themed settings can resemble "a madhouse on weekends" (especially Clark Street) with "long waits", and holdouts harangue the "hit-or-miss" experience is "not worth the hype and high prices."

Original Gino's East, The   22 | 13 | 15 | $19 |
2801 N. Lincoln Ave. (Diversey Pkwy.), 773-327-3737
633 N. Wells St. (Ontario St.), 312-943-1124
1807 S. Washington St. (bet. Foxcroft & Redstart Rds.), Naperville, 630-548-9555
15840 S. Harlem Ave. (159th St.), Orland Park, 708-633-1300
1321 W. Golf Rd. (Algonquin Rd.), Rolling Meadows, 847-364-6644

(continued)

(continued)

Original Gino's East, The

8725 W. Higgins Rd. (bet. Cumberland & River Rds.), Rosemont, 773-444-2244

Tin Cup Pass Shopping Ctr., 1590 E. Main St. (Tyler Rd.), St. Charles, 630-513-1311

315 W. Front St. (West St.), Wheaton, 630-588-1010

www.ginoseast.com

While none is the original 'Original', "the legend lives on" at these chain outposts for lovers of "scrumptious" "traditional Chicago deep-dish" pie with "cornmeal crust" ("nice thin-crust" too) and salads that are "just as good"; contributors call the rendition in the River North "tourist area" a "good place to take out-of-towners" to "write on" the "graffiti-laden walls" (they "were moved" from the "character-filled former" flagship), but doubters demand that management "take 'Original' the hell off the sign"; N.B. some sites are privately owned.

ORIGINAL PANCAKE HOUSE, THE 23 | 14 | 18 | $15

22 E. Bellevue Pl. (bet. Michigan Ave. & Rush St.), 312-642-7917 ⊽

2020 N. Lincoln Park W. (Clark St.), 773-929-8130 ⊽

Village Ctr., 1517 E. Hyde Park Blvd. (bet. 51st St. & Lake Park Blvd.), 773-288-2323 ⊽

5148 W. 159th St. (bet. Laramie & Le Claire Aves.), Oak Forest, 708-687-8282 ⊽

954 Lake St. (Forest St.), Oak Park, 708-524-0955

www.originalpancakehouse.com

WALKER BROS. ORIGINAL PANCAKE HOUSE

825 W. Dundee Rd. (bet. Arlington Heights Rd. & Rte. 53), Arlington Heights, 847-392-6600

620 Central Ave. (bet. Green Bay Rd. & 2nd St.), Highland Park, 847-432-0660

Lake Zurich Theatre Development, 767 S. Rand Rd. (Rte. 22), Lake Zurich, 847-550-0006

200 Marriott Dr. (Milwaukee Ave.), Lincolnshire, 847-634-2220

153 Green Bay Rd. (bet. Central & Lake Aves.), Wilmette, 847-251-6000

www.walkerbrosoph.com

"Loosen the belt a notch" before a visit to this chain of "quintessential" American pancake "joints" that's "exactly what it's supposed to be" — namely, "the standard-bearer" for "gimongous", "coma-inducing breakfasts" most "any time of day"; like the hours and credit-card policy, the settings vary by location, ranging from "worn-out" "diner" to "stained glass and wood", but the "long lines don't lie" about the "high-quality" and "reasonable prices"; P.S. though all are considered "egg-cellent", the Walker Bros. operation appears to have the edge decorwise.

Osteria Via Stato   21 19 21 $47
620 N. State St. (Ontario St.), 312-642-8450; www.leye.com
A "boffo" "family-style" Italian dining experience is on the
table at this Lettuce Entertain You "all-you-can-eat free-
for-all" in River North, where "you pick the main dish" from
"just a few choices" and "the food just keeps coming"; the
"stone-and-dark-wood decor provides a warm atmosphere", made even more "cozy" by "some communal
seating", but respondents who feel "rushed" gripe that the
"gimmick" is "too much circus" and say "service is a
work-in-progress"; P.S. if the fare seems "overpriced",
"eat at the much-cheaper enoteca in front."

Oysy   21 17 18 $31
50 E. Grand Ave. (bet. Rush St. & Wabash Ave.), 312-670-6750
888 S. Michigan Ave. (9th St.), 312-922-1127
315 Skokie Blvd. (Dundee Rd.), Northbrook, 847-714-1188
www.oysysushi.com
Enthusiasts explain that "everything's fresh and tasty" at
these "stylish and hip" South Loop, River North and North
Shore spots with "succulent sushi" and a "good selection"
of cooked Japanese fare, including "nice small plates",
served in a "beautifully minimal" "space-age environment"; lauders also love the "lunch specials", but some
suggest that the "pleasant but not very knowledgeable
servers" could provide "much better service."

Pacific Blue   ∇ 25 19 20 $35
536C Crescent Blvd. (Main St.), Glen Ellyn, 630-469-1080;
www.pacificbluerestaurant.com
"Succulent", "sophisticated and fresh seafood" appeals
to West Suburbanites who reel in the "reasonably priced
menu and wine list" and "conversation-friendly" beach-
house atmosphere (complete with "great" "live jazz on the
weekends") at this "nice neighborhood place" in Glen
Ellyn; N.B. a children's menu is available.

Palm, The   23 19 22 $56
Swissôtel, 323 E. Wacker Dr. (bet. Lake Shore Dr. &
Michigan Ave.), 312-616-1000
Northbrook Court Shopping Ctr., 2000 Northbrook Ct.
(Lake Cook Rd.), Northbrook, 847-239-7256
www.thepalm.com
"Filled with celebs and wannabes", these "venerable" Loop
and North Suburban "meat-palace" "classics" are known
for "excessive portions (at excessive prices)" of "prime
steaks" and "huge lobsters", plus "excellent service" and
"clubby, dark" decor "with nostalgia dripping from the
walls"; nonetheless, a contingent of contentious carnivores concludes there are "better options" "in a town with
a surplus of great steakhouses"; P.S. wallet-watchers
"love the family-style menu" special that feeds three,
available Sunday–Thursday (Northbrook only).

Pancho Viti's Mexican Cantina   12   15   16 $29
431 Temple Ave. (bet. Lauretta Pl. & Waukegan Ave.),
Highland Park, 847-433-5550; www.panchoviti.com
"When the garage doors open in the summer, you feel like
you are being served on a sidewalk in Mexico City" at this
"casual" North Suburban "hangout" from Gabe 'Pancho' Viti
(Gabriel's, Miramar); patient patrons are willing to "wait a
while for the recipes and staff to reach speed", but sour surveyors who report "bland food" and "weak drinks" say
"sorry, Gabe", pegging this "poor attempt" as his "only dud."

Pane Caldo   24   20   22 $57
72 E. Walton St. (bet. Michigan Ave. & Rush St.), 312-649-0055;
www.pane-caldo.com
"Genuinely interesting and well-prepared" Northern
Italian cuisine from a constantly changing menu and a
"wine list to die for" are presented by a "very good" staff
at this "serious", "sophisticated" Gold Coast "find" with
an "intimate" (i.e. "elbow-to-elbow") feel; penne-pinchers
warn, though, that it's "way overpriced", making it "a luxury to go here."

Papa Milano   18   12   18 $25
951 N. State St. (bet. Oak St. & Walton Pl.), 312-787-3710
"A dive" "but a classic", this Gold Coast Southern Italian
"neighborhood" "red-sauce" "joint" is a "throwback to
the '50s" (literally, as it opened in 1951) that stays perpetu-
ally "packed" thanks to "huge portions, good pizza and
friendly service" – plus "super prices" help make it a
"great place to bring the family"; P.S. efficiency experts
"wish they would [take] reservations."

Pappadeaux Seafood Kitchen   20   18   19 $33
798 W. Algonquin Rd. (Golf Rd.), Arlington Heights, 847-228-9551
921 Pasquinelli Dr. (Oakmont Ln.), Westmont, 630-455-9846
www.pappas.com
These sister suburbanite "chain"-sters lure fin-fans with
their "diverse menus" of "delicious", "fresh" fish with a
Louisiana "flair" – the "blackened dishes" have many
boosters – and "big, fun seafood-shack" interiors that are
pretty much "always deafening"; "large portions and fair
prices make them winners with families", but faultfinders
figure the food is "faux Cajun" and the "service is sometimes shaky"; P.S. "live [Saturday night zydeco] music is an
added feature" at the Westmont branch, and Arlington
Heights does a Sunday brunch buffet.

Parkers' Ocean Grill   21   21   21 $44
1000 31st St. (Highland Ave.), Downers Grove, 630-960-5701;
www.selectrestaurants.com
Serving "simple preparations" of "great seafood" in a
"lovely" "country-club atmosphere", this "large" West
Suburban "fish house" is "upscale without the snob ap-

peal", though a passel of parsimonious pollsters perceives it as "a bit too pricey" "for the delivered goods"; N.B. there's live music on weekends and a patio in season.

Park Grill

19 | 20 | 18 | $36

Millennium Park, 11 N. Michigan Ave. (bet. Madison & Washington Sts.), 312-521-7275; www.parkgrillchicago.com
"Amazing Millennium Park" is home to this "awesomely located New American" whose "menu with lots of variety will please upscale tourists and locals alike" (the "great burgers" get the most raves), as will the "fun view of the [ice] skaters" and "nice fireplace" in winter and "fabulous outdoor area in summer"; picky eaters postulate the "pretty good" "but expensive" "food isn't up to the challenge", though, making the "beautiful scenery" "the real star here", and advise that "service is uneven" since the "staff is stretched too thin."

Parlor ◐

19 | 19 | 20 | $33

1745 W. North Ave. (bet. Hermitage Ave. & Wood St.), 773-782-9000
"An interesting take" on "well-prepared", "down-home" Traditional American "comfort foods" ("e.g. meatloaf and hamburgers") and "a fun", "albeit small, bar" with "good wines by the glass" and retro cocktails make this "classy" "1940s"-inspired "joint" with a "comfy vibe" a "great new" addition to the Wicker Park neighborhood; N.B. since opening they've added a patio.

Parrot Cage, The ◪

– | – | – | M

South Shore Cultural Ctr., 7059 S. Shore Dr. (71st St.), 773-602-5333
A proving ground for its staff of Washburne Culinary Institute students (their classes are held upstairs), this New American on the Far South Side offers a reasonably priced seasonal menu in a white-tablecloth setting; the parrot theme is carried out in the tropical color scheme, with picture windows providing lake views.

Parthenon ◐

20 | 15 | 18 | $26

314 S. Halsted St. (bet. Jackson Blvd. & Van Buren St.), 312-726-2407; www.theparthenon.com
"Old-fashioned Greek" goodies are offered at "value" prices at this "unpretentious", "reliable and boisterous" Greektown bastion that "delivers what one expects" – "amazing" flaming saganaki ("watch your eyebrows!"), "homemade gyros" and "lamb, lamb, lamb"; it's "fun" "family-style dining", and there's also "free valet parking", even if more finicky factions figure fans of its "heavy food" and "gruff service" "must be into nostalgia."

Pasta Palazzo

22 | 15 | 18 | $17

1966 N. Halsted St. (Armitage Ave.), 773-248-1400
"Keep it on the down-low" cry coveters of the "cheap, good eats" at this Lincoln Park Italian "hideout", saying you're

"guaranteed a tasty meal" from a "simple but complete menu" of "fast-food pasta"; you can dine in the "cool, urban" space ("where you may share a long table with strangers") "if you don't mind the cramped" confines – otherwise, avail yourself of the "great takeout"; N.B. they now accept credit cards.

Pasteur　　　　　21 20 18 $36
5525 N. Broadway St. (bet. Bryn Mawr & Catalpa Aves.), 773-878-1061

With plans for its rumored remodeling closure indefinitely delayed, this "upscale" Edgewater New French–Vietnamese continues to offer its "unusual", "wonderful" cuisine within an "atmospheric" "colonial setting" with "high ceilings, large windows, tropical plants, rattan chairs, white tablecloths and slow-churning ceiling fans"; there are those, however, who "preferred the old Pasteur before it went upscale", saying "the food, while solid, is simply not worth the tariff"; N.B. a casual Rogers Park spin-off, Viet Bistro, is in the works.

Pegasus ◖　　　　　22 20 20 $28
130 S. Halsted St. (bet. Adams & Monroe Sts.), 312-226-4666
Pegasus on the Fly
Yorktown Ctr., 203 Yorktown Shopping Ctr. (Highland Ave.), Lombard, 630-424-1441
Midway Int'l Airport, 5700 S. Cicero Ave. (55th St.), 773-581-1522 ◖
www.pegasuschicago.com

"More upscale than some Greektown establishments", this "consistent" "favorite" "goes beyond the typical gyros or souvlaki" with "never-ending choices" of "hubcap-sized" Hellenic plates presented with "warm service" in a "bright, decorated room" – or "in summer" you can "sit on the rooftop deck" "overlooking Downtown", either "for drinks" or to order from "a smaller menu"; P.S. the airport stand is "a great quick meal at Midway" (and now there's one in the food court at Lombard's Yorktown Shopping Center).

Penang ◖　　　　　19 14 17 $22
2201 S. Wentworth Ave. (Cermak Rd.), 312-326-6888

"A nice break from the mainstream", this "reasonably priced" outpost in the "heart of Chinatown" features a "good mix" of "very tasty" Southeast Asian food on its "exotic menu", which includes "both Chinese Malaysian and ethnic Malay" fare, as well as some Thai and sushi offerings; still, some noshers needle that you "need to order well"; N.B. they've added a karaoke lounge upstairs, and insomniacs appreciate that they're open till 1 AM.

Penny's Noodle Shop　　　　　19 12 17 $13
1542 N. Damen Ave. (North Ave.), 773-394-0100
3400 N. Sheffield Ave. (Roscoe St.), 773-281-8222

(continued)
Penny's Noodle Shop
950 W. Diversey Pkwy. (Sheffield Ave.), 773-281-8448
www.pennysnoodleshop.com
1130 Chicago Ave. (Harlem Ave.), Oak Park, 708-660-1300;
www.pennysnoodleshopoakpark.com
Oodles of slurpers support these "no-frills" noodleries as
"nice to have in the neighborhood" for their "great selection" of "amazingly affordable" "quickie Asian" eats,
which are "tasty" (if "not haute cuisine") and offered in
"casual", "packed" digs with "quick service" (for many,
the chain's also a "regular on the takeout-restaurant rota-
tion"); skeptics, though, sigh "same old, same old", saying
"everything's bland" at these "run-of-the-mill" eateries
"for beginners"; N.B. they all serve beer and wine except
Wrigleyville, which is BYO.

People Lounge ◑   – | – | – | M
1560 N. Milwaukee Ave. (Damen Ave.), 773-227-9339;
www.peoplechicago.com
The small-plate craze hits Wicker Park with this Spaniard
housed in a former liquor store and serving a limited-
but-growing menu of seasonal tapas (e.g. an emphasis on
cold items in summer); global tunes from live acts and DJs
fill the warm, wood-accented room that features massive
iron chandeliers, a 30-ft.-long bar and communal tables
with bench seating.

Pepper Lounge ◑   22 | 23 | 22 | $33
3441 N. Sheffield Ave. (Clark St.), 773-665-7377;
www.pepperlounge.com
"A fun little find" for a "night-in-the-city experience", this
"sophisticated", "gay-friendly" New American is also
"one of the few non-cheesy places in" Wrigleyville, with
its "well-presented", "creative and flavorful" fare, some of
the "best French and chocolate martinis in town", "great
background music" and a "gorgeous patio" (and they do
brunch too); a few faultfinders, however, feel the "food can
be hit-or-miss."

Pete Miller's   21 | 20 | 20 | $45
Seafood & Prime Steak
1557 Sherman Ave. (bet. Davis & Grove Sts.), Evanston,
847-328-0399 ◑
412 N. Milwaukee Ave. (Dundee Rd.), Wheeling,
847-243-3700
www.petemillers.com
"Mouthwatering" "thick steaks" and "great fish" "served
up with a healthy portion of live jazz" most nights keep
these "solid" North Suburban seafood-steakhouse "joints
jumping"; a retinue of raters relies on the "dark and
classy" yet "informal atmosphere" (the newer Wheeling
location is "more stylish") for a "relaxed meal" or some

billiards with a "very good burger", but others' enthusiasm peters out over service "delays" and "overpriced" fare with "low-octane flavor."

Petterino's   19 20 20 $38
Goodman Theatre Bldg., 150 N. Dearborn St. (Randolph St.), 312-422-0150; www.petterinos.com
Loop locals and Goodman Theater-goers feel "welcome" at this "convenient", "consistent" Traditional American with "old-fashioned, fun" fare (some Italian) and "caricatures of celebs" in a "red-velvet" "'40s" "supper-club" setting (granted, it gets "hectic before a show", but they "really hustle to make sure you make the curtain"); tougher critics, however, lower that curtain on this "cliché" "attempt at Rat Pack" "retro", saying "lackluster food" makes it "one of the least interesting of the Lettuce Entertain You restaurants."

P.F. CHANG'S CHINA BISTRO   20 20 19 $28
530 N. Wabash Ave. (Grand Ave.), 312-828-9977
2361 Fountain Square Dr. (bet. Butterfield & Meyers Rds.), Lombard, 630-652-9977
1819 Lake Cook Rd. (Northbrook Court Dr.), Northbrook, 847-509-8844
Woodfield Mall, 5 Woodfield Mall (Frontage & Golf Rds.), Schaumburg, 847-610-8000
www.pfchangs.com
Flatterers of this "friendly" foursome favor its "nontraditional", "varied" Mandarin-style munchables made from "fresh", "identifiable ingredients", plus its "excellent cocktails" and Great Wall of Chocolate dessert ("as big as" the real thing) offered in "upscale-casual" confines with "tasteful decor"; but while adherents assert they "look for" outposts of the "consistent chain" "in every city", foes find the feel "formulaic" and fault the fare as "faux Chinese", saying it's "not for purists."

Philander's Oak Park   ∇ 21 23 21 $44
Carleton Hotel, 1110 Pleasant St. (bet. Maple Ave. & Marion St.), Oak Park, 708-848-4250; www.carletonhotel.com
"Cozy", "clubby" and "charming", this "intimate" "white-tablecloth" dining experience "in an old hotel in scenic Oak Park" includes "great" New American cuisine, "attentive service" and a "hot middle-aged bar scene" with live "music at the piano" nightly; all told, it's a "great place to hang out."

Phil & Lou's ⊠   ∇ 17 19 17 $29
1124 W. Madison St. (bet. Halsted St. & Racine Ave.), 312-455-0070; www.philandlous.com
Cohorts of this "comfortable" West Looper purport it's a "perfect match for the neighborhood", saying they like to

"kick back and relax" over its "dependable", "down-home" American food or even kick up their heels at the retro DJ dance party on Friday nights; others with "bad experiences" to report berate it as "boring", but most insist it's "a safe place to eat before a game."

Philly G's   22 19 21 $35
(fka Gilardi's)

1252 E. Hwy 45 (Rte. 21), Vernon Hills, 847-634-1811
Retaining its "proud family" heritage, this Northwest Suburban "casa de garlic" is now owned and operated by scion Phil Gilardi Jr., and is still serving "good roadhouse-y Italian" (including "great veal") within the "beautiful, comfortable rooms" of a restored home; the "charming" patio and weekend entertainment help make it "a nice date restaurant", but some judges jot "the jury is still out" on this new incarnation.

Phil Stefani's 437 Rush ⌦   21 18 22 $44
437 N. Rush St. (Hubbard St.), 312-222-0101;
www.stefanirestaurants.com
"Well-prepared" "classic Italian steakhouse" cooking in "grand proportions" is the draw at this "clubby", "comfortable" River Norther "with old-time service" and a "lively", "large bar area" (it's also "great for a business lunch or dinner"); still, raters who rank it "reliable but never spectacular" – with prices that are "a bit high" – assign it "secondary" status on their personal lists.

Phoenix   22 13 16 $21
2131 S. Archer Ave., 2nd fl. (Wentworth Ave.),
312-328-0848
Patrons of this Chinatown chow-palace are pleased by its "great variety, freshness and service", pronouncing it "one of the best places for daily dim sum" (offered from carts until 2:30 PM) and deeming "dinner a gracious experience" as well, with a "menu that focuses on Mandarin cuisine"; an abundance of "families adds to the cheer" of its "relaxed, open" space, though at peak hours "its popularity can be a bit daunting" due to the resulting "long lines and crowded rooms."

Piazza Bella   21 18 20 $28
2116 W. Roscoe St. (bet. Damen & Western Aves.),
773-477-7330; www.piazzabella.com
"Romantic, candlelit and casual", this Roscoe Village "neighborhood Italian trattoria" is "well-frequented" for its "classic dishes", such as "cracker thin–crusted pizzas and various" "nice pastas", plus "good steak and fish as well" ("the specials are usually impressive" too); a "welcoming staff" and "nice wine list" further enhance the "happy atmosphere"; P.S. "if you want to sit outside", be warned that the patio gets "very crowded in the summer."

Piece   22   15   15 $18

1927 W. North Ave. (bet. Damen & Wolcott Aves.),
773-772-4422; www.piecechicago.com

If you believe "beer and pizza [are the] staples of life" and
"you're not in the mood for traditional Chicago" pie, check
out this "large, industrial" Bucktowner – its "great New
Haven–style" thin-crust 'za "with interesting combinations" of toppings, plus "excellent large salads" and
"tasty" microbrews, appeal to a "young, hip" crowd, making it a favorite place to "watch a game" or cut loose on
the "loud", "wacky karaoke nights" (Thursdays, and with a
live band on Saturdays).

Pierrot Gourmet   21   20   20 $30

Peninsula Hotel, 108 E. Superior St. (bet. Michigan Ave. &
Rush St.), 312-573-6749; www.peninsula.com

"Traditional French bistro" fare served in a "quaint" "informal" setting (especially "for a top-level hotel") makes this
River Norther a "favorite" "place for a quick, quality
bite" – from "great coffee and breakfast pastries" to "a
light lunch" with a glass of wine from a "pretty decent list"
to "afternoon tea" to "outdoor cafe dining on Rush Street"
(and even "for meeting people at the communal tables");
"inconsistent service" is a concern to some, however, and
"lower prices would have [others] returning more often."

Pine Yard   20   11   15 $20

1033 Davis St. (Oak St.), Evanston, 847-475-4940;
www.pineyardrestaurant.com

"Very good", "straightforward" Szechuan and Mandarin
"dishes done with careful attention" create converts to
the cause of this North Suburban "standby" ("lunch is a
deal", and beer and wine are served); those unwilling to
overlook the "prickly" personnel and "cheesy decor",
though, say "you may want to take out", while purists take
a pass, purporting the provender "puts the American back
in Chinese-American cuisine."

Ping Pong ⬤   21   15   16 $18

3322 N. Broadway (bet. Aldine Ave. & Buckingham Pl.),
773-281-7575; www.eatpingpong.com

This Boys Town BYO plates "quality" Pan-Asian "fusion"
fare and dishes it out in an "ultramodern" space, "complete with pulsating beats", that strikes supporters as
"cute as a button – and not much bigger than one" (they
take no reservations, but the "great crowd-watching in
summer makes the wait almost enjoyable"); still, wags
wonder "if minimalist white counts as decor", while sensitive sorts suggest that "good food doesn't entirely offset
the slow service" from certain "snippy" staffers.

PITA INN   24   10   16 $11

9854 N. Milwaukee Ave. (Golf Rd.), Glenview, 847-759-9990

(continued)
PITA INN
3910 W. Dempster St. (Crawford St.), Skokie, 847-677-0211
122 S. Elmhurst Rd. (Dundee Rd.), Wheeling, 847-808-7733
www.pitainn.com
The "fabulous", "plentiful", "healthy and tasty Middle-Eastern" and "Med favorites" accompanied by "fresh-out-of-the-oven pita" are a "different", "high-quality" "fast food" at this North Suburban trio with "quick service"; the "unassuming location" ("who needs decor when the food is so great?") is "packed every night of the week" with "every type of person" (it's "great for vegetarians") – after all, who wouldn't want to "eat like a king [on] a pauper's budget"?

Pizza Capri 19 13 15 $18
1501 E. 53rd St. (Harper Ave.), 773-324-7777
1733 N. Halsted St. (Willow St.), 312-280-5700
962 W. Belmont Ave. (Sheffield Ave.), 773-296-6000
www.pizzacapri.com
"Unique pizza" "that is a little more grown-up" thanks to "interesting toppings" (some "love the BBQ chicken" variety, while others say "try the rosemary potato" version), as well as "solid pastas", "great sandwiches" and "terrific salads" have surveyors saying this "unpretentious", "efficiently run" Italian trio "is excellent for what it aims to be"; P.S. the Lincoln Park branch "mostly does takeout and delivery", while the Hyde Park location is separately owned.

Pizza D.O.C. 22 14 17 $24
2251 W. Lawrence Ave. (Oakley Ave.), 773-784-8777;
www.pizza-doc.com
"Wonderful", "refined" "Italian-style pizzas" with "cracker-like crust" from a "wood-burning oven", plus "always-fresh" pastas, "terrific" antipasto and a "nice wine list" woo lovers of this "casual" Lincoln Square "neighborhood place"; still, emergency meal technicians swear the pie "sometimes comes out more soggy than crisp", and say both the "lacking service" and "rustic" "interior could use some work" (though "the open kitchen cozies up the space").

Pizzeria Uno ◗ 22 14 15 $20
29 E. Ohio St. (Wabash Ave.), 312-321-1000
Pizzeria Due ◗
619 N. Wabash Ave. (bet. Ohio & Ontario Sts.), 312-943-2400
www.unos.com
"Prepare to be rolled out on a dolly" after dining at either of these Chicago "originals" with lots of "history behind" them, as you'll be "so full" with "one of the better deep-dish pies" around; diehards aren't dissuaded by "workmanlike service", "scrunched-in tables" and "long waits due to heavy tourist traffic", insisting "this is still Chicago's pizza" and advising "accept no substitutes" – these "classics" "bear little or no resemblance to the national chain they spawned."

P.J. Clarke's　　　　　　17 | 15 | 17 | $24
*Embassy Suites Hotel, 302 E. Illinois St. (Columbus Dr.),
312-670-7500*
1204 N. State Pkwy. (Division St.), 312-664-1650
www.pjclarkeschicago.com
"Lively" and "crowded", these Gold Coast and Streeterville
"watering holes" serving "standard" Traditional American
provender are "popular" "for a casual beer and burger",
"watching a game", "good people-watching on weekdays
for the after-work crowd" and as "meeting spots" for
"over-35 singles"; rueful raters, however, report that the
original on State, a "once-great neighborhood haunt",
now "reminds [them] of a chain" with "ho-hum" eats —
though both branches are unrelated to and "without the
history of the NY original."

Platiyo　　　　　　　20 | 20 | 19 | $31
*3313 N. Clark St. (bet. Buckingham Pl. & School St.),
773-477-6700; www.platiyo.com*
Though now under new ownership, this "friendly", "funky"
Lakeview cantina still "does for Mexican what [its former
cousin next door] Mia Francesca has done for Italian",
serving up "fresh" "modern" fare with a "gourmet touch"
(such as "interesting, very tasty moles and sauces" as
well as "amazing margaritas") and "vibrant surroundings"; N.B. they also offer Sunday brunch, patio dining and
live music some nights.

Poag Mahone's Carvery &　　17 | 14 | 14 | $18
Ale House ☒
*175 W. Jackson Blvd. (bet. LaSalle & Wells Sts.), 312-566-9100;
www.poagmahone.com*
The "better-than-average" Traditional American "pub
grub" at this Loop location includes a "damn good burger",
which "you can eat in peace" at lunch — as opposed to "after work", when it's "packed to the gills" with "painfully
loud" patrons who perhaps find it funny that the name
means 'kiss my ass' in Gaelic; a minority maligns it as "a
pseudo pub in an office building", with "mediocre", "cookie-
cutter food and decor", but barflies bellow "after a happy-
hour double scotch on the rocks, who really cares?"

Pompei Bakery　　　　　20 | 14 | 16 | $15
2955 N. Sheffield Ave. (Wellington Ave.), 773-325-1900
1531 W. Taylor St. (bet. Ashland Ave. & Laflin St.), 312-421-5179
17 W. 744 22nd St. (Summit Ave.), Oakbrook Terrace, 630-620-0600
7215 W. Lake St. (Harlem Ave.), River Forest, 708-488-9800
*1261 E. Higgins Rd. (bet. Meacham Rd. & National Pkwy.),
Schaumburg, 847-619-5001*
www.pompeibakery.com
First opened in Little Italy in 1909 (though at a different
location from that nabe's current branch, today a rater
"favorite"), this "cheap, dependable" chain of "solid"

"cafeteria-style Italian" installations issues "very good pizzas" that qualify as "comfort by the slice", plus "unique
sandwiches" and "great soups and salads"; it's "not quite
fast food – but service is quick", making it an "easy" stop
with kids; N.B. the River Forest branch opened post-*Survey*.

Potbelly Sandwich Works   20 | 15 | 18 | $9

508 N. Clark St. (bet. Grand Ave. & Illinois St.), 312-644-9131
2264 N. Lincoln Ave. (bet. Belden & Webster Aves.), 773-528-1405
3424 N. Southport Ave. (Roscoe St.), 773-289-1807
190 N. State St. (Lake St.), 312-683-1234
One Illinois Ctr., 111 E. Wacker Dr. (Michigan Ave.),
312-861-0013 ⊠
The Shops at North Bridge, 520 N. Michigan Ave., 4th fl.
(Grand Ave.), 312-644-1008
175 W. Jackson Blvd. (bet. Financial Pl. & Wells St.),
312-588-1150 ⊠
303 W. Madison St. (Franklin St.), 312-346-1234 ⊠
55 W. Monroe St. (Dearborn St.), 312-577-0070 ⊠
1422 W. Webster Ave. (Clybourn Ave.), 773-755-1234
www.potbelly.com
Additional locations throughout the Chicago area
"There's a reason the lines are out the door" at this beloved
bevy of "fast-food" "favorites" "at the top of their game"
with "tasty, toasty sandwiches" that "satisfy" "addicts"
from "vegetarians to the biggest carnivore"; though some
"first-time"-ers complain of a "confusing ordering sys-
tem", most insist the "unbelievably speedy" counter staff
has it "down to a science", ensuring "you'll never waste a
lot of time getting your food."

Prairie Grass Cafe   21 | 18 | 19 | $40

601 Skokie Blvd. (bet. Dundee & Lake Cook Rds.), Northbrook,
847-205-4433; www.prairiegrasscafe.com
"Chefs [Sarah] Stegner and [George] Bumbaris bring their
Ritz-Carlton pedigree to everyday family" dining at this
North Suburban "neighborhood benchmark", where the
"wonderful, upscale" New American "comfort food"
showcases "high-quality ingredients and simple, straightforward preparations" ("don't miss the shepherd's pie");
ayes also appreciate the "nod to Chicago's history" in the
"cavernous", "polished, prairie-style setting", but nays
note it's "noisy" – and "disappointed" deserters "expected more from such talented chefs."

P.S. Bangkok   20 | 13 | 17 | $19

3345 N. Clark St. (bet. Aldine Ave. & Roscoe St.), 773-871-7777;
www.psbangkok.com
P.S. Bangkok 2
2521 N. Halsted St. (bet. Fullerton Pkwy. & Wrightwood Ave.),
773-348-0072
Separately owned, these fraternal Siamese twins dish up
"delicious", "consistently good" Thai "with great versions

of classics as well as regional" treats, plus an "outstanding" Sunday buffet at Wrigleyville (which serves beer and wine – Lincoln Park is BYO); their "casual" settings, however, are marred by what some Thai-rants target as "tired" decor and "inconsistent service", making them take-out and "delivery favorites."

Puck's at the MCA　　　20 | 21 | 16 | $23
Museum of Contemporary Art, 220 E. Chicago Ave.
(Mies van der Rohe Way), 312-397-4034; www.mcachicago.org
"You get to enjoy the Museum of Contemporary Art's atmosphere, plus a fabulous terrace with a lake view", at this "airy", "ultramodern" Wolfgang Puck place "with just the right touch of snob appeal" as well as New American "gourmet sandwiches", "salads and entrees" (plus "you can eat here without paying the museum admission"); P.S. it's "only open for lunch", its "great Sunday brunch buffet" and during the 'Tuesdays on the Terrace' live "jazz evenings in summer."

PUMP ROOM, THE　　　21 | 24 | 23 | $56
Ambassador East Hotel, 1301 N. State Pkwy. (Goethe St.),
312-266-0360; www.pumproom.com
Fans "half expect Sinatra to walk in the door and order a martini" at "this Gold Coast grande dame" in the Ambassador East Hotel, where you can "experience the splendor" of "a bygone era" (it opened in 1938) "via photographs of the day's great celebrities on the walls"; a recent change in ownership and a series of chef shifts have muddied the culinary water, though, with some surveyors swearing the New American fare "is better again" but others insisting "the food and service lack what they once had."

Quartino ☻　　　　　– | – | – | M
626 N. State St. (Ontario St.), 312-698-5000;
www.quartinochicago.com
From the Gibsons gang comes this River North Italian where chef John Coletta (ex Caliterra, Carlucci) offers an extensive small-plates menu full of intriguing variations on bruschetta, antipasto, risotto and cured meats from the in-house *salumeria*; the earthy, bustling setting boasts a big bar area and an open kitchen, which serves until 1 AM; N.B. the name comes from the quarter-liter *quartinos* in which the 21 house wines are served.

Raj Darbar　　　　　20 | 12 | 16 | $23
2660 N. Halsted St. (Wrightwood Ave.), 773-348-1010
"Quality Indian fare", including "excellent lentil dishes" and "authentic paneer", makes this subcontinental a "popular local choice in the heart of Lincoln Park", especially for those "not feeling up to the trek to Devon"; some assess the food as "not the greatest" of the genre, and others feel the "reasonable prices" are undercut by the

"portion size, especially for delivery or carryout", but at least the "good" fixed-price Sunday buffet is all you can eat.

RA Sushi
19 | 19 | 19 | $30

1139 N. State St. (Elm St.), 312-274-0011
2601 Aviator Ln. (Patriot Blvd.), Glenview, 847-510-1100
www.rasushi.com

"Great choices of creative rolls" plus "many delicious noodle dishes" – and a "good lunch menu as well" – find favor with fans of this "fun" Gold Coast Japanese chain outpost with an "amazing happy hour on weekdays" and an "excellent crowd on Friday/Saturday nights" (some say the "great people-watching", "decor and scene are really the reason to come"); the "outside seating is nice in the summer" and they serve a late-night bar menu until 1:30 AM; N.B. the Glenview location opened post-*Survey*.

Redfish
16 | 15 | 15 | $30

400 N. State St. (Kinzie St.), 312-467-1600;
www.redfishamerica.com

Partakers "pass the Mardi Gras beads and fried green tomatoes" at this "kitschy, casual" Cajun seafood spot in River North with "fun food and music" (live jazz and blues Wednesday–Saturday); some raters reckon it's "convenient for business lunches", while others "go there to socialize" at the "packed bar", but a raft of rabble-rousers boos the "blah service" and berates the "boring" bounty for being "as close to Bayonne as it is to New Orleans."

Red Light
23 | 23 | 20 | $42

820 W. Randolph St. (Green St.), 312-733-8880;
www.redlight-chicago.com

"Upholding high food standards", "incredible" chef "Jackie Shen works her magic" at this "intoxicating", "hopping" Market District fusion "fantasy" where "Pan-Asian meets the club scene"; "delighted" denizens who "never tire of dining" on her "creative, "high-quality" cuisine, accompanied by "refreshing mango martinis" and served in a "flashy, over-the-top" setting, admit it's "expensive" but insist it's "still a value in the see-and-be-seen category."

Red Lion Pub
16 | 18 | 18 | $18

2446 N. Lincoln Ave. (Fullerton Pkwy.), 773-348-2695;
www.theredlionpub.com

"More authentic than many", this "classic British pub" in Lincoln Park possesses an "intimate" "dive" atmosphere that matches its "good draughts", "cider on tap" and "traditional English fare at a reasonable price" (seems "every patron in the place is eating the fish 'n' chips"); there's also the promise of "fun, intelligent conversation with the bartender and patrons", plus the "friendly" "servers are always willing to tell of their experiences with the ghosts" that "supposedly" inhabit the premises.

Red Star Tavern 14 17 15 $24
1700 S. Randall Rd. (County Line Rd.), Algonquin, 847-458-4500
Chicago Premium Outlets Mall, 1650 Premium Outlets Blvd.
(Farnsworth St.), Aurora, 630-978-8800
Deerfield Commons, 695 Deerfield Rd. (Waukegan Rd.),
Deerfield, 847-948-9700
Geneva Commons, 1602 Commons Dr. (bet. Bricher &
Randall Sts.), Geneva, 630-845-0845
1800 Tower Dr. (Aviator Rd.), Glenview, 847-486-0099
www.redstartavern.net
"With lots of dark wood and dim lighting", these outposts
of an expanding family are "more than sports bars", with
an "all-encompassing menu" of Traditional American
"comfort food" and an "impressive list of beers"; still,
many tavern-goers tell of "inconsistent", "institutional pub
grub disguised as neighborhood fare", staffers that "just
don't have their service down yet" and interiors that "look
like a chain restaurant – even blindfolded."

Retro Bistro ⊠ 25 18 23 $42
Mt. Prospect Commons, 1746 W. Golf Rd. (Busse Rd.),
Mt. Prospect, 847-439-2424; www.retrobistro.com
A "favorite among in-the-know" Northwest suburbanites,
this French bistro confers a touch of "old Paris" via "consistently" "exceptional, top-quality food" accompanied by
a "very good wine selection" ("ask for the reserve list") at
prices that make it a "really nice value" – especially the
"prix fixe bargain"; "welcoming" staffers who really
"know the menu" are another asset, and while the setting
says "strip mall" in both "location and decor", the "food
will make you think you're somewhere else."

Reza's 19 15 18 $24
5255 N. Clark St. (Berwyn Ave.), 773-561-1898 ◗
432 W. Ontario St. (Orleans St.), 312-664-4500 ◗
40 N. Tower Rd. (Butterfield Rd.), Oak Brook, 630-424-9900
www.rezasrestaurants.com
"Relaxed" and "reliable", these sister "best buys" harbor
a "huge selection" of "delicious Middle-Eastern cuisine"
to "satisfy carnivores and veg heads" alike, making them
"perfect for large groups with differing tastes on a moder-
ate budget"; the "plentiful servings" include "enough dill
rice to feed all of Persia" plus "free-flowing tea", but that's
not enough for naysayers who negate it as "not a gourmet
experience" (merely "a cut above a buffet") and suggest
that "service can be lackluster."

Rhapsody 21 22 20 $45
Symphony Ctr., 65 E. Adams St. (bet. Michigan & Wabash Aves.),
312-786-9911; www.rhapsodychicago.com
The "seasonal offerings" of "innovative but restrained"
New American cuisine are "music to the taste buds" at this
Loop "lovely" in the Symphony Center with a "tranquil",

"staid" dining room, "lively bar" and "gorgeous patio"; proponents pick it as "the perfect overture" to a concert or Art Institute visit (and a "power-lunch" spot too), though dissidents detect dissonance in the form of "unpolished" service; N.B. hours are per the concert schedule, and performance-night "reservations are a necessity."

Ribs 'n' Bibs ●   22 | 6 | 13 | $15 |
5300 S. Dorchester Ave. (53rd St.), 773-493-0400
You'll be "planning another pilgrimage" after your first visit to this Hyde Park "carry-out place" where the "aroma of barbecue" makes for "great advertising" ("walk downwind and savor the smell"); "you get an entire bucket" of "real ribs vs. Northside counterparts" "slathered in great sauce", "each one as delicious as the next", but be aware that management "doesn't mess around with decor" ("you really can't sit in the place") – and "don't come for the service, unless you call 'take-a-number' service."

Riccardo Trattoria ⊠   – | – | – | M |
2119 N. Clark St. (bet. Dickens & Webster Aves.), 773-549-0038
Chef-owner Riccardo Michi (ex Bice), a native of Milan, proudly prepares many of his mother's recipes at this casually elegant, affordably priced Tuscan trattoria in Lincoln Park's erstwhile Via Emilia space; N.B. the BYO policy helps keep costs down.

Rinconcito Sudamericano   ∇ 17 | 6 | 16 | $23 |
1954 W. Armitage Ave. (Damen Ave.), 773-489-3126
"Traditional" and "authentic", this Bucktown BYO is home to "huge portions of very comforting and tasty" South American fare, including "Peruvian specialties", that have takers testifying "your taste buds will thank you" – and your wallet as well, as it's "a value"; still, the unsatisfied insinuate the fare is "uninspired", the "atmosphere is so-so" and the "service is not as good" as it once was; N.B. a spin-off in the same neighborhood is in the works.

Ringo   ∇ 22 | 11 | 20 | $23 |
2507 N. Lincoln Ave. (bet. Fullerton Pkwy. & Wrightwood Ave.), 773-248-5788; www.rin-go.us
Raw-fish lovers cheer this Lincoln Park local "treasure" serving "fresh", "tasty rolls", "terrific specials" and "good rice-bowl dishes"; there's "not much atmosphere", and the "food may lack some imagination, but this is a great entry-level sushi house", and you "can't beat the BYO policy, friendly service" and "bargain" prices; N.B. at *Survey* time, efforts were underway to expand and add a sushi bar.

Rioja   21 | 18 | 19 | $29 |
5101 N. Clark St. (Carmen Ave.), 773-275-9191;
www.jackjonesrestaurants.com
"If you're looking for a twist on tapas", look no farther than this "lively", "upscale yet comfortable" Andersonville

"date spot" in the "former Atlantique" space, where the seasonal Spanish small plates are "not your standard offerings" (the "seafood dishes are highly recommended"); its "fun, young crowd" also appreciates the "affordable wine list" and "phenomenal specialty martinis", and even grazers who grade the service as "uneven" hope the staffers "will hit their stride."

Riques
21 | 10 | 19 | $18 |

5004 N. Sheridan Rd. (Argyle St.), 773-728-6200;
www.riqueschicago.com

"Wonderful, fresh" and "authentic Mexican food" – "not just burritos and tacos" – served "at a great price" in an "out-of-the-way" Uptown location ("don't be put off by the neighborhood") has contributors crowing they "can't get enough of" this "friendly" (and "vegetarian-friendly") BYO; P.S. you can "travel Mexico" without leaving town via chef-owner Enrique Cortes' "regional cuisine on Saturday nights."

Rise
20 | 18 | 14 | $33 |

3401 N. Southport Ave. (Roscoe St.), 773-525-3535;
www.risesushi.com

An "outstanding menu" of "beautiful, fresh" fish "and enough non-sushi" Japanese fare for landlubbers is coupled with a "creative drink menu", "cool decor", "good people-watching" and "fun" "open-air dining" at this "clubby" Wrigleyville spot; despite these attributes, though, regulars report it "has fallen off recently" (as have its ratings, across the board), perhaps because those who feel they've "given it too many chances" are "less impressed every time" with "glitz over substance" and "painful service" from an "arrogant", "surly" staff.

ristorante we
18 | 20 | 17 | $44 |

W Hotel, 172 W. Adams St. (LaSalle St.), 312-917-5608;
www.ristorantewe.com

Contributors seem conflicted about this Loop Northern Italian that's tempering the steaks 'n' sauces trend with a Tuscan twist – some say it's a "trendy and upbeat" "minimalist's paradise" with an "interesting menu" of "good" eating that's "worth every penny" ("nice service" too), while others opine it's an "uppity", "hotel restaurant" where "the food doesn't quite measure up" and the staff is "confused"; N.B. a DJ entertains nightly except Sunday.

Ritz-Carlton Café
22 | 22 | 24 | $41 |

Ritz-Carlton Hotel, 160 E. Pearson St., 12th fl. (Michigan Ave.),
312-573-5160; www.fourseasons.com

"Convenient for hotel guests" and "great for locals", this "always-classy" Streeterville venue is a "solid" option "any time of day", whether for a "great breakfast", "awesome Sunday brunch" or "relaxing" New American "meal after shopping"; a "well-trained" staff works the "lovely gardenlike surroundings", which offer an "open vista across the vast lobby" with a "soothing fountain", making it a "nice alternative to the very expensive Dining Room" – though some feel its "prices are ritzier than the food warrants."

RITZ-CARLTON DINING ROOM　27 | 27 | 28 | $80 |

Ritz-Carlton Hotel, 160 E. Pearson St., 12th fl. (Michigan Ave.), 312-573-5223; www.fourseasons.com

"Elegant, excellent" and "expensive", this "epitome of gracious dining" in the Ritz is a Streeterville "culinary oasis" where "top-tier" New French fare meets an 800-bottle wine list that might "make you weep (and Amex jump for joy)"; the "beautiful" setting is "grand" and "romantic", and the "professional staff is extremely helpful", contributing to a "special-event experience extraordinaire"; N.B. rumblings of "inconsistency" reflect a series of chef changes, the latest being the post-*Survey* departure of chef Kevin Hickey for Seasons and promotion of former sous-chef Mark Payne.

Riva　18 | 20 | 17 | $46 |

Navy Pier, 700 E. Grand Ave. (Lake Shore Dr.), 312-644-7482; www.stefanirestaurants.com

Supporters see "something for everyone on the menu" – from American "fresh-fish" dishes to "Italian seafood" preps to "great steaks" – at this "huge" but "lovely" Streeterville destination where, "from the right tables", the "spectacular" lakefront views are worth braving the "carnival atmosphere" of Navy Pier for; still, antis insist "the locale's the star", the ambiance "depends on how loud the tourists" are and the prices are "ridiculous" "for what you get" – namely "lackluster food" and "nonchalant service."

R.J. Grunts　19 | 16 | 18 | $21 |

2056 N. Lincoln Park W. (Dickens Ave.), 773-929-5363; www.leye.com

"Sentimental" surveyors trust this "loud, crowded" Lincoln Park "classic" – "the first 'Lettuce' restaurant" – known for "hearty" American fare served by "cheeky" staffers in a setting dominated by "groovy music" and "photos of staffers over the years"; it "still feels very '70s", and perhaps it's "not up with the latest things people like to eat", but for every dismisser who dubs it "dated" there's a diehard declaring "try and close it and I'll chain myself to the doors in protest."

RL　22 | 26 | 23 | $49 |

115 E. Chicago Ave. (Michigan Ave.), 312-475-1100; www.rlrestaurant.com

"Wear something cashmere" to Ralph Lauren's "see-and-be-seen" Gold Coast American that "delivers what it should – straightforward", "old-school" fare "and cold martinis" amid ambiance likened to "an old hunting club" with "portraits on the walls" instead of "dead animals" (or "your grandfather's study, if your grandfather was unbelievably rich"); peopled with "blue blazers", "hungry shoppers", "little old ladies with gloves" and "conceited" "Bitsy and Mitsy types", it's also "loved" for its "especially cozy bar", "pretentious" vibe and "glib waiters"; P.S. "great for people-watching from the patio."

Robinson's No. 1 Ribs　　19 6 14 $21
Union Station, 225 S. Canal St. (bet. Adams St. & Jackson Blvd.), 312-258-8477
655 W. Armitage Ave. (Orchard St.), 312-337-1399; www.ribs1.com
940 W. Madison St. (Clinton St.), Oak Park, 708-383-8452; www.rib1.com
"Falling-off-the-bone ribs", "tender chicken" and "BBQ pork sandwiches (mmmmm)" slathered in "rich, spicy sauce" prompt plentiful "finger lickin'" at this "no-frills" threesome; gourmands are grateful that they're "not as tourist-oriented" as some "chain" competitors and are generally willing to ignore the "nonexistent decor" – though most nevertheless "order delivery or take it home."

Rock Bottom Brewery　　16 15 16 $22
1 W. Grand Ave. (State St.), 312-755-9339
28256 Diehl Rd. (Winfield Rd.), Warrenville, 630-836-1380
www.rockbottom.com
For some, "the beers are the reason to stop by" these "crowded, noisy", "comfortable" Traditional American "gathering places", but in addition to the "great microbrews" (including "amusing flights" and "seasonal" choices) there's "a nice variety" of "comfort food"; still, critics wonder "why go for chain conformity in a town with great watering holes?", contending the "run-of-the-mill" "pub fare" and service are "unremarkable"; P.S. River North's rooftop deck "is quite a swinging singles joint."

Rockit Bar & Grill ●　　19 19 16 $28
22 W. Hubbard St. (bet. Dearborn & State Sts.), 312-645-6000; www.rockitbarandgrill.com
A "fun" "30-and-under" crowd of "frat" types and "eye candy in skimpy outfits" convenes at this "rockin'" River North Traditional American "sandwich-and-easy-meal place", a "much-needed happy-hour destination" and "pre-partying" staging area with "above-average bar food" and a Bloody Mary cart that's becoming "one of the great Chicago brunch traditions"; diners who "don't quite understand all the hubbub" are "disappointed by the food" and "overpriced drinks", and say the staff is sometimes "overwhelmed."

RODITYS ●　　22 17 20 $25
222 S. Halsted St. (bet. Adams St. & Jackson Blvd.), 312-454-0800; www.roditys.com
One of the Greektown "classics", this "authentic" "fave" "holds its own" and "can always be counted on" for "con-

sistently good", "quality" "Greek food" at a "value" served
in a "family-style atmosphere that will have you swilling
ouzo and breaking plates (well, almost)"; N.B. they're open
till midnight, 1 AM on weekends.

Ron of Japan
18 | 17 | 18 | $37

230 E. Ontario St. (bet. Fairbanks Ct. & St. Clair St.), 312-644-6500
633 Skokie Blvd. (Dundee Rd.), Northbrook, 847-564-5900
Aficionados of tabletop-cooked Japanese steakhouse
sustenance assert these Streeterville and North Suburban
"throwbacks" are "as good as always" and "fun for a big
group", with "usually personable" "show"-men and "good
food"; others advise that these teppanyaki "tourist traps"
are "getting tired", with "stale" chefs and "outdated decor", adding "you stink when you leave"; P.S. "prepare to
sit with strangers" at the communal tables.

RoSal's Italian Kitchen ⊠
24 | 16 | 22 | $29

1154 W. Taylor St. (Racine Ave.), 312-243-2357; www.rosals.com
"Excellent", "hearty" Southern Italian and a "staff that
makes you feel at home" lure loyalists to this "quaint" Little
Italy "storefront space" with "a lot of charm" and "a real
family-owned feeling"; P.S. the "Sicilian wine is a wonderful surprise", and they serve a bargain lunch buffet.

Rose Angelis
22 | 20 | 21 | $28

1314 W. Wrightwood Ave. (bet. Racine & Southport Aves.),
773-296-0081; www.roseangelis.com
Enthusiasm runs high from eaters who enjoy the "hearty
portions" of "dependably good" "homemade Italian" (including "veggie-friendly" selections)" and "incredible
value" at this "sweet, romantic" Lincoln Park "institution"
in a "cozy" townhouse "with tons of character"; it can be
"tough to get into as they don't take reservations", and dubious diners "don't know why people tolerate the long
waits" (especially "when you can get takeaway") for what
they consider "heavy" fare.

ROSEBUD, THE
21 | 18 | 19 | $36

1500 W. Taylor St. (Laflin St.), 312-942-1117
ROSEBUD OF HIGHLAND PARK
1850 Second St. (Central Ave.), Highland Park, 847-926-4800
ROSEBUD OF NAPERVILLE
48 W. Chicago Ave. (Washington St.), Naperville, 630-548-9800
ROSEBUD ON RUSH
720 N. Rush St. (Superior St.), 312-266-6444
ROSEBUD THEATER DISTRICT ⊠
3 First National Plaza, 70 W. Madison St. (bet. Clark &
Dearborn Sts.), 312-332-9500
www.rosebudrestaurants.com
"Consistently good", "old-fashioned" Italian is served
"by the barrel" at these "crowded", "touristy", "high-
energy spots" (especially the "classic Chicago" "legend"

in Little Italy) that are "a real trip back in time" – complete with "Sinatra playing in the background"; service runs from "pleasant" to "surly", though, and peeved paisanos posit "piggy portions don't hide that the food" is a "throwback to the old days before Americans knew what real Italian food is."

Rosebud Steakhouse

| 23 | 21 | 22 | $51 |

192 E. Walton St. (Mies van der Rohe Way), 312-397-1000; www.rosebudrestaurants.com

Gold Coast locals like to "see and be seen" at this purveyor of "hearty" "Italian specialties along with gargantuan steaks" and one of the "best burgers in the city", all served "in a great location" that's "like going to a" "laid-back" "private club"; the "staff are real pros" who "take good care of you, especially if you are a regular", and "portions are stupidly big" – "but they're good about splitting"; P.S. if you find the interior "unbearably noisy", try the "charming outdoor seating."

Roy's

| 24 | 21 | 23 | $50 |

720 N. State St. (Superior St.), 312-787-7599; www.roysrestaurant.com

"Close your eyes and you'll think you're in Hawaii" enjoying "a fantastic meal" of "innovative" "upscale" regional cuisine at this River North outpost of "one of the best high-end chains out there", where "beautifully presented" "signature dishes" featuring a "unique assortment" of "extremely fresh seafood" are enhanced by an "interesting and good-value wine list" and a "fun cocktail menu"; veterans of the Honolulu original, however, lament "like all branch restaurants with nonresident chefs, the food suffers from the separation."

Ruby of Siam

| 20 | 13 | 16 | $18 |

1125 Emerson St. (Ridge Ave.), Evanston, 847-492-1008
Skokie Fashion Sq., 9420 Skokie Blvd. (Gross Point Rd.), Skokie, 847-675-7008
www.rubyofsiam.com

Insiders insist "if you live near" a branch of this BYO duo, "you don't really have to bother finding any other place for Thai" in the Northern Suburbs, since each offers "a huge menu" of "reliable selections" from a "kitchen willing to substitute", making them "frequent destinations for vegetarians" and "good places to take kids with an adventurous palate"; add in "fabulous value", and you can see why touters tolerate "average atmosphere" and "iffy service."

Rumba ⌧

| 18 | 22 | 18 | $40 |

351 W. Hubbard St. (bet. Kingsbury & Orleans Sts.), 312-222-1226; www.rumba351.com

"For a fun night of dinner and dancing", this "moderately priced" River North Nuevo Latino offers a "different dining experience", with "true Latin American tastes" and "great drinks" served in an "upbeat", "upscale setting" (though foodies feels the fare "needs to catch up with the decor"); P.S. "the noise level increases greatly as you progress through the evening", especially on weekends when they offer free salsa lessons.

Rushmore ⊠   20 | 18 | 18 | $44
1023 W. Lake St. (Carpenter St.), 312-421-8845;
www.rushmore-chicago.com
For an "upscale" perspective on "solid" "New American comfort food", surveyors suggest this "classy spot" in the Market District ("try the grilled blue cheese sandwich and roasted tomato bisque for a twist on an old standby", and the "cookie-dough eggroll for dessert"); its "inconvenient" but "cool" "storefront" location "under the el" tracks is a touch of "vintage Chicago" that appeals to nostalgics, but some nevertheless note that it's "not as good as it used to be."

Russell's Barbecue   18 | 10 | 13 | $15
1621 N. Thatcher Ave. (North Ave.), Elmwood Park, 708-453-7065
2885 Algonquin Rd. (bet. Carriageway & Newport Drs.),
Rolling Meadows, 847-259-5710
www.russellsbarbecue.com
This "no-nonsense" West Suburban "institution", a "trusty old BBQ stop" that's "been there forever" (since 1930), is "a favorite for pulled pork and beef sandwiches and fallin'-off-the-bone tender smoked ribs"; even fans who feel the fare "is great" admit the "decor and service aren't", while tepid tasters "think you had to grow up with this food" "to really appreciate" it; N.B. at a mere 25 years of age, the Rolling Meadows location is a relative newcomer.

Russian Tea Time   22 | 20 | 21 | $36
77 E. Adams St. (bet. Michigan & Wabash Aves.), 312-360-0000;
www.russianteatime.com
"A real culinary trip" "right in the heart of" the Loop, this "cozy" "hideaway" presents a "menu that reads like a Russian novel, with a story explaining the history of each" "interesting choice" of "trusty" Russian fare; red-heads also revere the "old-world service", "burgundy-and-brass" interior "filled" with "lovely flowers", "samovars and velvet", "nice afternoon tea" and "flights" of "great infused vodkas", calling it "the best choice if you are bound for the symphony or Art Institute."

RUTH'S CHRIS STEAK HOUSE   24 | 20 | 23 | $57
431 N. Dearborn St. (Hubbard St.), 312-321-2725
Renaissance Hotel, 933 Skokie Blvd. (Dundee Rd.), Northbrook,
847-498-6889
www.ruthschris.com
These River North and North Suburban steakhouse outposts hew to the "proven formula" of their "reliable chain", of-

fering "always the same great meal" – "sizzling platters" of "scrumptious" prime beef with "lots of butter", plus "seafood options that provide a nice balance to the red meat", amid "comfortable", "classy" "dark-wood" decor; even so, chompers with "sticker shock" state "for what I pay here, I expect something [more] memorable", while the home team harps that they're "not very Chicago."

Sabatino's ● 23 17 22 $30
4441 W. Irving Park Rd. (bet. Cicero & Pulaski Aves.), 773-283-8331
"A time warp" of "old Chicago Italian" dining, this Northwest Side "classic" does an "excellent job with the standard menu" (plus "great specials") served in "plentiful portions" that "preclude even the contemplation of dessert"; the "warmly bustling" setting is "like stepping into an old-time movie", "with the baby grand piano [played live on weekends], dim lighting, booths tucked into corners and behind pulled curtains" – part of why it "draws crowds" ranging from "families with kids" to "older" folks.

Sabor do Brasil – – – E
15750 S. Harlem Ave. (157th St.), Orland Park, 708-444-2770; www.sabor-do-brasil.com
Churrascaria-style chowhounds head to this Southwest Suburban for all-you-can-eat rotisserie meats, including numerous varieties of beef, pork, lamb, chicken and sausage – just be careful not to fill up on all the heavy sides; it's certainly not cheap, but its menu is priced below the city competition and served in a warmly lit space accented with exposed brick, dark wood, golden walls and an authentic-looking adobe facade.

Sage Grille 🖾 – – – M
260 Green Bay Rd. (Highwood Ave.), Highwood, 847-433-7005
Urban dining descends on suburban Highwood with this moderately priced New American offering ingredient-driven culinary creations, plus simple steaks and chops (with the increasingly de rigueur choice of sauce) and desserts by Trotter's/Trio alum Tamara White; the comfortably upscale setting is a hybrid of city chic and bistro ease; N.B. a kids' menu is available.

Sai Café 24 15 21 $33
2010 N. Sheffield Ave. (Armitage Ave.), 773-472-8080; www.saicafe.com
"For the love of maki, just go" to this "wonderful neighborhood sushi bar" that's "been around Lincoln Park for [20] years" urge enthusiasts of its "nice, large cuts" of "fresh fish" "and other Japanese preparations" "prepared by super chefs"; with its "homey", "relaxing" feel, it's "not as flashy" "as the trendy places", but most agree it's a "value" – so "plan ahead to get a table" or expect "lengthy

waits on weekend nights"; N.B. the Decor score may not reflect a recent partial remodeling.

Sal & Carvão Churrascaria   23 20 24 $54
739 N. Clark St. (Superior St.), 312-932-1100
3008 Finley Rd. (Butterfield Rd.), Downers Grove, 630-512-0900
801 E. Algonquin Rd. (Roselle Rd.), Schaumburg, 847-925-0061
www.salecarvao.com
Sated surveyors are "still full" after visits to this Brazilian meat three-peat in the city and suburbs, where the "roving" "service begins immediately", "tempting you constantly with skewers of meat" that amount to a "well-prepared" "feast"; to "get your money's worth", experts advise go "easy on" the "extensive, beautiful salad bar" and choose "carefully", as "the offerings vary in quality" – for though this is a "fun experience", it's also "an expensive one" ("lunch is a much better deal").

SALBUTE ⊠   26 16 22 $41
20 E. First St. (bet. Garfield & Washington Sts.), Hinsdale, 630-920-8077; www.salbute.com
Scoring highly for its "excellent, authentic regional Mexican cuisine", this "quaint", "modest storefront" in the West Suburbs accompanies its daily menu of "mouth-wateringly spectacular" food with "margaritas that will knock your socks off"; even admirers, though, admit it's "expensive" and say the "tiny" space can sometimes feel "cramped" ("better make a reservation").

Saloon Steakhouse, The   23 19 23 $51
Seneca Hotel, 200 E. Chestnut St. (bet. Lake Shore Dr. & Michigan Ave.), 312-280-5454; www.saloonsteakhouse.com
A Streeterville "locals'" "secret" that "does just what it should do", this "clubby" steakhouse serves "some of the finest beef", including "succulent wagyu" (prized by patrons as "on the money") and "fine, fine martinis too" in "classy", "pleasant surroundings" (the "perfect place for a business lunch"); the "nice" "older" clientele values the "friendly", "professional staff" and also likes that this "Chicago meat and potatoes" "standby" is "less crowded and noisy than nearby competitors" – and "without the attitude."

Salpicón   24 19 22 $42
1252 N. Wells St. (bet. Goethe & Scott Sts.), 312-988-7811; www.salpicon.com
"Every dish seems new and inventive and delicious" at this "colorful" Old Town "gem" showcasing Priscila Satkoff's "haute", "authentic" "Mexican with elegant presentation and savory sauces", plus "tons of tequila options" and a "surprisingly" "great wine list"; surveyor service assessments seesaw from "fabulous" to "snooty", and budgeters believe it's "a bit pricey", but it's a "must for anyone who likes their Mex with a modern twist."

Saltaus ◑▨ ▽ 19 25 16 $48

1350 W. Randolph St. (Ada St.), 312-455-1919; www.saltaus.com
The departure of onetime chef-partner Michael Taus
(Zealous) shortly after its opening occasioned a kitchen
switch to the current Eclectic menu, an "interesting fusion"
of modern Mediterranean and Asian, which may explain why
this "trendy [Market District] newcomer" is still "finding its
way"; positive signs include a "top-notch crowd", an "ample
wine collection", "spare" yet "sophisticated decor", "a hip
lounge upstairs" and a "warm host-owner"; N.B. a DJ spins
on weekends, and there's Zen garden seating in season.

Salvatore's Ristorante ▽ 21 20 20 $36

525 W. Arlington Pl. (Clark St.), 773-528-1200;
www.salvatores-chicago.com
For nearly 30 years, this "hidden" Lincoln Park Northern
Italian "tucked away on a side street" has "charmed"
chowhounds who favor "old-fashioned, quiet" dining (it's
"not the place to see and be seen") on "underpriced" edibles with "good sauces", which are served in a "romantic"
"ballroom"-like setting or on the "terrace overlooking a
garden" (it's "popular for weddings and special events"); on
the other hand, modernists maintain it's "outdated."

Samah ◑ – – – M

3330A N. Clark St. (Buckingham Pl.), 773-248-4606;
www.samahlounge.com
Dreamlike ambiance awaits visitors to this late-night
Wrigleyville Middle Eastern lounge whose interior includes multiple seating areas draped and cushioned with
luxurious fabrics; classic fare such as falafel and shish kebab is complemented by a range of coffee and tea drinks,
belly dancing (Thursdays and Fridays) and optional hookah-
puffing, but don't expect a tipple with your toke – no alcohol is served, or allowed in.

San Gabriel Mexican Cafe 20 16 18 $28

Bannockburn Green Shopping Ctr., 2535 Waukegan Rd.
(Half Day Rd.), Bannockburn, 847-940-0200
"A nicely balanced menu" of "very good, fresh Mexican"
fare "with some interesting specials", plus "great tableside guacamole" and a "good tequila selection (especially
for the [Northern] Suburbs)" appeal to amigos of this "casual" "strip-mall" spot; some surveyors, though, can't get
past certain "ups and downs" they perceive, most notably
in relation to the "uneven service"; N.B. a mariachi band
makes music on Thursdays.

Sangria Restaurant & Tapas Bar 16 18 14 $29

901 W. Weed St. (Fremont St.), 312-266-1200;
www.sangriachicago.com
As you'd guess, this "colorful", "happening" Nuevo Latino
"hangout" in Lincoln Park has a "great sangria selection",

but it also serves "fun" small plates; still, the consensus is that "the point of going here is not the food" (most find the "average" offerings "uninteresting") or service (which many feel "is worse than a coffeehouse"), but rather "the cool atmosphere and beautiful people" – though management and chef changes simultaneous with our *Survey* may make a difference.

San Soo Gab San ◑ ▽ 21 8 16 $24
5247 N. Western Ave. (Foster Ave.), 773-334-1589
This "great" Northwest Side "Korean BBQ joint" "should be on every night person's 'A' list", as it offers an "amazing all-night grilled-meat extravaganza" and "huge assortment of *panch'an*" (the savory, spicy and pickled little extras); it's "always crowded", partly because it's such a "good bargain", and you can have "great fun figuring out what the heck the items are", "but service is choppy" so "go with someone with experience."

Santorini ◑ 21 19 20 $32
800 W. Adams St. (Halsted St.), 312-829-8820;
www.santorinichicago.com
If you "need an evening in the Greek Islands", try this "more upscale" and "enlightened" "white-tablecloth" Hellenic "specializing in seafood" with "tableside filleting" (they "do the other specialties equally well"); veterans vow that the "very comfortable, almost elegant" environs are "quieter" and "not so touristy" as "most of its [Greektown] neighbors", and it's especially "warm and inviting by the fireplace" "on a cold night", though some say "service is hit-or-miss."

Sapori Trattoria 22 17 20 $30
2701 N. Halsted St. (Schubert Ave.), 773-832-9999
It's "always packed" at this "charming" Lincoln Park "favorite", so "reserve for sure" for a "warm and friendly", "authentic" "trattoria experience" with "fresh Italian food" including "homemade pastas" (habitués are "hooked" on both the pumpkin and lobster ravioli) and "delicious specials" that are "so good, you always feel like you're getting such a deal" (there's also an "extensive list of wines at reasonable prices"); P.S. garden seating helps alleviate the "crowded", sometimes "noisy" conditions inside.

Sayat Nova 20 14 19 $27
157 E. Ohio St. (bet. Michigan Ave. & St. Clair St.), 312-644-9159;
www.sayatnovachicago.com
The "authentic Armenian fare" is a "great value" at this "cozy", "family-run" Streeterville "treasure tucked away just off Michigan Avenue", an "offbeat choice for something out of the ordinary", with "interesting" if "somewhat seedy decor"; most of the time it's a "quiet hideaway", but DJs and hookahs heat up the scene two Saturdays a month.

Schwa ⊠   ▽ 26 | 14 | 24 | $54

1466 N. Ashland Ave. (LeMoyne St.), 773-252-1466;
www.schwarestaurant.com

Prescient patrons predict chef Michael Carlson "will be a star someday" as they "dream of [their] next meal" of his "spectacular" "seasonal" New American cuisine, "artfully presented" within the "minimalist, unpretentious atmosphere" of "the smallest dining room and kitchen imaginable" (formerly Lovitt and Savoy Truffle) on Lincoln Park's western edge; bargain-hunters find it "a bit pricey", but supporters swear this "little-restaurant-that-could" is "a must"; P.S. "plan ahead, given the" space limitations, "and inquire about the daily menu, since it's BYO."

Scoozi!   21 | 19 | 20 | $35

410 W. Huron St. (bet. Kingsbury & Orleans Sts.), 312-943-5900;
www.leye.com

"Still fun" and "consistent", this River North "crowd-pleaser" "never gets tired" to surveyors supportive of its "solid execution" of "down-to-earth, identifiable" "Americanized Italian" fare served at "fair prices" by a "happy" staff within a "huge", "noisy" and "rustic" warehouse" setting; tarter tongues tell us this "typical Lettuce operation" "is a bit passé" and there's "nothing original" on its "generic" menu, but it's "good" "for the whole family" ("especially on Sundays when kids can make pizza"); P.S. there's a "hopping" "happy-hour scene."

Scylla   25 | 20 | 24 | $49

1952 N. Damen Ave. (Armitage Ave.), 773-227-2995;
www.scyllarestaurant.com

When "craving something from the sea", this "is the place to be" rhyme ravers who relish Stephanie Izard's "terrific" "cutting-edge" "fresh fish" dishes with "unusual" Mediterranean treatments at this Bucktown yearling (the "savvy servers" also rate a special mention); perhaps its "intimate" setting in a "funky" "little house" is a tad "too cozy" for claustrophobes, but it's nevertheless earning itself a reputation as "a force to be reckoned with."

SEASONS   26 | 27 | 27 | $78

Four Seasons Hotel, 120 E. Delaware Pl., 7th fl. (bet. Michigan Ave.
& Rush St.), 312-649-2349; www.fourseasons.com

A "classic" "for all seasons", this Gold Coast "formal" "fine-dining" destination treats guests "like royalty", with "pampering" service, a "magnificent", "refined" setting seen as "one of Chicago's prettiest rooms" and "excellent" New American cuisine augmented by an "amazing wine selection"; those who suggest "the food is sometimes a little less than expected for the price" may not have visited since "new chef" Kevin Hickey (ex Ritz-Carlton) "came on board" during this *Survey*; P.S. for many, the "out-of-this-world" "Sunday brunch is the reason to head here."

SEASONS CAFÉ ◗   25 | 25 | 26 | $45
Four Seasons Hotel, 120 E. Delaware Pl., 7th fl. (bet. Michigan Ave. & Rush St.), 312-649-2349; www.fourseasons.com
Eaters who know to expect most "everything you get at Seasons for [nearly] half the price" – namely "excellent food and service" – savor this Gold Coast "feel-good experience", where you can "check your shopping bags" and "relax" over a "simple menu" of Traditional American fare ("the lobster club is to die for") in a "tasteful", "civilized setting."

1776 ☒   24 | 19 | 22 | $41
397 Virginia St./Rte. 14 (bet. Dole & McHenry Aves.), Crystal Lake, 815-356-1776; www.1776restaurant.com
"A [New] American revolution" in the "far Northwest" suburbs, this "out-of-the-way" Crystal Lake "jewel" proffers "unique", "fine food" (including "wild game"), and owner Andy Andresky "knows his vintages well", making it "a great choice for wine lovers"; "the building used to house a KFC" and is "not long on atmosphere", but it's "comfortable", and the "service will make you feel at home"; P.S. don't miss the "excellent early-birds, theme dinners and tapas nights."

Shallots Bistro   ▽ 21 | 19 | 21 | $46
4741 W. Main St. (Skokie Blvd.), Skokie, 847-677-3463; www.shallotsbistro.com
Laura Frankel's North Suburban French-Med bistro "serves the orthodox community" with "innovative", "high-end" kosher food, including a "nice selection of meats and fish, great desserts" and a "good wine list" (plus "seasonal tasting menus add variety"); "good service", an "intimate setting" and "alfresco dining" add to the appeal; P.S. they keep "short hours" (service ends at 8:30 most nights, and they're closed on Fridays and summer Saturdays).

SHANGHAI TERRACE ☒   24 | 26 | 25 | $57
Peninsula Hotel, 108 E. Superior St., 5th fl. (bet. Michigan Ave. & Rush St.), 312-573-6744; www.chicago.peninsula.com
"Attention to detail and interesting flavors" are hallmarks of this "exceptional", "marvelously appointed temple of outstanding Pan-Asian cuisine" in the Peninsula that "transports" raters with the "refined elegance" of its "gorgeous" River North setting and its "quality service" – whether "for special occasions" or "expense-account" dining (fans also praise its rooftop terrace as "the most beautiful Zen garden in the city" and "the ideal summer date venue"); a minority, however, finds it "pricey above its merit."

SHAW'S CRAB HOUSE   23 | 19 | 21 | $46
21 E. Hubbard St. (bet. State St. & Wabash Ave.), 312-527-2722
1900 E. Higgins Rd. (Rte. 53), Schaumburg, 847-517-2722
www.shawscrabhouse.com
"Plain, simple fresh fish" and "surprisingly good sushi too" make these River North and Northwest Suburban "stand-

bys" a "Chicago seafood tradition", with "professional" service and "a choice between formal and casual dining rooms" (many patrons "prefer the informality" of the "oyster bars, with their great selection, throwback atmosphere" and "live music"); still, others opine that its somewhat "pedestrian" profferings have "gotten rather pricey."

Shine & Morida
20 | 18 | 19 | $30

901 W. Armitage Ave. (Fremont St.), 773-296-0101;
www.shinemorida.com
"One-stop Chinese-Japanese" dining from a "unique, diverse menu" "has earned a loyal following" of "dual"-minded Lincoln Park "locals" for this "upscale" "hybrid" serving "solid" Mandarin meals – some say this is the "better" option – and "very fresh sushi" (it's also "a great spot for takeout or delivery"); a "family crowd dominates" the side-by-side "modern" environments in the "early hours – until the sleeker singles and couples take over later on."

Shiroi Hana
18 | 8 | 17 | $20

3242 N. Clark St. (Belmont Ave.), 773-477-1652
A "standby", this 21-year-old Lakeview Japanese "budget-sushi" spot satisfies seekers of a "good variety" of "fresh" "standards" that are "not as expensive as" the raw-fish fare at more "yuppified places"; it's "always full, but [there's] seldom a wait" – though be warned it's "not for romantics" as the "decor is awful."

Shula's Steakhouse
20 | 19 | 19 | $62

Sheraton Chicago, 301 E. North Water St. (Columbus Dr.),
312-670-0788
Wyndham Northwest Chicago, 400 Park Blvd. (Thorndale Ave.),
Itasca, 630-775-1499
www.donshula.com
"If you like the 1972 Dolphins, you'll like" these two members of a national team of "upscale" "sports-themed steakhouses celebrating Shula's splendid career"; the defense deems them "well done", with "great service and food", ("huge" "aged steaks" and seafood too), but the offense scores them "too expensive for the quality" (the "black Angus offerings can't stand up to the prime cuts" elsewhere) and thinks "the coach should have stuck with football."

Sidebar Grille
– | – | – | M

221 N. LaSalle St. (Wacker Dr.), 312-739-3900;
www.sidebargrille.com
This Loop Eclectic serves moderately priced American faves (ribs, steaks, Cobb salad, turkey club) and a mix of global goodies (Thai beef salad, quesadilla, fish tacos) in a comfy, carpeted space appointed with leather booths, walnut tables and multiple TVs airing sports or the stock ticker; there's also a big smoke-free bar area and a cafe for morning coffee or a quick lunch.

SIGNATURE ROOM 18 27 20 $54
John Hancock Ctr., 875 N. Michigan Ave., 95th fl.
(bet. Chestnut St. & Delaware Pl.), 312-787-9596;
www.signatureroom.com

With "better views than the [John Hancock Center's] actual observation deck", this Streeterville New American is "the greatest place to bring" "out-of-towners" for a "gargantuan Sunday brunch", a "reasonable lunch buffet" or just "a drink in the bar", but veterans with "vertigo and wallet cramps" advise "go somewhere else" for dinner because this "overpriced" "towering tourist trap" "can afford to under-perform" with its "pedestrian" food and service; N.B. live jazz spices up weekends.

Silver Cloud Bar & Grill 18 14 17 $19
1700 N. Damen Ave. (Wabansia Ave.), 773-489-6212;
www.silvercloudchicago.com

This "quintessential neighborhood place" in Bucktown qualifies as a "low-key hangout" and "hangover place" with "homey", "artery-clogging" Traditional American "comfort food" reminiscent of "elementary school" – "go for the sloppy joes or the grilled cheese and tomato soup" – and a "great drink selection"; it "looks like a trashy diner" with "lots of '70s sparkle furniture inside", plus there's "great outdoor seating" ("you can bring your dog", though Fido has to stay outside the fence).

Silver Seafood ● ▽ 22 7 17 $23
4829 N. Broadway St. (Lawrence Ave.), 773-784-0668

"It almost takes longer to read the menu than to eat" at this "Cantonese-style" Chinese seafood spot where Uptowners turn up for "delicious", "authentic", "fresh" fare (some of the fodder is "live" when you arrive, so "you can watch it swim before you" consume it); still, frustrated fish lovers fault the "horrible" setting and feel that management "needs to have a proficient English speaker on staff."

Slice of Life/Hy Life Bistro ⊄ ▽ 13 12 13 $25
4120 W. Dempster St. (bet. Crawford Ave. & Keeler St.),
Skokie, 847-674-2021

Filling a Suburban North niche "for the orthodox" diner, this double-kitchen duo (one mainly vegetarian, the other Eclectic) draws diverse comments for its "wide selection" of fare – some cite "good kosher pizza" in its support, whereas others insist only a "captive audience" "would put up with such poor food"; P.S. hours vary by season.

Smith & Wollensky 22 20 20 $55
318 N. State St. (Wacker Dr.), 312-670-9900;
www.smithandwollensky.com

"Bone or no bone, that is the question" at this "classic" River North steakhouse that "ranks high for a chain" on the strength of "excellent slabs" of prime dry-aged meat "with the expected accompaniments", "a kick-ass" if "expensive" "wine list" and "fabulous martinis" in a "fantastic" "riverside location"; fans find it "pricey but worth it" and say the cafe "downstairs is a bargain" (and "open late"), though moderates who muse "there are better places" "in the steak race" cite "attitude issues" and "inconsistent" service.

Smoke Daddy
| 20 | 12 | 15 | $19 |

1804 W. Division St. (bet. Ashland & Damen Aves.),
773-772-6656; www.thesmokedaddy.com
Fans of "good, smoky flavor" "love the great ribs, sweet potato fries" and "yummy pulled pork" at this Wicker Park "local hangout" serving "just plain ol'" "bodacious" BBQ; supporters also like its "barlike" setting decorated with vintage Chicago photos and guitars on the walls and say another "plus" is that there's "a live band every night with no cover", though some suggest "the bands are hit-or-miss" and "service is slow."

socca
| 21 | 18 | 20 | $34 |

3301 N. Clark St. (Aldine Ave.), 773-248-1155;
www.soccachicago.com
"They're happy to have you" at this "elegant" but "unpretentious" "gourmet" "surprise" "amid the hustle and bustle" of Lakeview/Wrigleyville, where the "simple, rustic" French-Italian bistro fare features "high-quality ingredients" (with "a touch of the unexpected thrown in") and the decor includes "amazing windows"; fence-sitters, however, perceive some "odd combinations" that "don't quite work", and purport that the "painfully loud room mars an otherwise friendly and appealing restaurant" – though the "side patio is nice and relaxing."

Soiree Bar & Restaurant, The
| – | – | – | M |

4539 N. Lincoln Ave. (bet. Sunnyside & Wilson Aves.),
773-293-3690
Daniel Vogel, a former Wolfgang Puck apprentice, creates moderately priced, foodie-friendly New American fare featuring many organic ingredients and world-traveler accents – French, Asian, Italian, Latin – at this Lincoln Park storefront (formerly She She), a cozy little space with a tin ceiling, leopard-print chair cushions and paper tablecloths; the bar biz carries on until 2 AM, and unusual brunch fare is served à la carte on Sundays.

Sola 🗷
| – | – | – | M |

3868 N. Lincoln Ave. (Byron St.), 773-327-3868
Carol Wallack split from Deleece to launch this Lakeview New American with Asian and Hawaiian accents and reasonable prices that extend to the wine list; the soft, modern space is done in warm yellows and browns and lit by a 'sea' of pendant light fixtures, a wall of windows and a double-sided fireplace set in a stone room divider; N.B. no

you're not lost – despite its address, the restaurant entrance is really on Byron St.

Souk ⌧
▽ 17 | 19 | 15 | $34

1552 N. Milwaukee Ave. (bet. Division St. & North Ave.), 773-227-1818; www.soukrestaurant.com

"If you love dancing", this "funky" Wicker Park Middle Eastern eatery with "fun" harem decor "is a can't-miss hot spot on the weekends" and Wednesdays, when it hosts a band and belly dancing; it's also a "great place to smoke a hookah" all week long, and fans "could live off the appetizers", but critics take a pass on what they consider "so-so food" and "slow service."

South
▽ 19 | 17 | 18 | $32

5900 N. Broadway (Rosedale Ave.), 773-989-7666; www.southinchicago.com

"The vibe is welcoming and the customers are from all walks of life" at this Edgewater eatery now serving Eclectic cuisine (it's "not as Southern as it used to be"); loyal fans favor the "very good", "innovative" eats and "great atmosphere", but "nothing special"-ists nag it "still hasn't decided what to be when it grows up" and "liked it better when it was The Room" – though they're "happy it's remained BYO."

South Gate Cafe
18 | 18 | 19 | $34

655 Forest Ave. (Deerpath Ave.), Lake Forest, 847-234-8800

Set on Lake Forest's Market Square, this "upscale local hangout" serves a "varied American menu" of "tasty" food; insiders favor the "clubby" interior with fireplace, while fresh-air fiends say "summertime out in the courtyard is how to enjoy this place" – still, some middlers maintain they've "never had a bad meal here, but never a great one either", while foes simply "don't get the attraction."

South Water Kitchen
17 | 17 | 17 | $31

Hotel Monaco, 225 N. Wabash Ave. (Upper Wacker Dr.), 312-236-9300; www.southwaterkitchen.com

Traditional American "home cooking" (including a "good breakfast") "with modern twists" and a "cute" "high-ceiling room" have some Loop denizens grading this a "great place for a quick and hearty" lunch, a "drink after work" or a "pre-theater" dinner, but "uneven" food and "hit-or-miss service" sour surveyors who note it's "not great in any category" – though it's "convenient if you're staying at the hotel."

Speakeasy Supperclub
22 | 21 | 20 | $36

1401 W. Devon Ave. (Glenwood Ave.), 773-338-0600; www.speakeasysupperclub.com

Co-owned by restaurateur Jody Andre (South, ex Tomboy) and crooner Michael Feinstein, this "cool", "cozy" Edgewater Eclectic "has brought life to a barren stretch of

Devon Avenue"; fans "can't say enough about" its "great concept": combine an "interesting menu" of "inventive food" and an "intimate atmosphere" with regular "live-music" entertainment; some suggest that the service is "inconsistent", but pragmatists pen that its BYO status "is a great thing", as it "helps to soften the bill."

SPIAGGIA
26 27 25 $80

One Magnificent Mile Bldg., 980 N. Michigan Ave., 2nd fl. (Oak St.), 312-280-2750; www.spiaggiarestaurant.com

Expect a "peak dining experience" at this "honed-to-perfection", "luxury" Gold Coaster boasting a "sumptuous" setting with "spectacular views" of the Michigans (both Lake and Avenue), chef Tony Mantuano's "sublime", "incomparable Italian" cuisine, an "excellent", "extensive wine list" and "superlative service"; most maintain it's "one of the few places where the high price tag is worth it", though a segment of surveyors submits that the staff's "snooty" and the "small portions" are "overpriced" ("lunch is a lot less expensive"); N.B. jackets required.

Spoon Thai
22 12 16 $17

4608 N. Western Ave. (Wilson Ave.), 773-769-1173; www.spoonthai.com

"Not at all the usual Thai fare", this Lincoln Square BYO's "interesting", "authentic and aromatic" chow — including "edgy dishes" such as its "unique catfish curry with eggplant" — makes it a "cheap-eats" "favorite" that has devotees declaring the "owners should charge double (but we're glad they don't)"; if you find the decor "a little depressing", remember that it's "great for pickup or delivery."

SPRING
27 25 25 $59

2039 W. North Ave. (Damen Ave.), 773-395-7100; www.springrestaurant.net

Shawn McClain's "incredible creations" of "perfectly prepared" New American seafood "with a slight Asian slant" inspire acolytes to inquire "is it impolite to lick the plate?" at this "hip" Wicker Parker that's "as fresh and exciting as the season it's named after"; the "quietly elegant setting" "in a converted bathhouse" is "beautiful and peaceful", the service is "polished but not overwhelming" and there's an "outstanding wine list", all of which adds up to "a wonderful experience" — so if you don't have a "special occasion, just come up with one."

Square Kitchen
18 18 18 $26

4600 N. Lincoln Ave. (Wilson Ave.), 773-751-1500; www.squarekitchen.com

"Equally good for brunch and dinner", this "solid Lincoln Square establishment" proffers "just-real-good" Traditional and New American eats in a "funky space" that's "casual", "comfortable" and "kid-friendly"; regulars grouse the "limited menu" "gets a little boring" and "could use a bit more creativity", but it's nevertheless "a great staple to have around."

Stained Glass Wine Bar Bistro   23   20   22 $42
1735 Benson Ave. (bet. Church & Clark Sts.), Evanston, 847-864-8600; www.thestainedglass.com
"Fun flights" and an "interesting modern American menu, served well" by a "knowledgeable", "unpretentious" staff, make this "reliable" "little" restaurant "tucked between Evanston storefronts" equally "great for a fancy dinner or just a bite after a movie" – especially given the "inventive wine pairings" from its "wide-ranging list" and its "warm" space, which "looks better after" a recent "renovation."

Stanley's Kitchen & Tap   19   13   15 $19
1970 N. Lincoln Ave. (Armitage Ave.), 312-642-0007; www.stanleysrestaurant.com
"A good neighborhood joint" for "down-home" Traditional American eating, "drinking and hanging out", this "fun" "fake roadhouse" and "family restaurant hidden in a bar" in Lincoln Park slings "classic mac 'n' cheese", "better meatloaf than mom's" and a "maximum-cholesterol" weekend brunch that gets "very crowded" – especially "during football season."

Starfish   23   19   20 $41
804 W. Randolph St. (Halsted St.), 312-997-2433; www.starfishsushi.com
"Delectable sushi" (including "wonderful rolls" that are "artistic and original in preparation and presentation") draws maki-munchers to this "romantic" Market District Japanese serving a "wide variety of sake choices" and "really fun martinis" – plus assessors also appreciate that it's "worth the price."

Star of Siam   20   14   18 $18
11 E. Illinois St. (State St.), 312-670-0100; www.starofsiamchicago.com
"Cheap and cheerful", this River North old-timer (opened in 1984) is "a humble choice" serving "reliably delicious" Thai with "no surprises" – "simply good stuff" that "they'll spice up if you request it hot"; in addition to "traditional tables and chairs", the "simple setting" offers "cubby holes to sit in (a fun departure)", and "fast service" makes it a "great" place to "grab a quick lunch" – though some surveyors score it as strictly "serviceable."

State   –   –   –   M
935 W. Webster Ave. (Bissell St.), 773-975-8030; www.statechicago.com
With one of the longest menus in memory, this tech-y Lincoln Park New American offers a vast selection of moderately priced, all-day eats (salads, burgers, wraps, entrees,

etc.) in a former grocery store; the electronic amusements include WiFi access, dozens of plasma screens, 20 free-access computer workstations and laptop rentals.

Stetson's Chop House 23 19 20 $49

Hyatt Regency, 151 E. Wacker Dr. (bet. Michigan & Stetson Aves.), 312-239-4495; www.hyatt.com

"Impressed" diners declare "don't dismiss" this "solid steakhouse" just "because it's in a tourist-filled [Loop] hotel", as it sizzles up "huge portions" of prime "dry-aged" beef in a "casual" setting with a "nice bar"; holdouts tally it a trifle "typical", though, and title it "a good steakhouse in a great steak town"; N.B. there's live jazz nightly except Sundays.

Stir Crazy 19 16 17 $21

Northbrook Court Shopping Ctr., 1186 Northbrook Ct.
(bet. Skokie Blvd. & Waukegan Rd.), Northbrook, 847-562-4800
Oakbrook Center Mall, 105 Oakbrook Ctr. (Rte. 83), Oak Brook, 630-575-0155
Woodfield Mall, 5 Woodfield Mall (Frontage & Golf Rds.), Schaumburg, 847-330-1200
28252 Diehl Rd. (Windfield Rd.), Warrenville, 630-393-4700
www.stircrazy.com

Frequent fryers find "nothing more fun than choosing your own ingredients, heaping them as high as possible in a bowl", then "watching" as they're "cooked fresh in front of you" at this "convenient and friendly" clan of Asian stir-fry stations with "many menu options" (including "prepared dishes"); it's "quick" and "good for kids", though some raters rank the results "run-of-the-mill" and the settings sometimes "hectic" and "noisy enough to drive you stir crazy."

Sullivan's Steakhouse 23 22 22 $50

415 N. Dearborn St. (Hubbard St.), 312-527-3510
244 S. Main St. (bet. Jackson & Jefferson Aves.), Naperville, 630-305-0230
www.sullivanssteakhouse.com

"They do a really nice job" "for either business or romance" at this "polished", "clubby" duo in River North and the Western Suburbs, where the certified Angus steaks are "excellent", "the onion rings are as big as doughnuts and the broccoli is as big as a small tree"; some respondents regard it as "a notch below some of the other places" due to "disappointing service", but others observe "the jazz and the great bar set it apart" – plus it's "a bit less expensive"; P.S. "the pineapple martinis are addictive."

SUPERDAWG DRIVE-IN 22 16 18 $9

Midway Int'l Airport, 5700 S. Cicero Ave. (55th St.), 773-948-6300
6363 N. Milwaukee Ave. (Devon Ave.), 773-763-0660 ●⊘⊄
www.superdawg.com

An "icon" of "Americana" on the Northwest Side, this "true drive-in" "of the 1950s era" delivers "dawgs to die for" in

"amusing little boxes" plus "deeelicious" shakes and fries –
all the ingredients of "perfect summer evenings" (and
travelers can get a taste at the Midway Airport outpost);
besides, you "gotta love the two flirting hot dogs on the roof",
though smart alecks "don't understand why there isn't a little" cocktail weenie up there too, since the couple's "been
standing there for years – perhaps they should lie down!"

Sushi Ai ⊠

– | – | – | M

710 W. Euclid Ave. (Parkside Dr.), Palatine, 847-221-5100
'Sushi love' swoops down on the Northwest 'burbs via this
sophisticated Japanese, where a master sushi chef creates unique maki in conjunction with a thorough roster of
the raw and the cooked, all served alongside a generous
sake selection in an intimate Asian-chic setting that belies
its strip-mall location; N.B. the lunch boxes are a bargain.

Sushi Naniwa

21 | 12 | 20 | $33

607 N. Wells St. (bet. Ohio & Ontario Sts.), 312-255-8555;
www.sushinaniwa.com
An "authentic sushi bar" "without all the fluff" of some
newer competitors, this River North Japanese from owner
Bob Bee (of Bob San fame) is known for "reliable", "very
fresh fish" "at a reasonable price"; perhaps the "standard", "no-frills" decor is "not particularly memorable",
but the service is "attentive without being annoying" and
there's "great outdoor seating in the summer" – plus it's
also "good for takeout."

SUSHISAMBA RIO

21 | 26 | 17 | $48

504 N. Wells St. (bet. Grand Ave. & Illinois St.), 312-595-2300;
www.sushisamba.com
"Super-cool atmosphere" wins the day at this "jumping"
"Asian-Latin–themed" River Norther with a "wild" "nightclub feel" ("PartySamba Rio!"), "amazing roof bar" and "lots
of pretty people" using "interesting" "coed bathrooms";
surveyors are split on whether the sushi–South American
amalgam is "unique and exciting" or "schizophrenic", but
those with the "sneaking suspicion" they're "not hip enough
to be in the room" posit it "provides that Miami touch that
nobody was really asking for", advising "be sure to get
glammed up to get the respect of" the "uninformed" staff.

SUSHI WABI

26 | 18 | 19 | $41

842 W. Randolph St. (bet. Green & Peoria Sts.), 312-563-1224;
www.sushiwabi.com
Drawing "a mostly younger crowd", this "swank, trendy"
Market District "spot serves a unique blend of new sushi
as well as the typical standby" stuff in "cool", "urban-
contemporary" confines with "loud music and low lighting"; the "killer" cuts and "creative maki rolls" ("fantastic
hot" Japanese fare too) can produce "killer waits", and
service strikes critics as "complacent."

Swordfish　　　　　　　▽ 25 | 22 | 23 | $37
207 N. Randall Rd. (McKee St.), Batavia, 630-406-6463;
www.swordfishsushi.com
"High-end, innovative sushi finally reaches the far
West Suburbs", prompting novices to note "now I know
why people like this stuff", at this "trendy" Japanese
sister of Starfish and Wildfish where "incredibly" "fresh
fish" – and "much more" – is served in a "subtle, modern"
setting that surveyors say will make you "feel like you're in
a Downtown restaurant"; P.S. it also offers a "thoughtfully
planned wine list."

Tagine ☒　　　　　　　　– | – | – | I
4749 N. Rockwell St. (Lawrence Ave.), 773-989-4340
Though the namesake slow-cooked stews are the specialty of the house, this bargain-priced Moroccan storefront in Ravenswood also dishes up variations on
couscous and kebabs, all served in a modern, pillow-
strewn space enlivened by juicy shades of mango and
grape; N.B. it's BYO.

Takkatsu　　　　　　　　– | – | – | M
161 W. Wing St. (Vail Ave.), Arlington Heights,
847-818-1860
Reincarnating the shuttered Winnetka spot of the same
name is this cozy Suburban Northwest hideaway in a new
condo building with a serene dining space and a bar proffering Japanese beer, sake and shochu; the moderately
priced Japanese menu emphasizes tonkatsu – the traditional breaded-and-fried pork cutlet.

TALLGRASS　　　　　　　28 | 24 | 25 | $69
1006 S. State St. (10th St.), Lockport, 815-838-5566;
www.tallgrassrestaurant.com
"Spectacular", "innovative" New French fare and a "deep
wine list" (600 labels strong) fuel this "venerable"
"foodie's paradise" "in the middle of nowhere" – aka historic Southwest Suburban Lockport – that's "well worth
the drive from anywhere"; gourmets gush they "would go
broke if they [lived] nearby", returning for chef-partner
Robert Burcenski's "fine haute cuisine" with "wonderful
presentation" in a "very private", "romantic" space;
N.B. jackets are suggested for gentlemen.

Tango　　　　　　　　　▽ 20 | 15 | 19 | $33
5 W. Jackson St. (Washington St.), Naperville,
630-848-1818
It's "lots of fun" to chow on "excellent" steaks or "sample
the tapas and sit on the roof" quaffing "homemade sangria" at this Argentinean "addition to Naperville's eclectic
choice of eateries"; in summer, your "wonderful evening"
might include "a great guitarist playing" and salsa nights
on Thursdays and Fridays.

TANGO SUR
| 24 | 16 | 18 | $27 |

3763 N. Southport Ave. (Grace St.), 773-477-5466

"It's all about" the "obscenely large, delicious cuts" of "succulent, flavorful meat" at this "lively" Wrigleyville BYO Argentinean steakhouse in a "dark, intimate" "storefront"; it's seemingly "always packed" with "locals" who "line up out the door" since it's "an absolute steal", though critics contend the "quality isn't first rate" and the "earnest service" can be "unreliable", adding that management "should improve" the "unassuming" interior – though you can "eat outside on a nice night."

Tank Sushi
| 21 | 20 | 18 | $35 |

4514 N. Lincoln Ave. (Sunnyside Ave.), 773-769-2600;
www.tanksushi.com

"Sleek" and "spiffy" for Lincoln Square, this "indulgent" Japanese "pleasure" combines "clever maki rolls" made from "fresh ingredients" – "if you're looking for traditional sushi, this isn't the place" – with "brilliant drinks, beautiful presentation and surroundings" that "can be very loud" ("ambient club music"); some feel it's "service-challenged", and tight-fisted tipsters say it's "slightly overpriced", so "go before 7" PM on weekends for the "half-price deal."

Tapas Barcelona
| 20 | 19 | 17 | $26 |

The Northshore Hotel Retirement Home, 1615 Chicago Ave.
(bet. Church & Davis Sts.), Evanston, 847-866-9900;
www.tapasbarcelona.com

"Eat communally to savor the most sensations" at this "festive" Spaniard serving North Suburbanites "very good" tapas, "great sangria" and the "best sherry selection" in the vicinity; pleased patrons praise it as "perfect in summer for dining in the pretty garden" "but also fun in the noisy exciting dining room" done up in "lots of cool tiles and colors", though some warn of "rough service" and say the food "never really surprises or wows" – "but the price is right."

Tarantino's
| 21 | 20 | 20 | $35 |

1112 W. Armitage Ave. (Seminary Ave.), 773-871-2929

John Tarantino's "upscale Lincoln Park" establishment is a "cozy place for a simple dinner or a romantic night out" over "quality Italian" fare that's "consistently" "solid and fresh" – "without the high price tag"; some say "service can be on or off" and feel there are "probably better options out there", but more maintain it's "everything one could want in a neighborhood restaurant"; P.S. "have a martini at the bar", as there's a "great list" to choose from.

Tasting Room, The ●◖☒
| 18 | 20 | 19 | $32 |

1415 W. Randolph St. (Ogden Ave.), 312-942-1313;
www.tlcwine.com

"A tasting adventure" awaits visitors to this "laid-back" "yet still trendy" Market District "hideaway" boasting "a breadth of [Eclectic] appetizers that many wine bars seem to lack" plus "staffers who know the inventory and can describe with accuracy each" option from the "fantastic selection" ("at good prices"); the "convivial atmosphere" of its "roomy" space lures loungers to the "leather couches" and "chairs in the open loft upstairs", where they're wowed by an "unrivaled" "city-skyline view."

Tavern 🛇   ▽ 23 25 25 $59
519 N. Milwaukee Ave. (bet. Cook Ave. & Lake St.),
Libertyville, 847-367-5755
North Suburban fans who "feel very lucky" to have this "local" New American "favorite" "so close" swear it serves the "best steaks in" the area, "excellent fresh seafood" and an "ample list of fine wines", all within a setting sporting "extra special and unique" decor – no wonder so few mind that it's "a bit pricey"; P.S. "the dessert list is satisfyingly sweet."

Tavern on Rush ●   19 19 19 $45
1031 N. Rush St. (Bellevue Pl.), 312-664-9600;
www.tavernonrush.com
A "great celeb hot spot", this "consistent", "no-nonsense" Traditional American steakhouse has a "crowded, lively" "bar downstairs" and "dining above", where "you can sit and watch the action on Rush" (it's also a "wonderful place to sit outside for lunch in the summer"); still, some say the "prime people-watching takes your mind off" the "disappointing service" and "high cost", while others see it as a "singles bar" for the "Viagra-triangle crowd" "looking for love in all the wrong places"; N.B. weekend brunch is also served.

Tecalitlan ●   ▽ 23 16 19 $17
1814 W. Chicago Ave. (Wood St.), 773-384-4285
"Holy" "big burrito!" hail honchos who hanker for the "generous portions" of "delicious", "authentic Mexican food" and "great value" at this "laid-back", "retro" West Town "original"; it's "open very late" – until 3 AM on weekends – and it's "always full", plus there's "takeout" available, too.

Ted's Montana Grill   17 17 17 $26
1811 Tower Dr. (Chestnut Ave.), Glenview, 847-729-1117;
www.tedsmontanagrill.com
"Authentic Old West flair" comes to the North Suburbs via this "friendly" member of Ted Turner's Traditional American herd, where the menu offers "great options for adults and kids alike" (the "gigantic onion rings are a must", and "try the bison burger"); the interior's "warm colors make for a relaxing dining experience", and the "nice bar" helps with the waits, which "can be daunting on weekend evenings", but some rustlers still rate the overall experience "disappointing."

Tempo ◑≠ 19 | 11 | 17 | $16
6 E. Chestnut St. (State St.), 312-943-4373
"Open 24 hours to better serve the late, late crowd", this "nice, Greek" Gold Coast "landmark" is a "classic diner" that's "great morning, noon and night" for "wonderful, enormous omelets" and other "tasty" "coffee-shop" fare; there's "pleasant sidewalk dining in season", but "expect to wait for breakfast/brunch on the weekends", when it's "a zoo" – though it can be "dead at dinner"; P.S. yep, it's still "cash only."

Terragusto Italian Café – | – | – | M
1851 W. Addison St. (bet. Ravenswood & Wolcott Aves.), 773-248-2777
Theo Gilbert (ex Trattoria No. 10, Spiaggia) created this intimate, reasonably priced Italian BYO to showcase his devotion to organic, sustainable and local ingredients; salads are served with handmade vinegars, pasta is made fresh and the limited entree list is simplicity itself (including a daily fish seared and roasted); the casually elegant, tablecloth-free Roscoe Village setting also serves frittatas and crespelle for breakfast and panini for lunch, and there's a small 'local market' area vending farm-fresh ingredients – from produce, flour and eggs to sauces and cheeses.

Texas de Brazil Churrascaria ⊠ – | – | – | E
Woodfield Mall, 5 Woodfield Mall (Frontage & Golf Rds.), Schaumburg, 847-413-1600; www.texasdebrazil.com
Southern Brazil comes to the Suburban Northwest via this upscale churrascaria chain with a touch of Texas hospitality (it's a Dallas import); all-you-can-eat meat (just don't fill up on the huge salad bar) is served by a swashbuckling staff wielding skewers like cutlasses in the rugged Southwestern setting.

Thai Classic ∇ 23 | 15 | 18 | $20
3332 N. Clark St. (bet. Belmont Ave. & Roscoe St.), 773-404-2000; www.thaiclassicrestaurant.com
It may "look like a standard neighborhood Thai place", but its "extensive menu" of "high-quality", "authentic" preparations and "cheap" prices (aided by a BYO policy) have raters raving over this "excellent spot" in Lakeview with a "friendly and efficient staff" and a "fantastic buffet on Saturday and Sunday"; P.S. some like it "especially for takeout or delivery."

Thai Pastry 22 | 10 | 14 | $18
4925 N. Broadway St. (bet. Argyle St. & Lawrence Ave.), 773-784-5399; www.thaipastry.com
"If you like Thai, don't miss" the "authentic" "awesome, cheap" eats with "fresh, vibrant flavors" and "some different offerings than most" at this Uptown Siamese where "BYO is a big plus"; most are "forgiving of the atmosphere"

(those who feel it "brings the food down" "order for takeout or have it delivered"), but others opine that "the only letdown is the service, which can be slow and inattentive" – "but not rude."

Think Café | 24 | 18 | 23 | $33 |

2235 N. Western Ave. (Lyndale St.), 773-394-0537;
www.think-cafe.com

The "best secret of Bucktown" may be this Italian "gem" and "BYO bargain" that's "more sophisticated than you would think", having "grown into a very good restaurant" with "a nice balance of traditional items", "unique creations" and "not-to-be-missed desserts", all at "great prices"; rapt raters have "no second thoughts about returning" to the "quaint", "romantic" space, where "friendly owners" and "charming staffers" who "take what they do very seriously" provide "wonderful service."

Three Happiness ◗ | 22 | 10 | 17 | $19 |

209 W. Cermak Rd. (20th St.), 312-842-1964

"A Chinatown classic" that's "been there forever" (since 1971), this "family-run casual Chinese kitchen" with Cantonese "home cooking" and "steam-cart dim sum" is "always packed" with folks who come for the "great food" (especially "late-night eats", as it's open 24 hours on the weekend, and only closed from 6–9 AM on weekdays), not the "lacking atmosphere" or "spotty service"; P.S. it's unrelated to the bigger, more visible New Three Happiness on the corner.

312 Chicago | 19 | 19 | 19 | $38 |

Hotel Allegro, 136 N. LaSalle St. (Randolph St.), 312-696-2420;
www.312chicago.com

Dialers declare this "convenient" "class act" in the Loop's Hotel Allegro a "good spot for breakfast", a "power lunch", or an "after-work or pre-theater bite" thanks to a "nice, varied menu" of "delicious" Italian-American cooking that's "better than typical hotel dining room" fare, plus "great people-watching" – all "without breaking the bank"; still, some skeptics give it static, nagging about "noise", "pedestrian" provender and "rushed service" "before a show."

Thyme Café | 23 | 18 | 21 | $34 |

1540 N. Milwaukee Ave. (North Ave.), 773-227-1400;
www.thymechicago.com

Wicker Parkers "want to go back thyme and thyme again" to this "casual", "comfortably sophisticated" New American–New French (little sister to the former Thyme, now Timo), a "fun and yummy choice" thanks to "outstanding food" from chef-owner John Bubala served by an "accommodating" staff within a "warm", "welcoming" atmosphere; the "excellent brunch" features "an all-you-can-drink-mimosa option", and the "$25 three-course menu" is "the

best deal in the city" "for the quality" – plus simplicity-
seekers "love that the wine is all the same price."

Tiffin 　　　　　　　　　 22 | 15 | 17 | $25 |
2536 W. Devon Ave. (Maplewood Ave.), 773-338-2143
"Everything's great from soup to dessert" at this "upscale"
"jewel among the cheap eateries on Devon Avenue" in West
Rogers Park, where the Indian "menu is quite diverse"
(with plenty of "vegetarian options"), the interior is "comfortable", the staff is "helpful" and the prices are "very
reasonable" (the "weekday lunch buffet is a steal"); P.S. they
offer a "good wine selection" – and beer too.

Tilli's 　　　　　　　　　 16 | 17 | 15 | $24 |
1952 N. Halsted St. (bet. Armitage Ave. & Willow St.),
773-325-0044; www.tillischicago.com
With a "good drink" roster and "diverse" Eclectic eats (including "twists on old standbys"), this "upscale pub" in
Lincoln Park is "family-friendly by day" – the servers
"don't mind working around strollers" – and a "singles
scene by night", while "Sunday brunch is a popular option
for bleary-eyed" "hip locals"; still, dubious delegates who
dub the dining merely "decent" and suggest "service
could be better" "doubt the crowds are there for the food."

Timo 　　　　　　　　　　 – | – | – | M |
464 N. Halsted St. (Grand Ave.), 312-226-4300
After eight years, John Bubala has reconcepted his Near
West French-American pioneer, Thyme, and reopened it
as this Italian modernist with a well-crafted, midpriced
menu, served in a setting with stained glass–like murals on
the windows and contemporary light fixtures both indoors
and on the renowned landscaped patio; his existing small-
producer wine list will feature an expanded Italian section.

Timpano Italian Chophouse 🗷 　 – | – | – | M |
22 E. Chicago Ave. (Washington St.), Naperville, 630-753-0985;
www.timpanochophouse.net
An Orlando-based chain has stepped into the Western
'burbs space that formerly held Samba Room with this
swanky, big-city version of an Italian steakhouse; torch
songs and Sinatra-era crooning set a clubby mood amid
dark, handsome surroundings with leather booths, white
tablecloths and a martini lounge.

Tin Fish 　　　　　　　　 22 | 18 | 20 | $36 |
17 W. 512 22nd St. (Midwest Rd.), Oakbrook Terrace,
630-279-0808
Cornerstone Ctr., 18201 S. Harlem Ave. (183rd St.), Tinley Park,
708-532-0200
www.tf-tinfish.com
A school of surveyors savors this suburban seafood two-
fer for "extremely fresh" "edibles from the deep" "done
your way", a "fantastic raw bar" and "well-thought-out,

reasonably priced wine list"; the decor strikes some as "classy" and "clever", but a few fin-icky feeders feel both the "chain" ambiance and "'you guys' service" are "more casual than expected, considering the food quality" – also, some note "noise" issues, though boosters believe "the food makes up for it."

TIZI MELLOUL   21 | 25 | 20 | $41

531 N. Wells St. (Grand Ave.), 312-670-4338;
www.tizimelloul.com
"Come to the casbah" in River North, where "you can't help but feel cool" amid the "amazingly funky/exotic decor" with "different rooms to choose from" (including the "truly unique", "private" "round room"); to fully appreciate the "innovative flavors", "be adventurous" with the "unusual" and "high-quality" Middle Eastern–Mediterranean cuisine, then soak up the "fun drinks", "sexy vibe" and "occasional belly dancing" (on Sunday nights).

Toast   22 | 16 | 18 | $16

2046 N. Damen Ave. (Dickens Ave.), 773-772-5600
746 W. Webster Ave. (Halsted St.), 773-935-5600
Tasters toast this Traditional American twosome for "imaginative creations" such as "orgasmic stuffed French toast", "fluffy omelets" and "huge pancakes" "piled high with fresh fruit, granola and yogurt", all served within a "homey" "luncheonette" atmosphere; despite reports of "abrupt if not abusive service" and "hellish waits", hordes "still keep going back for the food"; P.S. "the Bucktown location has a nice back patio" but "no Bloody Marys [or other alcohol] . . . be warned!"

Tomboy ⊠   21 | 19 | 19 | $37

5402 N. Clark St. (bet. Balmoral Ave. & Clark St.),
773-907-0636; www.tomboyrestaurant.com
Andersonville appreciates this "classy"-"casual" "see-and-be-seen spot" where the New American "food and patrons are all yummy", the "great exposed-brick atmosphere" is "romantic" and "gay"-friendly, and the "recently acquired liquor license" hasn't obviated the "welcome BYO policy" (only a "$5 corkage" fee); still, a cadre of contributors considers the food "good but not haute cuisine" and the service "spotty"; N.B. there's live jazz on Thursdays.

Tony Rocco's River North ⊠   – | – | – | M

416 W. Ontario St. (bet. Kingsbury & Orleans Sts.),
312-787-1400
River North is home to this affordable rustic Italian ristorante that sounds like a chain but is actually a family-run independent named for the owner's son (her daughters and grand-daughters get menu items); think macaroni and meatballs, thin-crust pizzas and a giant antipasto-style salad for two, served in cozy confines with exposed brick and a whimsical

mural of Chicago; N.B. delivery within a two-mile radius means the luxury of brunch brought to your door.

Topo Gigio Ristorante | 20 | 17 | 19 | $34 |
1516 N. Wells St. (bet. Division St. & North Ave.), 312-266-9355
"Popular in the neighborhood", this "solid" Old Town "traditional Italian" performer "has become a classic" thanks to "delicious comfort food" (including seafood options such as "rich squid ink pasta" on Fridays), a "cute and kitschy atmosphere with images of Topo Gigio – the famous mouse – all over the place", "great outdoor eating" and "people-watching" in summer and "reasonable prices"; catty consumers, however, take a swipe at the bill of fare and staff, branding them "boring" and "bored", respectively.

TOPOLOBAMPO ⊠ | 27 | 23 | 25 | $57 |
445 N. Clark St. (bet. Hubbard & Illinois Sts.), 312-661-1434; www.fronterakitchens.com
"This is what the food in heaven must taste like" posit praisers of this "pinnacle" of Mexican *alta cucina* in River North, where "every bite" of "creative genius" Rick Bayless' cuisine is "utterly swoon-worthy", the tequila list is "to die for" and the "passionate staff" "pampers" patrons; most feel it's "more elegant than its attached sister restaurant, Frontera Grill", with fare that "really is better", even if a handful of heretics wonder "is it worth the price difference?"; P.S. "book well ahead", as getting "weekend reservations can take forever."

Trattoria D.O.C. | – | – | – | M |
706 Main St. (Custer Ave.), Evanston, 847-475-1111; www.trattoria-doc.com
A scaled-up cousin of Pizza D.O.C., this Evanstonian appeases appetites with an expanded selection of 30-some *pizze* (individual-sized thin crust with vegetarian, seafood and meat options), a full menu of hearty Italian offerings and a bar with a nice selection of wines and beers from The Boot – all in a snazzy storefront setting with a prominent brick wood-burning oven and wall of windows overlooking Main Street.

Trattoria Gianni | 18 | 15 | 20 | $38 |
1711 N. Halsted St. (bet. North Ave. & Willow St.), 312-266-1976; www.trattoriagianni.com
Raters regard this "friendly", "traditional trattoria" serving "simple, authentic" Italian fare as a "great neighborhood hangout" and "dependable pasta spot near the theaters" in Lincoln Park ("they always make sure you make your show"); sure, "the decor could be improved", but the "service is consistently very good" – and even those who find the experience "ordinary" admit it's "pleasant."

Trattoria No. 10 ⊠   23 20 21 $39

10 N. Dearborn St. (Madison St.), 312-984-1718;
www.trattoriaten.com
Considered a "quiet oasis" "in a hectic neighborhood", this
"charming", "consistent" "Loop classic" is a "favorite
of the theater" and "business-lunch" crowds, serving
up "a slice of real Italy in a sea of Americanized" versions
("homemade ravioli", "jump-at-you fresh fish") within a
"dark", "cozy", "underground" setting; some with sizable
stomachs growl over "high-ish prices [for] smallish portions", but the "value" "happy-hour buffet runs circles
around the competition."

Trattoria Roma   19 15 20 $30

1535 N. Wells St. (bet. North Ave. & Schiller St.), 312-664-7907;
www.trattoriaroma.com
"Authentic [Southern] Italian fare" earns this "wonderful
neighborhood spot" a loyal following of Old Town "locals"
who like the "great basic" food, "rustic grotto" atmosphere and "outdoor seating in the summer"; service comments conflict, though, with some praising the staff for
creating a "relaxed" environment "without the attitude"
but others quipping that the "speed of service is also authentic to Italy – leisurely."

Trattoria Trullo   19 14 18 $33

1700 Central St. (Eastwood Ave.), Evanston, 847-570-0093;
www.trattoriatrullo.com
"The real deal" for "very good Southern Italian cooking",
this "neighborhood favorite in Evanston" plates up "good
portions" "at reasonable prices", which are served by a
"friendly" staff "in the shadow of NU football"; the "storefront" space is "intimate", "but it can be noisy when full" –
so "go early or eat outside."

Tre Kronor   24 16 21 $18

3258 W. Foster Ave. (bet. Kedzie & Kimball Aves.),
773-267-9888; www.swedishbistro.com
"A taste of Sweden [and Norway] from the food to the
trolls on the walls" sums up this "off-the-beaten-path"
Scandinavian BYO "treasure" on the Northwest Side proffering "something decidedly different" with its "authentic",
"traditional" fare – such as "lots of herring" (at lunch) and
"great blueberry soup" for dessert – at "reasonable" prices
within a "cozy", "homelike atmosphere"; N.B. Christmas
brings live music, an extravagant all-you-can-eat dinner
and magicians for the kids (also on weekends in summer).

TRU ⊠   28 27 28 $117

676 N. St. Clair St. (bet. Erie & Huron Sts.), 312-202-0001;
www.trurestaurant.com
"Art and food meet and really, really like each other" at this
Streeterville "temple of excess" where chefs Rick Tramonto

("bravo!") and Gale Gand ("the goddess of the dessert") "amaze" with "progressive, daring" New French plates plus sommelier Scott Tyree's "divinely inspired" 1,400-bottle wine selection, all borne by a virtually "flawless" staff within a "stark, simple" setting sporting an "original Andy Warhol" and "a lovely little tuffet for Madame's handbag"; "sticker shock" aside, it's a "magical experience" that "will become a lasting memory"; N.B. jackets required.

Trucchi Italian Bistro — — — M

5141 Main St. (Curtiss St.), Downers Grove, 630-434-7700; www.trucchibistro.com

Its name is Italian for 'monkey business', and while this West Suburban trattoria features primate-themed decorative touches, it offers a fairly straightforward regional menu that, for the most part, eschews red sauce; an affordable wine list and carry-out pizza counter in the back round out the offerings; N.B. neighboring Comida Bebida shares the same owners, chef and kitchen.

T-Spot Sushi & Tea Bar — — — M

3925 N. Lincoln Ave. (Larchmont Ave.), 773-549-4500; www.tspotsushiandteabar.com

This Japanese newcomer in Lakeview combines creative rolls, raw-fish fare (including a create-your-own-tartare option) and a modicum of cooked seafood (no poultry or meat options) with a serious tea program offering about 35 selections by the cup or pot; the hip, nightclubby setting features black-and-yellow brick walls, a sushi bar and bright lounge furniture.

Tsuki 22 23 19 $39

1441-45 W. Fullerton Ave. (Janssen Ave.), 773-883-8722; www.tsuki.us

"Hip"-sters herald this Lincoln Park "standout in a crowded field" as "a showcase" for "wonderfully prepared Japanese cooked and raw dishes", both "traditional and contemporary", including "novel sushi and interesting small dishes", conveyed in a "clublike but serene space" by a "good" staff; tougher tipsters tell us it's "too trendy", though, from its clientele to its "techno-chic decor"; P.S. "go early for the kids' bento boxes – Hello Kitty" for girls, a train motif for boys.

Tsunami 20 17 17 $39

1160 N. Dearborn St. (Division St.), 312-642-9911; www.tsunamichicago.com

A relative old-timer at 10 years of age, this "solid sushi choice" on the Gold Coast slices "delicious basics" of raw-fish fare and other Japanese faves ("stay for the tempura and udon noodles"); some suggest its offerings seem "less innovative" now, with nothing "unique or off-the-wall", while others assess the "aging" dining room as

"nothing special" (as evidenced by the Decor score drop),
but "romantics" suggest the sofas "upstairs near the fireplace" "for a relaxed experience", or avail yourself of the
"great patio seating."

Tucci Benucch   18 17 18 $29
900 N. Michigan Ave., 5th fl. (Walton St.), 312-266-2500;
www.leye.com
The "hearty", "convenient, middle-of-the-road family"
Italian fare (including the "best baked spaghetti around")
"holds its own" at this Lettuce Entertain You offering in the
Gold Coast's Bloomingdale's building; "regulars love it" for
a "relatively cheap" "shopping lunch or informal dinner"
with "relaxed service" and "cozy", "villa-esque decor",
but cranky shoppers who deem it merely "decent" dub it
"Disneyland meets Tuscany."

Tufano's Vernon Park Tap ⊅   21 12 19 $25
1073 W. Vernon Park Pl. (bet. Harrison & Racine Sts.),
312-733-3393
"Run, don't walk" – and "take cash" – to this "old-time"
"classic" on the Near South Side known since 1930 for
"huge amounts of cheap", "homestyle" Southern Italian
dishes (made from recipes handed down from the current
owner's grandmother) and a "casual", "fun family atmosphere"; if for no other reason, it's "worth visiting because
there are not a lot of places like this left."

Turquoise   21 16 17 $29
2147 W. Roscoe St. (bet. Damon & Western Aves.), 773-549-3523;
www.turquoisedining.com
"More than just the bar it appears to be", this "nice" entry
offers restless Roscoe Villagers a Turkish tour via the
"bright Mediterranean flavors" of its "reasonably priced
fare", including "flavorful meats and seafood"; some suggest the "genial" "though unpolished" staff sometimes
provides "splintered service", but at least "there's a
friendly atmosphere", and "the owners try hard to make
you feel welcome."

Tuscany   22 18 19 $33
3700 N. Clark St. (Waveland Ave.), 773-404-7700
1014 W. Taylor St. (Morgan St.), 312-829-1990
1415 W. 22nd St. (Rte. 83), Oak Brook, 630-990-1993
550 S. Milwaukee Ave. (bet. Dundee & Hintz Rds.), Wheeling,
847-465-9988
www.stefanirestaurants.com
"Tuscan before Tuscan was cool", these "lively", "dependable Phil Stefani outlets" – the Little Italy *pater*
familias and its various offspring – dish out "hearty"
"traditional" Northern Italian fare plus "original dishes"
("two words: pear ravioli"); each manages to seem "elegant and homey at the same time", though "every location

is a little different", and the original has a "cool throwback bar", but assets aside, some type it as "typical" and say "service can be slow."

Tweet ⌷ | 21 | 16 | 20 | $28 |

5020 N. Sheridan Rd. (Foster St.), 773-728-5576;
www.tweet.biz

"Go for the early-*bird* special" at this "Uptown gem" featuring an "arty" vibe, "fab staff" and "Eclectic menu" of "funk-a-licous" "seasonal" "contemporary Americana" made from "fresh, high-quality" and "organic" ingredients; it can be "noisy and crowded", especially at the "outstanding" weekend brunch, while some little birdies tell us of "uneven food (some dishes make it but some just don't cut it)" and cheep that "the whole cash-only thing is really inconvenient."

Twin Anchors | 22 | 13 | 18 | $27 |

1655 N. Sedgwick St. (bet. Eugenie St. & North Ave.),
312-266-1616; www.twinanchorsribs.com

"Delicious but divey (and therefore great)", this "quintessential" BBQ in Old Town (opened in 1932) "should be declared a historical landmark" say supporters who swear by its "succulent", "fall-off-the-bones" "ribs basted in a zesty sauce" – and "good chicken, burgers, chili and salad" too; with a "fun Wisconsin-like" "tavern" feel and "atmosphere to spare", it's constantly "crowded" with "friendly, sometimes rowdy" folk enjoying the "good juke-box" and "TV sports", so expect a "possibly lengthy wait" ("they don't accept reservations").

Twist | 22 | 18 | 18 | $26 |

3412 N. Sheffield Ave. (Clark St.), 773-388-2727

"The most inventive" Eclectic small plates, "good seasonal specials" and "traditional" Spanish tapas all fit in this "little" Lakeview lair with "a lot of character"; add "awesome sangria" and "efficient servers" and it's a "fun place to start the night" and "a great group dining destination" – but it's "small and the tables are cramped" so "get there early to avoid a wait."

Twisted Spoke ◑ | 18 | 17 | 17 | $17 |

3369 N. Clark St. (Roscoe St.), 773-525-5300
501 N. Ogden Ave. (Grand Ave.), 312-666-1500
www.twistedspoke.com

Roar up to these Near West and Wrigleyville "upscale dives" for some "big, big burgers and cold, cold beer" plus other "better-than-average" Traditional American "pub fare" and even some "respectable salads" served in a "pseudo–biker bar" setting with "metal tabletops, motorcycle parts everywhere" and "gruff service"; some say the "food's better with a hangover" – especially at the "great brunch" starring "killer bloody Marys" – and the weekly

"Smut and Eggs [event] at midnight on Saturdays" is "a must-see" for "porn" fanciers.

Udupi Palace
▽ | 23 | 11 | 17 | $16 |

2543 W. Devon Ave. (bet. Maplewood Ave. & Rockwell St.), 773-338-2152
Market Sq., 730 E. Schaumburg Rd. (Plum Grove Rd.), Schaumburg, 847-884-9510
www.udupipalace.com

To Southern Indian seekers, this West Rogers Park "favorite" and its Northwest Suburban sib are "bona fide dosai palaces" supplying "great vegetarian" entrees plus "a few meat dishes for carnivores" in "huge portions" and at "extremely reasonable prices"; perhaps the settings are "not fancy", but some nevertheless find them "interesting"; N.B. the city spot is BYO.

Uncommon Ground
21 | 20 | 19 | $20 |

3800 N. Clark St. (Grace St.), 773-929-3680;
www.uncommonground.com

"In the midst of the Wrigleyville madness", this "recently expanded" "coffee shop/bar/restaurant" is a "favorite hangout" for a "diverse clientele", providing "room upon room" of "entertainment options", including "some of the best live acts", plus "yummy" Eclectic eats incorporating some "organic" ingredients (including "excellent brunches" all week long); loungers label the "laid-back atmosphere" "addictive", with some preferring the "front room with fireplace" and others heading for the "nice patio" – "it's the bomb."

Uno Di Martino
21 | 11 | 20 | $26 |

2122 W. Lawrence Ave. (Hamilton Ave.), 773-878-1326

"Giving it a very personal touch, the brothers who own" this "quirky" Lincoln Square BYO, chefs Martino and Geronimo Ontiveros, create "fresh", "authentic and homey Italian" fare that's served by a "warm and savvy staff"; the "stunningly strange" interior is done up as a "faux castle" (a reminder of "the space's previous occupant", "a medieval restaurant"), but the "bizarro decor" "shouldn't deter you" – just know that it gets "noisy because of the stone walls."

VA PENSIERO
26 | 23 | 25 | $51 |

Margarita Inn, 1566 Oak Ave. (Davis St.), Evanston,
847-475-7779; www.va-p.com

A "long-standing" destination for "distinctive, quality Italian" that's "both satisfying and imaginative", this "upscale" "old-world" North Suburbanite in a "quaint" "residential" hotel "enchants" with "wonderful service" – including "knowledgeable" "wine assistance" with the "fantastic", "handpicked" "all-Italian" list – and a "soothing", "romantic" setting complete with a "lovely" "terrace";

true, it's "not cheap", but it's still "one of Evanston's great special-occasion restaurants."

Venus Greek-Cypriot Cuisine ▽ 19 17 22 $33

820 W. Jackson Blvd. (bet. Green & Halsted Sts.), 312-714-1001; www.venuschicago.com

Admirers of this "lovely", "adventurous" "addition to Greektown" delight in its "delicious and unique twist" on Hellenic fare, as it serves "not only Greek" cuisine but also dishes with a wider "Mediterranean flair", including "some typically Cypriot dishes"; it's "an interesting variation in a neighborhood where each place [serves] the same food", and there's also a lunch buffet and live weekend entertainment; P.S. "follow the waiter's suggestions" – but don't miss "the slow-cooked lamb."

Vermilion 21 19 19 $46

10 W. Hubbard St. (bet. Dearborn & State Sts.), 312-527-4060

"An interesting mix of foodies" finds "delicious" "new things to try" on the "intriguing menu" of "cutting-edge" "Indian-Latin fusion" cuisine at this "hip", "intimate" River Norther with "simple but sexy decor"; still, some traditionalists assert that the "unique concept" "doesn't quite work" (and comes with a "steep price tag" to boot), adding that the "stark" setting can be "noisy"; N.B. the ratings may not reflect a post-*Survey* redecoration and menu revamp.

Via Carducci 20 17 17 $30

1419 W. Fullerton Ave. (Southport Ave.), 773-665-1981; www.viacarducci.com

Enjoy "quality" Southern Italian (including "wonderfully done traditional offerings" and "authentic specials") "without breaking the bank" at this "very intimate", "bustling" spot "nestled in Lincoln Park"; it's "always packed" with allies who applaud its "casual", "uncomplicated approach", though on the other side of the via, opponents peg it as "uninspired" and wonder if management "could squeeze any more tables into the dining room"; N.B. its adjacent wine bar, Via Due, serves a slightly different menu.

Viand Bar & Kitchen ▽ 23 20 21 $32

155 E. Ontario St. (St. Clair St.), 312-255-8505; www.viandchicago.com

"Hidden in the Marriott Courtyard" in Streeterville, this "little gem" is seen as "funky and cool", from its "unique menu offerings" of New American "small plates that actually go a long way" (some organic ingredients) to its "avant-garde decor" ("interesting table settings") and "innovative cocktails"; partakers are also pleased by the "well-priced, thoughtful list" of vino and "half-price wine night on Wednesdays", plus there's sidewalk seating.

Viceroy of India　　20 12 17 $24

2520 W. Devon Ave. (bet. Campbell & Maplewood Aves.),
773-743-4100

19W 555 Roosevelt Rd. (Highland Ave.), Lombard,
630-627-4411

www.viceroyofindia.com

"All the basics are covered well" at this "popular"
West Rogers Park and West Suburban pair that some
reporters rate as a "safe bet" for "tasty" Indian food
that's definitely "the real thing" – and "reasonably priced",
to boot; still, those who see them as "nothing special"
submit that the fare "is adjusted for the hoi polloi", the
"banquet setting" is somewhat "cheesy" and the staff
is sometimes "unfriendly."

Victory's Banner　　23 13 18 $14

2100 W. Roscoe St. (Hoyne Ave.), 773-665-0227;
www.victorysbanner.com

This 100 percent "vegetarian hot spot" in Roscoe Village is
a "favorite" "retreat" for conscientious consumers craving "unconditionally good" Eclectic fare made from "the
freshest" ingredients – including a "wonderful
breakfast" that's one of "the best around" – and served
by a "devoted" staff; some say the "meditative" setting
is "heavenly" and "rejuvenating", while others warn you
have to "overlook the odd decor and messages praising
the swami", but it's "always crowded" – and "worth the
wait"; N.B. no dinner service.

VIE 🅉　　27 23 23 $55

4471 Lawn Ave. (Burlington Ave.), Western Springs,
708-246-2082; www.vierestaurant.com

"Wow"-ed West Suburbanites feel "lucky to have" this
New American in the "quaint", "sleepy" town of Western
Springs, where chef-owner "Paul Virant brings many of
his Blackbird sensibilities" to his "haute" "seasonal"
"dishes with excellent flavor combinations", paired with a
"very interesting wine list"; just "steps from the train station", it's even "worth the reverse commute for adventurous Chicagoans", though some call the "modern,
minimalist" decor "cold" and others purport it would be
"perfect" "if the service could catch up with the brilliance
of the food."

Vien Dong 🅉　　– – – I

3227 N. Clark St. (Belmont Ave.), 773-348-6879

"Although you might not expect authentic Vietnamese
food to be found in Lakeview", this "legit" "family-owned
BYO" is a "reliable" source for a "great variety" of dishes
that are "as real as it gets" ("the lemongrass beef skewers
are highly recommended"), "including an excellent array
of pho", all served in an "unpretentious neighborhood"
environment – plus "you can't beat the price."

Village, The ◗　　　19　20　20　$32

Italian Village, 71 W. Monroe St., 2nd fl. (bet. Clark & Dearborn Sts.), 312-332-7005;
www.italianvillage-chicago.com
The "last of the [Loop] survivors" "from days gone by", this "sentimental favorite" of the Italian Village trio is "filled with old-school" "nostalgia and charm" and plates "plentiful servings" of "predictable satisfying fare" (including "the best chicken Vesuvio") in a "wonderful interior" where "couples can enjoy private booths" with "twinkling lights" supplying the "stars"; modernists who find it "tired", however, say service swings from "charming" and "efficient" to "rushed" and "indifferent", and foodies find the fare "fancy eatin' for kids and tourists."

Vinci　　　22　20　21　$40

1732 N. Halsted St. (Willow St.), 312-266-1199;
www.vincichicago.com
Satisfied surveyors say that the "quiet, dignified Italian dining" "never goes out of style" at this "upscale" Lincoln Park "favorite" where "Paul LoDuca continues to create a warm place with excellent food" (props for the "amazing polenta with mushrooms"), a "good wine list and equitable pricing" in a "convenient" location that's "wonderful" for theatergoers; P.S. it's also a "great place for Sunday brunch" and "monthly wine dinners" that represent "a fantastic deal."

Vive La Crepe　　　▽　20　14　15　$19

1565 Sherman Ave. (bet. Davis & Grove Sts.), Evanston, 847-570-0600; www.vivelacrepe.com
A "really interesting twist on crêpes" – "not filled" but with "delicious" sauces and ingredients "poured on top" – characterizes the "cheap" Eclectic–New French fare at this "cute little spot" in Evanston; its "nice" savory options and "yummy dessert" varieties are a "taste of France" that's "fun for a change", even if a few feel they're "not fantastic"; N.B. check out the signature hard cider served in a tea cup.

Vivere ☒　　　21　21　21　$47

Italian Village, 71 W. Monroe St. (bet. Clark & Dearborn Sts.), 312-332-4040; www.italianvillage-chicago.com
Loyal Loopers look for la dolce vita at this "funky-upscale" spot, the "hippest" of the Italian Village triumvirate with "quite good" seasonal contemporary Italian fare (backed by an "extensive wine list") and a "most accommodating" staff, especially to "business lunch"-ers and "theater and concertgoers"; still, those for whom the "food just misses the mark" and the "futuristic Italian spaceship" "decor is getting tired" feel "the upscale price isn't warranted considering the value" and "schmaltzy charm" of its siblings in the same complex.

Vivo
21 | 20 | 19 | $40

838 W. Randolph St. (bet. Green & Peoria Sts.), 312-733-3379;
www.vivo-chicago.com

"Still a solid player" despite all the "new places in the area", this Market District pioneer continues to please with "excellent Italian cuisine" – including "heavenly gnocchi and fettuccine" and "outstanding fish specials" – served "in a trendy loft setting" that's "crowded, yet cozy"; it's "too loud sometimes but otherwise enjoyable" some surveyors say, adding that "service can be a bit uneven"; P.S. many "love eating in the elevator shaft", whose table seats six.

Volare
23 | 16 | 22 | $34

201 E. Grand Ave. (St. Clair St.), 312-410-9900;
www.volarerestaurant.com

A taste of "true *Italiano*" "hidden away off Michigan Avenue" in Streeterville, this "friendly", "bustling" "backstreet trattoria" with "the feel of an old-fashioned neighborhood Italian supper club" puts out "big portions" of "delicious" "classics", including some of "the best osso buco and risotto" around and "well-prepared fresh seafood selections" – thus a visit here is "very enjoyable", except for the "close tables" and "terrible waits"; P.S. "the patio is wonderful."

Volo Restaurant & Wine Bar
20 | 19 | 21 | $36

2008 W. Roscoe St. (Damen Ave.), 773-348-4600;
www.volorestaurant.com

The "cool mood" comes with "fun and creative wine flights to match the creative" and "delectable" New American small plates at this "hip wine bar" in Roscoe Village, where the "welcoming atmosphere" includes "conviviality", "great background music" and a "huge wine list" with "nice descriptions" that help you choose; it can be "packed", but outdoor seating "practically doubles the number of tables"; still, some point out that it's "not vegetarian-friendly", as the non-meat "options are very limited."

Vong's Thai Kitchen
21 | 20 | 19 | $37

(aka VTK)

6 W. Hubbard St. (State St.), 312-644-8664;
www.leye.com

"Interesting" Thai fare with an "upscale", "metro flair" finds favor at this River North Lettuce Entertain You partnership with famed chef Jean-Georges Vongerichten, a "value" considering the "quality", "good service" and "serene" "Far East" decor; diners who are "disappointed" by "the more casual food and presentation" at "the most down-market Vong there is" would "just as soon go to a neighborhood" Siamese and "save money" (though the "$1 dessert menu [at lunch] is the best concept ever").

Wave 20 24 18 $48

W Chicago Lakeshore, 644 N. Lake Shore Dr. (Ontario St.),
312-255-4460; www.waverestaurant.com

"Cool, modern decor" complements the "beautiful-
people" patrons at this "stylish" Streeterville spot for "innovative and delicious" Mediterranean small plates within
the "hipster's paradise" of the W hotel; "the price is a little
steep", considering what some call the "lack of 'wow' factor" in the food (and no one's raving about the service), but
wave-runners reckon the "movie-set" scene and view
"out to the Navy Pier Ferris wheel" make it "perfect for a
somewhat special occasion."

Weber Grill 19 16 18 $34

Hilton Garden Inn, 539 N. State St. (Grand Ave.),
312-467-9696
2331 Fountain Sq. Dr. (Meyers Rd.), Lombard,
630-953-8880
1010 N. Meacham Rd. (American Ln.), Schaumburg,
847-413-0800
www.webergrillrestaurant.com

"Authentic American BBQ" aficionados who "camp out" at
these "tourist-friendly" city and suburban sizzlefests –
where virtually "everything" is grilled on "huge Weber
kettles" – believe they bring "basic meat and potatoes" "to
the highest level", making them a "lower-cost alternative
to the high-priced steakhouses"; still, "char"-red chewers
who chastise them for "generic chain" grub, "weak service" and "noisy atmospheres" brag "my backyard is
much better"; N.B. the Wheeling branch closed post-*Survey.*

Webster's Wine Bar ● 17 21 20 $28

1480 W. Webster Ave. (bet. Ashland Ave. & Clybourn St.),
773-868-0608; www.websterwinebar.com

"Black-clad patrons pose, chatter and sip their Gigondas
appreciatively" at this "casually elegant" Lincoln Park
wine-bar "gem" where the "huge, fairly priced wine list"
is paired with a "small but well-done menu" of Eclectic
seasonal small plates; service is "knowledgeable" (if
sometimes "slow") in the "laid-back" "living-room" setting, "a place for a first date or to hang out with friends"
"after movies at Webster Place" – plus they have a "late
kitchen" (1 AM on weekends), though some gourmets "go
for the flights, not the food."

West Town Tavern ⌧ 23 20 21 $41

1329 W. Chicago Ave. (Throop St.), 312-666-6175;
www.westtowntavern.com

Drew and Susan Goss "pay attention to everything" at
their "deservedly popular" West Towner that's "more upscale than its name would suggest" considering the "high-
quality", Traditional American "comfort food" ("best pot
roast this side of my mother's"), "winning wines" and

"wonderful beer selection"; a "friendly" staff works the "warm", "hip", "exposed-brick interior", which strikes supporters as "low-key" and "carefree" – though some report it can get "crowded and noisy."

White Fence Farm
21 | 18 | 19 | $22

11700 Joliet Rd. (2 mi. south of I-55), Lemont, 630-739-1720; www.whitefencefarm.com

Born in 1954, this Southwest Suburban American "blast from the past" "beats the cluck out of typical fast-food chicken joints" with its "awesome" "crispy-fried" bird, "unbelievably delicious" corn fritters and "kitschy relish trays", and its "half *Hee Haw,* half elegant plantation house" setting – including a "big museum with old cars and much more" and a petting zoo – "has to be seen to be believed"; P.S. "don't forget to check out your physique in the funny mirrors while you wait."

Wiener's Circle, The ●▵⊄
20 | 6 | 13 | $7

2622 N. Clark St. (Wrightwood Ave.), 773-477-7444

"Gimme a charred red hot dammit!" demand "rude"-sters who relish the "funny, filthy-mouthed" "late-night" shtick (engaged in by customers and staff) as much as the "outstanding Chicago dogs", "amazing cheeseburgers" and "great shakes" at this "one-of-a-kind" Lincoln Park "sitcom-in-waiting"; still, be warned that "all the love goes in the bun, not in the decor" and there's "almost nowhere to sit" – plus some say "never go here sober."

WILDFIRE
23 | 21 | 21 | $40

159 W. Erie St. (bet. LaSalle & Wells Sts.), 312-787-9000
1300 Patriot Blvd. (Lake Ave.), Glenview, 847-657-6363
235 Parkway Dr. (Milwaukee Ave.), Lincolnshire, 847-279-7900
Oakbrook Center Mall, 232 Oakbrook Ctr. (Rte. 83), Oak Brook, 630-586-9000
1250 E. Higgins Rd. (National Pkwy.), Schaumburg, 847-995-0100
www.wildfirerestaurant.com

Spreading like their namesake, this "insanely popular" passel of Traditional American steakhouses from the "Lettuce Entertain You group" keeps carnivores "coming back" with "hearty Midwest-sized portions" from a "crowd-pleasing menu" of "awesome wood-fired" fare ("juicy" steaks and chops), "delicious chopped salad" and "great martini flights" in a "classy", "clubby" "'40s-style" setting; salivating surveyors swear it's "worth the wait" ("even with reservations"), but wet blankets rank these "noisy" "madhouses" "really rather ordinary, just on a grand scale."

Wildfish
∇ 25 | 22 | 20 | $39

Arlington Town Sq., 60 S. Arlington Heights Rd. (Northwest Hwy.), Arlington Heights, 847-870-8260

"A great selection of traditional and contemporary sushi as well as [other] delicious dishes" delight denizens of this "hip" "city" Japanese "hidden in a [Northwest] Suburban mall"; maki lovers are also "surprised" by the "minimal", "sleek decor" with "terrific" "private booths" and say the service is "attentive", if "not especially friendly."

Wishbone 21 17 18 $20
3300 N. Lincoln Ave. (School St.), 773-549-2663
1001 W. Washington Blvd. (Morgan St.), 312-850-2663
www.wishbonechicago.com
"Boisterous" and "family-friendly", this West Loop/Roscoe Village duo dishes up "delicious", "homey" Southern and "sometime-Cajun" cooking with a side of "whimsy" ("note the 'chickeney' decor touches"); a sizable demographic deems it "dependable" for a "great brunch", plus "hearty and filling" lunches and "dinners as well", all at "tolerable prices", even if "sometimes the wait is a little long" and "service is hit-or-miss", but a faction feels the experience is "fair to middling."

Wolfgang Puck's Grand Café 18 17 17 $28
Century Theatre Complex, 1701 Maple Ave. (Church St.),
Evanston, 847-869-9653; www.wolfgangpuck.com
"Good for salads" and "satisfying, creative" "wood oven–fired pizzas", this "high-energy" Evanston "local chain site" "attached to the movie complex" tenders its "tasty" New American edibles amid a mix of "futurism and art deco" where "outdoor dining and people-watching are a plus"; puckish pens, however, say "service is spotty" and pronounce the provender "ordinary" and "a bit pricey for the result" – especially "when you expect so much more from the big name."

Woo Lae Oak ▽ 19 18 17 $35
3201 Algonquin Rd. (Newport Dr.), Rolling Meadows,
847-870-9910
"Very interesting" choices of "good Korean food" beyond the "simple kalbi/bulgoki grill" make this "consistent", "understated" and "entertaining" establishment in the Suburban Northwest "as close as you can get" to the real thing according to raters who "can't wait to go back."

X/O CHICAGO ◕ 22 24 21 $44
3441 N. Halsted St. (Newport Ave.), 773-348-9696;
www.xochicago.com
The "latest place to be seen in Boys Town", this "ultracool" spot dishes a "delightful variety" of "stylin'", "creative" "Eclectic" small plates with "many [wine] flights" plus "incredible champagne cocktails and martinis" in an atmosphere buzzing with "super energy" (aided by a "DJ on weekends"); "the staff offers an interesting mix of flirtation and standoffish haughtiness" to the "mixed" "straight-and-gay" crowd, and the "exotic", "romantic" patio is "divine" – though the experience can get "expensive."

Yard House
17 | 16 | 17 | $24

The Glen, 1880 Tower Dr. (Patriot Blvd.), Glenview, 847-729-9273;
www.yardhouse.com

With well "over 100 on tap", "from all over the world", there may be "too many beers to choose from" – and "what a great problem to have" swoon suds lovers smitten with this North Suburban "microbrewery-type chain" outpost that also offers a "varied, value-conscious menu" of Eclectic eats "for anytime, with or without kids"; the bonanza of brews, however, falls flat with those who perceive the provender as "pedestrian"; P.S. if the "lively" environs seem "loud", adjourn to the "great outside seating."

Yoshi's Café
23 | 17 | 22 | $42

3257 N. Halsted St. (Belmont Ave.), 773-248-6160;
www.yoshiscafe.com

Adherents allege this "super-cool" New French–Asian fusion pioneer "in the middle of Boys Town" is "much better than the über-trendy fly-by-nights that surround it" thanks to "imaginative", "high-quality food" (a "gourmet bargain") and "understated" "bistro" atmosphere blessed with a "warm crowd" and "seasoned vet servers" – plus chef-owner Yoshi Katsumura "is always on hand"; divergers detect "one too many ingredients" in his "different" dishes, though, and describe the decor as that of "a diner converted into a 'nice' place."

Zapatista
20 | 18 | 18 | $29

1307 S. Wabash Ave. (13th St.), 312-435-1307;
www.zapatistacantina.com

"Wonderful", "fresh Mexican" with "subtle flavors" is served "south of the border (Roosevelt Street, that is)" at this South Loop "hot spot" where the "funky party atmosphere" "is lively and the volume is loud enough to drown out a bullfight" ("but who cares when you're drinking" "potent", "tasty margaritas"?); deserters are undecided, though, saying the fare's "not revolutionary" and management's "still ironing out kinks with the service"; N.B. the Food rating may not reflect a post-*Survey* chef change.

ZEALOUS ⊠
24 | 26 | 23 | $71

419 W. Superior St. (Sedgewick St.), 312-475-9112;
www.zealousrestaurant.com

"Loftlike ceilings", a "bamboo grove" and a "stunning glass wine cellar in the center of the dining room" make for a "minimalist" milieu at this "serene", "sophisticated" spot, a "prime" River North locale for "a quiet meal" or a "special occasion" thanks to "touted chef" Michael Taus' "excellent", "edgy" New American cooking with "daring, unusual combinations" and the "personable" staff's "high standards of service"; still, opponents opine that the "gorgeous decor" "outpaces" the "overpriced" food, which they feel "falls a little short."

Zest   20 | 22 | 19 | $36

Hotel InterContinental, 525 N. Michigan Ave. (Illinois St.),
312-321-8766; www.chicago.interconti.com

"Great" Eclectic–New American "hotel dining" in "taste-
fully Euro" environs "looking out at Michigan Avenue" and
"great hospitality", "crowded or not", make this "nice"
Streeterville spot in the InterContinental a "good place"
for a "quality breakfast", a "time-efficient lunch" "or a
quick, convenient bite" "if you're shopping on the Mag
Mile all day" ("get a window seat" "for people-watching").

Zia's Trattoria   22 | 17 | 20 | $30

6699 N. Northwest Hwy. (bet. Harlem & Touhy Aves.),
773-775-0808; www.ziaschicago.com

"A real find" on Edison Park's "Restaurant Row", this
"bustling", "rustic Italian eatery" earns enthusiasm for its
"fresh, authentic cuisine" and "nice wines" served in a
"comfortable" "location for commuters and folk looking for a
fine-dining experience on the periphery of the city"; still, a
portion of patrons says it "can be very noisy", "service is
slow" sometimes and the no-reservations policy (except for
parties of five or more on weekends) "makes it a hassle."

Chicago
Indexes

CUISINES
LOCATIONS
SPECIAL FEATURES

CUISINES

Afghan
Kabul House

American (New)
Adelle's
Alinea
Allen's
Amber Cafe
Aria
Atwater's
Avenue M
Bank Lane Bistro
Bijan's Bistro
Bin 36/Bin Wine
Blackbird
Block 44
Blue Water Grill
BOKA
Brett's Café
Butter
Cab's Wine Bar
Café Absinthe
Cafe Selmarie
Canoe Club
Cereality Cereal
Charlie Trotter's
Chef's Station
Chestnut Grill
Cité
Courtright's
Crofton on Wells
Custom House
David Burke Prime
David's Bistro
Dine
Emilio's Sunflower
erwin cafe & bar
Feast
Fixture
Green Dolphin St.
Harvest
HB
Improv Kitchen
Ina's
Jack's on Halsted
Jacky's Bistro
Jane's
Jilly's Cafe
La Fette
Landmark
Lovell's/Lake Forest

Magnolia Cafe
May St. Market
Meritage Cafe
M. Henry
Milk & Honey
mk
Montarra
Naha
North Pond
One North
Park Grill
Parrot Cage
Pepper Lounge
Philander's
Prairie Grass Cafe
Puck's at MCA
Pump Room
Rhapsody
Ritz-Carlton Café
Rushmore
Sage Grille
Schwa
Seasons
1776
Signature Room
Soiree Bar
Sola
Spring
Square Kitchen
Stained Glass Wine
State
Tavern
Thyme Café
Tomboy
Tweet
Viand Bar
Vie
Volo
Wolfgang Puck
Zealous
Zest

American (Traditional)
American Girl Cafe
Ann Sather
Atwood Cafe
Bandera
Bar Louie
Billy Goat Tavern
Birch River Grill
Bongo Room

Boston Blackie's
Breakfast Club
Cheesecake Factory
Chicago Firehouse
Clubhouse, The
Dine
Drake Bros.' Steak
Edelweiss
Entourage
Finley's Grill
Flo
Gale St. Inn
Golden Budha
Goose Is. Brewing
Grace O'Malley's
Green Door Tavern
Grill on the Alley
Hackney's
Hard Rock Cafe
Hemmingway's
Hot Chocolate
J. Alexander's
Joey's Brickhouse
John's Place
Kroll's
Kuma's Corner
Lawry's Prime Rib
Lou Mitchell's
Lucca's
Lux Bar
L. Woods Lodge
Margie's Candies
Max & Benny's
Medici on 57th
Mike Ditka's
Miller's Pub
Millrose
Mity Nice Grill
Mrs. Park's Tavern
Next Door Bistro
Nookies
Oak Tree
Orange
Original Pancake
Parlor
Petterino's
Phil & Lou's
P.J. Clarke's
Poag Mahone's
Red Star Tavern
R.J. Grunts
RL
Rock Bottom Brewery
Rockit B&G

Seasons Café
Sidebar Grille
Silver Cloud B&G
South Gate Cafe
South Water Kitchen
Square Kitchen
Stanley's Kitchen
Tavern on Rush
Ted's Montana Grill
312 Chicago
Toast
Twisted Spoke
Weber Grill
West Town Tavern
White Fence Farm
Wildfire
Yard House

Argentinean
El Nandu
Tango
Tango Sur

Armenian
Sayat Nova

Asian
Alice & Friends
Big Bowl
Catch 35
China Grill
Chinoiserie
Flat Top Grill
Karma
Kevin
LuLu's Dim Sum
Opera
Ping Pong
Red Light
Shanghai Terrace
Stir Crazy
Yoshi's Café

Austrian
Glunz Bavarian
Julius Meinl Café

Barbecue
Carson's Ribs
Fat Willy's
Hecky's
Lem's BBQ
Merle's Smokehouse
Ribs 'n' Bibs
Robinson's Ribs

Russell's BBQ
Smoke Daddy
Twin Anchors
Weber Grill

Brazilian
Brazzaz
Fogo de Chão
Sabor do Brasil
Sal & Carvão
Texas de Brazil

British
Red Lion Pub

Cajun
Davis St. Fishmarket
Dixie Kitchen
Heaven on Seven
Pappadeaux Seafood
Redfish
Wishbone

Californian
Caliterra B&G

Chinese
(* dim sum specialist)
Ben Pao
Best Hunan
Chen's Chinese
Dee's
Dragonfly Mandarin
Emperor's Choice
Evergreen
Fornetto Mei
Golden Budha
Hai Yen
Happy Chef Dim Sum*
Koi
Lao Sze Chuan
Moon Palace
New Three Happiness*
P.F. Chang's
Phoenix*
Pine Yard
Shine & Morida
Silver Seafood
Three Happiness*

Coffeehouses
Julius Meinl Café
Uncommon Ground

Coffee Shops/Diners
Chicago Diner
Ed Debevic's

Eleven City Diner
Lou Mitchell's
Manny's
Milk & Honey
Nookies
Orange
Original Pancake
Tempo

Colombian
La Fonda Latino
Las Tablas

Continental
Café la Cave
Le P'tit Paris
Lobby, The

Costa Rican
Irazu

Creole
Heaven on Seven
Pappadeaux Seafood

Cuban
Cafe Bolero
Cafe 28
Miramar

Delis
Bagel, The
Cold Comfort Cafe
Eleven City Diner
Manny's
Max & Benny's

Eclectic
Aria
Bite
CHIC Cafe
Chinoiserie
Deleece
Di Pescara
Eatzi's
Flight
foodlife
Fundajo Grill
Grand Lux Cafe
Gulliver's Pizza
Heartland Cafe
Jane's
Kit Kat Lounge
Kitsch'n
Lula

Mj2 Bistro
Moto
Narcisse
Orange
Saltaus
Sidebar Grille
Slice of Life
South
Speakeasy
Tasting Room
Tilli's
Tweet
Twist
Uncommon Ground
Victory's Banner
Vive La Crepe
Webster's Wine Bar
X/O Chicago
Yard House
Zest

Ethiopian
Ethiopian Diamond
Mama Desta's

Filipino
Coobah

Fondue
Geja's Cafe
Melting Pot

French
Cafe Matou
Froggy's French
La Fette
la petite folie
Le P'tit Paris
Le Vichyssois

French (Bistro)
Barrington Bistro
Bêtise Bistro
Bin 36/Bin Wine
Bistro Banlieue
Bistro Campagne
Bistro Kirkou
Bistro 110
Bistrot Margot
Bistrot Zinc
Café Bernard
Cafe Central
Café le Coq
Cafe Pyrenees
Chez François

Chez Joël
Cyrano's Bistrot
D & J Bistro
Hemmingway's
Jacky's Bistro
KiKi's Bistro
La Crêperie
La Sardine
La Tache
Le Bouchon
Marché
Miramar
Mon Ami Gabi
Pierrot Gourmet
Retro Bistro
Shallots Bistro
socca

French (Brasserie)
Brasserie Jo

French (New)
Ambria
Atwater's
Avenues
Café des Architectes
Carlos'
CHIC Cafe
copperblue
Dining Rm. at Kendall
Dorado
Everest
Gabriel's
Jilly's Cafe
Kevin
L'anne
Le Français
Le Lan
Les Deux Autres
Les Nomades
Le Titi de Paris
Michael
Mimosa
NoMI
Oceanique
one sixtyblue
Pasteur
Ritz-Carlton Din. Rm.
Tallgrass
Thyme Café
Tru
Vive La Crepe
Yoshi's Café

German
Berghoff Cafe
Edelweiss

Glunz Bavarian
Mirabell

Greek
Artopolis Bakery
Athena
Costa's
Greek Islands
OPA Estiatorio
Parthenon
Pegasus
Roditys
Santorini
Venus Greek-Cypriot

Hamburgers
Billy Goat Tavern
Boston Blackie's
Ed Debevic's
Goose Is. Brewing
Hackney's
Pete Miller Sea/Steak
P.J. Clarke's
Poag Mahone's
Twisted Spoke
Wiener's Circle

Hawaii Regional
Roy's

Hot Dogs
Al's #1 Beef
Gold Coast Dogs
Hot Doug's
Superdawg Drive-In
Wiener's Circle

Indian
Essence of India
Gaylord Indian
Hema's Kitchen
India House
Indian Garden
Klay Oven
Mt. Everest
Mysore Woodland
Raj Darbar
Tiffin
Udupi Palace
Vermilion
Viceroy of India

Irish
Chief O'Neill's Pub
Grace O'Malley's

Irish Oak
Mrs. Murphy & Sons

Israeli
Hashalom
Old Jerusalem

Italian
(N=Northern; S=Southern)
Angelina (S)
Anna Maria Pasteria
Antico Posto
a tavola (N)
Aurelio's Pizza
Bacchanalia (N)
Bacino's
Balagio
Ballo
Basil Leaf Cafe (N)
Bella Notte (S)
Bruna's
Buona Terra (N)
Cafe Borgia (N)
Café Spiaggia
Caliterra B&G (N)
Campagnola
Carlucci (N)
Carmine's
Club Lago (N)
Club Lucky (S)
Coco Pazzo (N)
Coco Pazzo (N)
Dave's Italian (S)
Del Rio (N)
Dinotto
Di Pescara
EJ's Place (N)
Enoteca Piattini (S)
Erie Cafe
Extra Virgin
Filippo's
Follia (N)
Fornetto Mei (N)
Francesca's
Francesco's (S)
Gabriel's
Gene & Georgetti
Gio (N)
Gioco (N)
Grotto
Harry Caray's
Il Mulino New York
Jay's Amore (N)
La Bocca/Verità

La Cantina (N)
La Cucina/Donatella
La Donna
La Gondola
La Piazza (Forest Park)
La Piazza (Naperville)
La Scarola
La Strada
La Vita (N)
Leonardo's (N)
Lucia
Luna Caprese (S)
Maggiano's
Merlo (N)
Mia Cucina (N)
Mia Francesca
Mimosa
Next Door Bistro
Osteria Via Stato
Pane Caldo (N)
Papa Milano (S)
Pasta Palazzo
Philly G's
Phil Stefani's
Piazza Bella
Pizza Capri
Pizza D.O.C.
Pompei Bakery
Quartino
Riccardo Trattoria (N)
ristorante we (N)
RoSal's Kitchen (S)
Rose Angelis
Rosebud
Rosebud Steak
Sabatino's
Salvatore's (N)
Sapori Trattoria
Scoozi!
socca
Spiaggia
Tarantino's
Terragusto Cafe
Think Café
312 Chicago
Timo
Timpano Chophouse
Tony Rocco's
Topo Gigio
Trattoria D.O.C.
Trattoria Gianni
Trattoria No. 10
Trattoria Roma (S)
Trattoria Trullo (S)

Trucchi Italian
Tucci Benucch
Tufano's Tap (S)
Tuscany (N)
Uno Di Martino
Va Pensiero
Via Carducci (S)
Village, The
Vinci
Vivere
Vivo
Volare
Zia's Trattoria

Japanese
(* no sushi)
Agami
Akai Hana
Aki Sushi
Benihana
Bluefin
Bob San
Chen's Chinese
Chiyo
Coast Sushi
Dee's
Great Lakes Fish
Hachi's Kitchen
Heat
Indie Cafe
Itto Sushi
Izumi Sushi
Japonais
Kamehachi
Katsu Japanese
Kaze Sushi
Kizoku Sushi
Kohan Japanese
Koi
Kuni's
Kyoto
Matsuya
Matsu Yama
Meiji
Mirai Sushi
Mizu Yakitori
Oysy
RA Sushi
Ringo
Rise
Ron of Japan
Sai Café
Shine & Morida
Shiroi Hana

Starfish
Sushi Ai
Sushi Naniwa
SushiSamba rio
Sushi Wabi
Swordfish
Takkatsu*
Tank Sushi
T-Spot Sushi
Tsuki
Tsunami
Wildfish

Jewish
Bagel, The
Eleven City Diner
Manny's
Max & Benny's

Korean
(* barbecue specialist)
Jin Ju
Koryo
San Soo Gab San*
Woo Lae Oak*

Kosher
Shallots Bistro
Slice of Life

Lebanese
Fattoush
Kan Zaman
Maza

Malaysian
Penang

Mediterranean
Andies
Artopolis Bakery
Avec
Café des Architectes
copperblue
Cousin's I.V.
Extra Virgin
Isabella's Estiatorio
Lucca's
Naha
Pita Inn
Scylla
Shallots Bistro
Tizi Melloul
Turquoise
Venus Greek-Cypriot
Wave

Mexican
Adobo Grill
Brioso
Cafe 28
Comida Bebida
De Cero
Don Juan
Dorado
El Presidente
Fonda del Mar
Frontera Grill
Hacienda Tecalitlan
Hot Tamales
Irazu
La Bonita
La Cazuela Mariscos
Lalo's
La Taberna Tapatia
Lupita's
Maiz
Pancho Viti's Mex.
Platiyo
Riques
Salbute
Salpicón
San Gabriel Mexican
Tecalitlan
Topolobampo
Zapatista

Middle Eastern
Aladdin's Eatery
Andies
Babylon Kitchen
Pita Inn
Reza's
Samah
Souk
Tizi Melloul

Moroccan
Hashalom
Tagine

Nepalese
Mt. Everest

Noodle Shops
Joy Yee's Noodle
Penny's Noodle

Nuevo Latino
Carnivale
Coobah
Cuatro

Mambo Grill
Mas
Nacional 27
Olé Olé
Rumba
Sangria
Vermilion

Pacific Northwest
Meritage Cafe

Persian/Iranian
Noon-O-Kabab

Pizza
Art of Pizza
Aurelio's Pizza
Bacino's
Bricks
Chicago Pizza
Edwardo's Pizza
Gio
Giordano's
Gulliver's Pizza
La Gondola
Lou Malnati Pizza
My Pie Pizza
Nancy's Stuffed Pizza
O'Famé
Original Gino's
Piece
Pizza Capri
Pizza D.O.C.
Pizzeria Uno/Due
Pompei Bakery
Trattoria D.O.C.
Trucchi Italian
Wolfgang Puck

Polish
Lutnia

Russian
Russian Tea Time

Sandwiches
Al's #1 Beef
Bagel, The
Berghoff Cafe
Cold Comfort Cafe
Mr. Beef
Potbelly Sandwich

Scandinavian
Tre Kronor

Scottish
Duke of Perth

Seafood
Avenues
Bob Chinn's Crab
Canoe Club
Cape Cod Room
Catch 35
Chinn's Fishery
Davis St. Fishmarket
Devon Seafood Grill
Don Roth's
Dover Straits
Drake Bros.' Steak
Emperor's Choice
Erie Cafe
Fonda del Mar
Froggy's French
Fulton's
Great Lakes Fish
Half Shell
Harbour House
Hugo's Frog & Fish
Joe's Seafood/Steak
Keefer's
La Cantina
La Cazuela Mariscos
Lobby, The
McCormick & Schmick
Mitchell's Fish Market
Nick's Fishmarket
Nine
Oceanique
Pacific Blue
Pappadeaux Seafood
Parkers' Ocean Grill
Pete Miller Sea/Steak
Redfish
Riva
Santorini
Scylla
Shaw's Crab House
Shula's Steak
Silver Seafood
Spring
Tin Fish

Small Plates
(See also Spanish tapas specialist)
Avec (Mediterranean)
BOKA (New American)
Enoteca Piattini (S. Italian)

Extra Virgin (Italian)
Fixture (New American)
Flight (Eclectic)
Green Zebra (Vegetarian)
La Taberna Tapatia (Mexican)
Maza (Lebanese)
Quartino (Italian)
Sangria (Nuevo Latino)
Tango (Argentinean)
Viand Bar (New American)
Volo (New American)
Wave (Mediterranean)
Webster's Wine Bar (Eclectic)
X/O Chicago (Eclectic)

Soul Food
Army & Lou's

South American
La Peña
Rinconcito So. Am.
SushiSamba rio

Southern
Army & Lou's
Dixie Kitchen
Fat Willy's
House of Blues
Wishbone

Southwestern
Bandera
Flo

Spanish/Tapas
Arco de Cuchilleros
Cafe Ba-Ba-Reeba!
Café Iberico
del Toro
Emilio's Tapas
1492 Tapas
Haro
La Tasca
Mesón Sabika
People Lounge
Rioja
Tapas Barcelona
Twist

Steakhouses
Avenue M
Benihana
Bogart's Charhouse
Brazzaz
Capital Grille
Carmichael Steak
Chicago Chop Hse.
Chicago Prime Steak
David Burke Prime
Don Roth's
Drake Bros.' Steak
EJ's Place
El Nandu
Entourage
Erie Cafe
Fleming's Steak
Fogo de Chão
Fulton's
Gene & Georgetti
Gibsons Steak
Grill on the Alley
Grillroom, The
Grotto
Harry Caray's
Hugo's Frog & Fish
Keefer's
Kinzie Chophouse
Las Tablas
Lawry's Prime Rib
Magnum's Steak
Mike Ditka's
Montarra
Morton's Steak
Myron & Phil's Steak
Narra
Nine
Palm, The
Pete Miller Sea/Steak
Phil Stefani's
ristorante we
Ron of Japan
Rosebud Steak
Ruth's Chris Steak
Sabor do Brasil
Sage Grille
Sal & Carvão
Saloon Steak
Shula's Steak
Smith & Wollensky
Stetson's Chop Hse.
Sullivan's Steak
Tango
Tango Sur
Tavern
Tavern on Rush
Texas de Brazil
Timpano Chophouse
Wildfire

Swedish
Ann Sather

Thai
Amarind's
Arun's
Indie Cafe
P.S. Bangkok
Ruby of Siam
Spoon Thai
Star of Siam
Thai Classic
Thai Pastry
Vong's

Turkish
A La Turka
Turquoise

Vegetarian
(* vegan)
Aladdin's Eatery
Alice & Friends*
Andies
Blind Faith Café
Chicago Diner

Cousin's I.V.*
Ethiopian Diamond
Green Zebra
Heartland Cafe
Hema's Kitchen
Kabul House
Karyn's Cooked*
Karyn's Fresh Corner*
Lake Side Café*
Lula*
Mama Desta's
Maza
Mysore Woodland
Reza's
Slice of Life
Tiffin
Udupi Palace
Victory's Banner

Vietnamese
Hai Yen
L'anne
Le Colonial
Le Lan
Pasteur
Vien Dong

LOCATIONS

DOWNTOWN

Loop
Aria
Atwood Cafe
Berghoff Cafe
Billy Goat Tavern
Boston Blackie's
Catch 35
Cereality Cereal
China Grill
Everest
Giordano's
Gold Coast Dogs
Golden Budha
Grillroom, The
Heaven on Seven
La Cantina
La Strada
Miller's Pub
Morton's Steak
Nick's Fishmarket
One North
Palm, The
Park Grill
Petterino's
Poag Mahone's
Potbelly Sandwich
Rhapsody
ristorante we
Rosebud
Russian Tea Time
Sidebar Grille
South Water Kitchen
Stetson's Chop Hse.
312 Chicago
Trattoria No. 10
Village, The
Vivere

River North
Allen's
Al's #1 Beef
Avenues
Ballo
Bar Louie
Ben Pao
Big Bowl
Bijan's Bistro
Billy Goat Tavern
Bin 36/Bin Wine

Blue Water Grill
Brasserie Jo
Brazzaz
Café Iberico
Carson's Ribs
Chicago Chop Hse.
CHIC Cafe
Club Lago
Coco Pazzo
Crofton on Wells
Cyrano's Bistrot
David Burke Prime
Devon Seafood Grill
Ed Debevic's
Erie Cafe
Fogo de Chão
1492 Tapas
Frontera Grill
Fulton's
Gaylord Indian
Gene & Georgetti
Giordano's
Grand Lux Cafe
Green Door Tavern
Hard Rock Cafe
Harry Caray's
Heaven on Seven
House of Blues
India House
Joe's Seafood/Steak
Kamehachi
Kan Zaman
Karyn's Cooked
Keefer's
Kevin
KiKi's Bistro
Kinzie Chophouse
Kitsch'n
Kizoku Sushi
Klay Oven
Lalo's
Lawry's Prime Rib
Le Lan
Lobby, The
Lou Malnati Pizza
Maggiano's
Mambo Grill
Melting Pot
mk
Mr. Beef

Nacional 27
Naha
Narcisse
Original Gino's
Osteria Via Stato
Oysy
P.F. Chang's
Phil Stefani's
Pierrot Gourmet
Pizzeria Uno/Due
Potbelly Sandwich
Quartino
Redfish
Reza's
Rock Bottom Brewery
Rockit B&G
Rosebud
Roy's
Rumba
Ruth's Chris Steak
Sal & Carvão
Scoozi!
Shanghai Terrace
Shaw's Crab House
Smith & Wollensky
Star of Siam
Sullivan's Steak
Sushi Naniwa
SushiSamba rio
Tizi Melloul
Tony Rocco's
Topolobampo
Vermilion
Vong's
Weber Grill
Wildfire
Zealous

Streeterville
Bandera
Benihana

Billy Goat Tavern
Boston Blackie's
Caliterra B&G
Cape Cod Room
Capital Grille
Cheesecake Factory
Chestnut Grill
Cité
Coco Pazzo
copperblue
Drake Bros.' Steak
Emilio's Tapas
foodlife
Grill on the Alley
Indian Garden
Kamehachi
Le P'tit Paris
Les Nomades
Max & Benny's
Mity Nice Grill
Mrs. Park's Tavern
Original Pancake
P.J. Clarke's
Puck's at MCA
Ritz-Carlton Café
Ritz-Carlton Din. Rm.
Riva
Ron of Japan
Saloon Steak
Sayat Nova
Shula's Steak
Signature Room
Tru
Viand Bar
Volare
Wave
Zest

CITY NORTH

Andersonville/Edgewater
Andies
Ann Sather
Ethiopian Diamond
Francesca's
Indie Cafe
Jin Ju
La Donna
La Fonda Latino
La Tache
Leonardo's

M. Henry
Olé Olé
Pasteur
Reza's
Rioja
South
Speakeasy
Tomboy

Gold Coast
American Girl Cafe
Big Bowl

Bistro 110
Bistrot Zinc
Café des Architectes
Café Spiaggia
Carmine's
Edwardo's Pizza
Fornetto Mei
Gibsons Steak
Grotto
Hugo's Frog & Fish
Il Mulino New York
Le Colonial
Lux Bar
McCormick & Schmick
Merlo
Mike Ditka's
Morton's Steak
NoMI
Oak Tree
Pane Caldo
Papa Milano
P.J. Clarke's
Pump Room
RA Sushi
RL
Rosebud Steak
Seasons
Seasons Café
Spiaggia
Tavern on Rush
Tempo
Tsunami
Tucci Benucch

Lakeview/Wrigleyville

A La Turka
Angelina
Ann Sather
Arco de Cuchilleros
Art of Pizza
Bagel, The
Bar Louie
Cafe 28
Chen's Chinese
Chicago Diner
Coobah
Cousin's I.V.
Deleece
Duke of Perth
erwin cafe & bar
Flat Top Grill
Fundajo Grill
Giordano's
Goose Is. Brewing

Half Shell
HB
Improv Kitchen
Irish Oak
Jack's on Halsted
Joey's Brickhouse
Julius Meinl Café
Kit Kat Lounge
Koryo
La Crêperie
Lucca's
Mama Desta's
Matsuya
Matsu Yama
Mia Francesca
Mrs. Murphy & Sons
Nancy's Stuffed Pizza
Nookies
Orange
Penny's Noodle
Pepper Lounge
Ping Pong
Pizza Capri
Platiyo
Potbelly Sandwich
P.S. Bangkok
Rise
Samah
Shiroi Hana
socca
Sola
Tango Sur
Thai Classic
T-Spot Sushi
Tuscany
Twist
Twisted Spoke
Uncommon Ground
Vien Dong
X/O Chicago
Yoshi's Café

Lincoln Park/DePaul/ Sheffield

Aladdin's Eatery
Alinea
Ambria
Bacino's
Bar Louie
Basil Leaf Cafe
BOKA
Bricks
Cafe Ba-Ba-Reeba!
Café Bernard
Charlie Trotter's

Chicago Pizza
Dee's
Eatzi's
Edwardo's Pizza
El Presidente
Emilio's Tapas
Enoteca Piattini
Fattoush
Filippo's
Fixture
Geja's Cafe
Goose Is. Brewing
Green Dolphin St.
Hema's Kitchen
Itto Sushi
J. Alexander's
John's Place
Karyn's Fresh Corner
Kyoto
La Gondola
Lalo's
Landmark
Las Tablas
Lou Malnati Pizza
Luna Caprese
Maza
Merlo
Mon Ami Gabi
My Pie Pizza
Nookies
North Pond
O'Famé
Original Gino's
Original Pancake
Pasta Palazzo
Penny's Noodle
Pizza Capri
Pompei Bakery
Potbelly Sandwich
P.S. Bangkok
Raj Darbar
Red Lion Pub
Riccardo Trattoria
Ringo
R.J. Grunts
Robinson's Ribs
Rose Angelis
Sai Café
Salvatore's
Sangria
Sapori Trattoria
Schwa
Shine & Morida
Soiree Bar
Stanley's Kitchen

State
Tarantino's
Tilli's
Toast
Trattoria Gianni
Tsuki
Via Carducci
Vinci
Webster's Wine Bar
Wiener's Circle

Old Town
Adobo Grill
Bistrot Margot
Dinotto
Flat Top Grill
Heat
Kamehachi
La Fette
Mizu Yakitori
Nookies
Old Jerusalem
Salpicón
Topo Gigio
Trattoria Roma
Twin Anchors

Rogers Park/ West Rogers Park
Gold Coast Dogs
Gulliver's Pizza
Heartland Cafe
Hema's Kitchen
Indian Garden
La Cazuela Mariscos
La Cucina/Donatella
Lake Side Café
Mysore Woodland
Tiffin
Udupi Palace
Viceroy of India

Uptown/Lincoln Square
Agami
Alice & Friends
Andies
Anna Maria Pasteria
Bistro Campagne
Block 44
Brioso
Cafe Selmarie
Dorado
Essence of India
Glunz Bavarian
Gold Coast Dogs
Hai Yen

La Bocca/Verità
Magnolia Cafe
Pizza D.O.C.
Riques
Silver Seafood
Spoon Thai

Square Kitchen
Tank Sushi
Thai Pastry
Tweet
Uno Di Martino

CITY NORTHWEST

Bucktown
Babylon Kitchen
Bar Louie
Bluefin
Café Absinthe
Cafe Bolero
Cafe Matou
Club Lucky
Coast Sushi
Cold Comfort Cafe
del Toro
Feast
Hot Chocolate
Irazu
Jane's
La Bonita
Le Bouchon
Margie's Candies
Meritage Cafe
My Pie Pizza
Piece
Rinconcito So. Am.
Scylla
Silver Cloud B&G
Think Café
Toast

Humboldt Park
Maiz

Logan Square
Buona Terra
El Nandu
Fat Willy's
Fonda del Mar
Hachi's Kitchen
Kuma's Corner
Lula

Northwest Side/ Ravenswood
Arun's
Chief O'Neill's Pub
Chiyo
Gale St. Inn
Giordano's

Hashalom
Hot Doug's
Katsu Japanese
La Peña
Las Tablas
Lutnia
Margie's Candies
Mirabell
Nancy's Stuffed Pizza
Noon-O-Kabab
Sabatino's
San Soo Gab San
Superdawg Drive-In
Tagine
Tre Kronor

O'Hare Area/Edison Park
Berghoff Cafe
Big Bowl
Billy Goat Tavern
Café la Cave
Carlucci
David's Bistro
Don Juan
Fleming's Steak
Gibsons Steak
Giordano's
Gold Coast Dogs
Great Lakes Fish
Harry Caray's
Kamehachi
Lou Mitchell's
Morton's Steak
Nick's Fishmarket
Original Gino's
Original Pancake
Wildfire
Zia's Trattoria

Roscoe Village
Brett's Café
Kaze Sushi
Kitsch'n
La Taberna Tapatia
Piazza Bella
Terragusto Cafe

Turquoise
Victory's Banner
Volo
Wishbone

Wicker Park
Adobo Grill
Aki Sushi
Bin 36/Bin Wine
Bob San
Bongo Room
Francesca's

Lucia
Mas
Milk & Honey
Mirai Sushi
Parlor
Penny's Noodle
People Lounge
Smoke Daddy
Souk
Spring
Thyme Café

CITY SOUTH

Chinatown
Emperor's Choice
Evergreen
Happy Chef Dim Sum
Joy Yee's Noodle
Lao Sze Chuan
Moon Palace
New Three Happiness
Penang
Phoenix
Three Happiness

Far South Side
Army & Lou's
Lem's BBQ
Parrot Cage

Hyde Park/Kenwood
Bar Louie
Dixie Kitchen
Edwardo's Pizza
la petite folie
Medici on 57th
Original Pancake
Pizza Capri
Ribs 'n' Bibs

Near South Side
Lalo's
Tufano's Tap

Printer's Row
Custom House
Edwardo's Pizza
Hackney's

South Loop
Bar Louie
Billy Goat Tavern
Bongo Room
Chicago Firehouse
Cuatro
Eleven City Diner
Gioco
Grace O'Malley's
Kohan Japanese
Kroll's
Manny's
Opera
Orange
Oysy
Zapatista

Southwest Side
Bacchanalia
Bruna's
Giordano's
Gold Coast Dogs
Haro
Harry Caray's
Lalo's
Lou Malnati Pizza
Manny's
Pegasus
Superdawg Drive-In

CITY WEST

Far West
Amarind's

Greektown
Artopolis Bakery
Athena

Butter
Costa's
Giordano's
Greek Islands
Parthenon

Pegasus
Roditys
Santorini
Venus Greek-Cypriot

Little Italy/ University Village
Al's #1 Beef
Bar Louie
Chez Joël
Francesca's
La Vita
Pompei Bakery
RoSal's Kitchen
Rosebud
Tuscany

Market District
De Cero
Dragonfly Mandarin
Extra Virgin
Flat Top Grill
Follia
Izumi Sushi
Marché
Moto
one sixtyblue
Red Light
Rushmore
Saltaus
Starfish
Sushi Wabi
Tasting Room
Vivo

Near West
Avenue M
Bella Notte
Dining Rm. at Kendall

Hecky's
Japonais
La Scarola
May St. Market
Timo
Twisted Spoke

Ukrainian Village
a tavola
Bite
Hacienda Tecalitlan

West Loop
Avec
Bacino's
Billy Goat Tavern
Blackbird
Carmichael Steak
Carnivale
Dine
Gold Coast Dogs
Ina's
Jay's Amore
La Sardine
Lou Mitchell's
Meiji
Nine
Phil & Lou's
Robinson's Ribs
Wishbone

West Town
Breakfast Club
Flo
Green Zebra
Tecalitlan
West Town Tavern

SUBURBS

Suburban North
Akai Hana
Al's #1 Beef
Bagel, The
Bank Lane Bistro
Bar Louie
Benihana
Best Hunan
Bêtise Bistro
Blind Faith Café
Bob Chinn's Crab
Boston Blackie's

Cafe Central
Cafe Pyrenees
Campagnola
Carlos'
Carson's Ribs
Cheesecake Factory
Chef's Station
Chinoiserie
Dave's Italian
Davis St. Fishmarket
Del Rio
Di Pescara
Dixie Kitchen

Don Roth's
Dover Straits
Edwardo's Pizza
EJ's Place
Flat Top Grill
Flight
Francesca's
Francesco's
Froggy's French
Gabriel's
Gale St. Inn
Gio
Hackney's
Harbour House
Hecky's
Hot Tamales
Jacky's Bistro
J. Alexander's
Jilly's Cafe
Joy Yee's Noodle
Kabul House
Kamehachi
Karma
Koi
Kuni's
Kyoto
Lalo's
Le Français
Lou Malnati Pizza
Lovell's/Lake Forest
LuLu's Dim Sum
Lupita's
L. Woods Lodge
Maggiano's
Max & Benny's
Merle's Smokehouse
Mesón Sabika
Michael
Mimosa
Miramar
Mitchell's Fish Market
Mt. Everest
Myron & Phil's Steak
Narra
Next Door Bistro
Oceanique
OPA Estiatorio
Oysy
Palm, The
Pancho Viti's Mex.
Pete Miller Sea/Steak
P.F. Chang's
Philly G's
Pine Yard

Pita Inn
Prairie Grass Cafe
RA Sushi
Red Star Tavern
Ron of Japan
Rosebud
Ruby of Siam
Ruth's Chris Steak
Sage Grille
San Gabriel Mexican
Shallots Bistro
Slice of Life
South Gate Cafe
Stained Glass Wine
Stir Crazy
Tapas Barcelona
Tavern
Ted's Montana Grill
Trattoria D.O.C.
Trattoria Trullo
Tuscany
Va Pensiero
Vive La Crepe
Original Pancake
Wildfire
Wolfgang Puck
Yard House

Suburban NW

Al's #1 Beef
Aurelio's Pizza
Barrington Bistro
Benihana
Big Bowl
Birch River Grill
Bistro Kirkou
Boston Blackie's
Cheesecake Factory
Chicago Prime Steak
D & J Bistro
Dover Straits
Edelweiss
Entourage
Francesca's
Gaylord Indian
Hackney's
India House
Indian Garden
Lalo's
Lao Sze Chuan
La Tasca
Le Titi de Paris
Le Vichyssois
Lou Malnati Pizza

Maggiano's
Magnum's Steak
Melting Pot
Mia Cucina
Millrose
Mj2 Bistro
Montarra
Morton's Steak
Nancy's Stuffed Pizza
Original Gino's
Pappadeaux Seafood
P.F. Chang's
Pompei Bakery
Red Star Tavern
Retro Bistro
Russell's BBQ
Sal & Carvão
1776
Shaw's Crab House
Shula's Steak
Stir Crazy
Sushi Ai
Takkatsu
Texas de Brazil
Udupi Palace
Original Pancake
Weber Grill
Wildfire
Wildfish
Woo Lae Oak

Suburban South

Al's #1 Beef
Aurelio's Pizza
Balagio
Bogart's Charhouse
Cafe Borgia
Dixie Kitchen
Original Pancake

Suburban SW

Al's #1 Beef
Aurelio's Pizza
Balagio
Bar Louie
Bogart's Charhouse
Canoe Club
Courtright's
Hackney's
Original Gino's
Sabor do Brasil
Tallgrass
Tin Fish
White Fence Farm

Suburban West

Adelle's
Amber Cafe
Antico Posto
Atwater's
Aurelio's Pizza
Bar Louie
Benihana
Bistro Banlieue
Bistrot Margot
Cab's Wine Bar
Café le Coq
Carlucci
Catch 35
Cheesecake Factory
Chez François
Chinn's Fishery
Clubhouse, The
Comida Bebida
Costa's
Ed Debevic's
Edwardo's Pizza
Emilio's Sunflower
Emilio's Tapas
Finley's Grill
Flat Top Grill
Francesca's
Greek Islands
Harvest
Heaven on Seven
Hemmingway's
Hugo's Frog & Fish
Indian Garden
Isabella's Estiatorio
J. Alexander's
Joy Yee's Noodle
Kyoto
Lalo's
L'anne
Lao Sze Chuan
La Piazza (Forest Park)
La Piazza (Naperville)
Les Deux Autres
Lou Malnati Pizza
Maggiano's
Magnum's Steak
Melting Pot
Mesón Sabika
Mon Ami Gabi
Morton's Steak
Mysore Woodland
Nancy's Stuffed Pizza
Original Gino's
Original Pancake

Pacific Blue
Pappadeaux Seafood
Parkers' Ocean Grill
Pegasus
Penny's Noodle
P.F. Chang's
Philander's
Pompei Bakery
Red Star Tavern
Reza's
Robinson's Ribs
Rock Bottom Brewery
Rosebud
Russell's BBQ

Sal & Carvão
Salbute
Stir Crazy
Sullivan's Steak
Swordfish
Tango
Timpano Chophouse
Tin Fish
Trucchi Italian
Tuscany
Viceroy of India
Vie
Weber Grill
Wildfire

SPECIAL FEATURES

(Indexes list the best in each category. Multi-location restaurants' features may vary by branch.)

Breakfast

(See also Hotel Dining)
Ann Sather
Army & Lou's
Bagel, The
Bar Louie
Billy Goat Tavern
Bin 36/Bin Wine
Bite
Blind Faith Café
Bongo Room
Breakfast Club
Cafe Selmarie
Chicago Diner
Cold Comfort Cafe
David's Bistro
Davis St. Fishmarket
Dixie Kitchen
Ed Debevic's
Flo
foodlife
Hackney's
Harry Caray's
Heartland Cafe
Heaven on Seven
Ina's
Irazu
Kitsch'n
Lou Mitchell's
Lula
Manny's
M. Henry
Milk & Honey
Millrose
Nookies
Oak Tree
Orange
Original Pancake
Pegasus
Phoenix
San Soo Gab San
Slice of Life
Tecalitlan
Tempo
Three Happiness
Tilli's
Toast
Tre Kronor
Uncommon Ground
Viand Bar
Victory's Banner
Wishbone

Brunch

Adobo Grill
American Girl Cafe
Andies
Angelina
Ann Sather
Atwater's
Atwood Cafe
Bar Louie
Bêtise Bistro
Bistro 110
Bistrot Margot
Bistrot Zinc
Bite
Bongo Room
Brett's Café
Café des Architectes
Cafe Selmarie
Café Spiaggia
Cafe 28
Cheesecake Factory
Chicago Diner
Clubhouse, The
Coobah
Davis St. Fishmarket
erwin cafe & bar
Flo
Frontera Grill
Grand Lux Cafe
Hackney's
Heaven on Seven
Hemmingway's
House of Blues
Jack's on Halsted
Jane's
Jilly's Cafe
John's Place
Kitsch'n
La Crêperie
La Donna
La Tache
Lobby, The
Magnolia Cafe

Meritage Cafe
Mesón Sabika
M. Henry
Mike Ditka's
Milk & Honey
Millrose
North Pond
Orange
Pizza Capri
P.J. Clarke's
Platiyo
Pump Room
ristorante we
Ritz-Carlton Café
Ritz-Carlton Din. Rm.
RL
Salpicón
Seasons
Signature Room
Silver Cloud B&G
Smith & Wollensky
South Water Kitchen
Square Kitchen
Stanley's Kitchen
SushiSamba rio
Tavern on Rush
312 Chicago
Tilli's
Toast
Tre Kronor
Tweet
Twisted Spoke
Uncommon Ground
Viceroy of India
Vinci
Original Pancake
Wishbone
Yoshi's Café

Buffet Served
(Check availability)
Andies
Avenues
Clubhouse, The
Drake Bros.' Steak
Edwardo's Pizza
Essence of India
Flat Top Grill
Gale St. Inn
Gaylord Indian
Grace O'Malley's
Hackney's
Hemmingway's
House of Blues

India House
Indian Garden
Karyn's Fresh Corner
Klay Oven
La Fonda Latino
Lobby, The
Mt. Everest
Pappadeaux Seafood
P.S. Bangkok
Puck's at MCA
Raj Darbar
Reza's
Ritz-Carlton Din. Rm.
RoSal's Kitchen
Ruby of Siam
Seasons
Signature Room
Stanley's Kitchen
Thai Classic
Tiffin
Udupi Palace
Venus Greek-Cypriot
Viceroy of India

Business Dining
Alinea
Aria
Atwood Cafe
Avenues
Balagio
Ben Pao
Bistro Kirkou
Blackbird
Blue Water Grill
Brasserie Jo
Brazzaz
Café des Architectes
Caliterra B&G
Capital Grille
Carlucci
Carmichael Steak
Catch 35
Charlie Trotter's
Chez François
Chicago Chop Hse.
Chicago Prime Steak
Coco Pazzo
Crofton on Wells
Custom House
David Burke Prime
David's Bistro
Devon Seafood Grill
Dine
Drake Bros.' Steak

Erie Cafe
Everest
Finley's Grill
Fleming's Steak
Fogo de Chão
Fulton's
Gene & Georgetti
Gibsons Steak
Golden Budha
Grill on the Alley
Grillroom, The
Grotto
Harry Caray's
Il Mulino New York
Japonais
Joe's Seafood/Steak
Karma
Keefer's
Kevin
Kinzie Chophouse
Lawry's Prime Rib
Le Colonial
Le Français
Les Nomades
Le Titi de Paris
Lux Bar
Magnum's Steak
McCormick & Schmick
Michael
Mike Ditka's
mk
Morton's Steak
Mrs. Park's Tavern
Naha
Narra
Nick's Fishmarket
Nine
NoMI
One North
one sixtyblue
Palm, The
Park Grill
Petterino's
Phil Stefani's
Rhapsody
ristorante we
Ritz-Carlton Din. Rm.
RL
Roy's
Ruth's Chris Steak
Sal & Carvão
Saloon Steak
Seasons
Shaw's Crab House

Sidebar Grille
Slice of Life
Smith & Wollensky
South Water Kitchen
Spiaggia
Sullivan's Steak
Takkatsu
Ted's Montana Grill
312 Chicago
Timpano Chophouse
Topolobampo
Tuscany
Vivere
Vivo
Vong's
Weber Grill

BYO

Agami
Ann Sather
Babylon Kitchen
Bite
CHIC Cafe
China Grill
Chinoiserie
Coast Sushi
Cold Comfort Cafe
Courtright's
Cuatro
Don Roth's
Dorado
El Presidente
Fattoush
Fonda del Mar
Gibsons Steak
Giordano's
Hashalom
HB
Hecky's
Hema's Kitchen
Indie Cafe
Irazu
Joy Yee's Noodle
Kabul House
Kan Zaman
Karyn's Fresh Corner
La Cazuela Mariscos
La Cucina/Donatella
Las Tablas
Lucia
Matsu Yama
Medici on 57th
Melting Pot
M. Henry

Mizu Yakitori
Morton's Steak
My Pie Pizza
Mysore Woodland
Nookies
Old Jerusalem
Orange
Original Gino's
Parrot Cage
Penny's Noodle
Ping Pong
P.S. Bangkok
Rinconcito So. Am.
Ringo
Riques
Robinson's Ribs
Ruby of Siam
Schwa
South
Speakeasy
Spoon Thai
State
Tango Sur
Thai Classic
Thai Pastry
Think Café
Tomboy
Tre Kronor
Trucchi Italian
T-Spot Sushi
Udupi Palace
Uno Di Martino
Vien Dong
Yard House

Celebrity Chefs
(Listed under their
primary restaurants)
Alinea, *Grant Achatz*
Ambria, *Gabino Sotelino*
Arun's, *Arun Sampanthavivat*
Avec, *Koren Grieveson*
Avenues, *Graham Elliot Bowles*
Bistro Campagne, *M. Altenberg*
Bistro 110, *Dominique Tougne*
Blackbird, *Paul Kahan*
Café le Coq, *Stephen Chiappetti*
Cafe Matou, *Charlie Socher*
Charlie Trotter's, *Charlie Trotter*
Crofton on Wells, *Suzy Crofton*
erwin cafe & bar, *Erwin
    Drechsler*
Everest, *Jean Joho*
Frontera Grill, *Rick Bayless*

Hot Chocolate, *Mindy Segal*
Jack's on Halsted, *Jack Jones*
Keefer's, *John Hogan*
Kevin, *Kevin Shikami*
Le Bouchon, *J-C Poilevey*
Le Français, *Roland Liccioni*
Le Titi de Paris, *M. Maddox*
Le Vichyssois, *Bernard Cretier*
Mas, *John Manion*
Michael, *Michael Lachowitz*
mk, *Todd Stein*
Moto, *Homaro Cantu*
Nacional 27, *Randy Zweiban*
Naha, *Carrie Nahabedian*
North Pond, *Bruce Sherman*
one sixtyblue, *Martial Noguier*
Opera, *Paul Wildermuth*
Prairie Grass Cafe, *Sarah
    Stegner & George Bumbaris*
Red Light, *Jackie Shen*
Salpicón, *Priscila Satkoff*
Schwa, *Michael Carlson*
Spiaggia, *Tony Mantuano*
Spring, *Shawn McClain*
Tallgrass, *Robert Burcenski*
Timo, *John Bubala*
Topolobampo, *Rick Bayless*
Tru, *Rick Tramonto, Gale Gand*
West Town Tavern, *Susan Goss*
Zealous, *Michael Taus*

Child-Friendly
(Alternatives to the usual
fast-food places; * children's
menu available)
American Girl Cafe*
Ann Sather
Antico Posto*
Artopolis Bakery
Bandera*
Benihana*
Berghoff Cafe
Big Bowl*
Bob Chinn's Crab*
Bongo Room
Breakfast Club
Cafe Selmarie
Carson's Ribs*
Cereality Cereal
Cheesecake Factory*
Chicago Pizza
Dave's Italian
Davis St. Fishmarket*
Eatzi's

Ed Debevic's*
Edwardo's Pizza*
Flat Top Grill*
foodlife*
Gold Coast Dogs
Gulliver's Pizza*
Hackney's*
Hard Rock Cafe*
Harry Caray's*
Heaven on Seven*
Hecky's
Hot Doug's*
House of Blues*
Ina's*
John's Place*
Joy Yee's Noodle
Kitsch'n*
Lawry's Prime Rib*
Lou Malnati Pizza*
Lou Mitchell's*
LuLu's Dim Sum
Maggiano's*
Manny's*
Margie's Candies*
Mity Nice Grill*
Oak Tree
OPA Estiatorio
Orange*
Original Gino's*
Original Pancake*
Pegasus
P.F. Chang's
Pizza Capri*
Pizza D.O.C.
Pizzeria Uno/Due*
Potbelly Sandwich
R.J. Grunts*
Robinson's Ribs*
Rock Bottom Brewery*
Ron of Japan*
Russell's BBQ*
Sapori Trattoria
Scoozi!*
Sidebar Grille
Stanley's Kitchen*
Stir Crazy*
Ted's Montana Grill*
Tempo
Timo
Toast*
Trattoria D.O.C.
Tucci Benucch*
Tufano's Tap
Twin Anchors*

Uncommon Ground*
White Fence Farm*
Wishbone*

Cigars Welcome
Agami
Ballo
Carlucci
Carmine's
Chestnut Grill
Chicago Prime Steak
Cité
Clubhouse, The
D & J Bistro
Devon Seafood Grill
Erie Cafe
Fornetto Mei
Froggy's French
Gale St. Inn
Gene & Georgetti
Gibsons Steak
Goose Is. Brewing
Greek Islands
Green Dolphin St.
Green Door Tavern
Grillroom, The
Grotto
Hacienda Tecalitlan
Hackney's
Hard Rock Cafe
Harry Caray's
Hugo's Frog & Fish
Irish Oak
Karma
Kinzie Chophouse
Kizoku Sushi
La Strada
Lovell's/Lake Forest
Magnum's Steak
Narcisse
Palm, The
Parkers' Ocean Grill
Philly G's
Phil Stefani's
P.J. Clarke's
Red Star Tavern
Riva
Rosebud
Rumba
Ruth's Chris Steak
Saloon Steak
Silver Cloud B&G
Smith & Wollensky
Smoke Daddy

Souk
Stetson's Chop Hse.
Sullivan's Steak
Tavern
Tavern on Rush
Topo Gigio
Trattoria Roma
Tuscany
Twisted Spoke
Viand Bar
Weber Grill
Zia's Trattoria

Dancing
Ballo
Dover Straits
Fundajo Grill
Gale St. Inn
Hacienda Tecalitlan
Kizoku Sushi
La Peña
La Tasca
Lutnia
Nacional 27
Narcisse
Nine
Phil & Lou's
Pump Room
Rumba
Sayat Nova
Souk
Venus Greek-Cypriot

Delivery/Takeout
(D=delivery, T=takeout)
Adobo Grill (T)
Akai Hana (D,T)
Aladdin's Eatery (D,T)
A La Turka (T)
Andies (D,T)
Athena (T)
Bella Notte (D,T)
Benihana (T)
Berghoff Cafe (T)
Bijan's Bistro (T)
Bob Chinn's Crab (T)
Cafe Ba-Ba-Reeba! (T)
Café Spiaggia (T)
Coco Pazzo (T)
Crofton on Wells (T)
D & J Bistro (T)
Davis St. Fishmarket (T)
Don Juan (T)
Emilio's Tapas (T)

erwin cafe & bar (T)
Filippo's (T)
foodlife (D,T)
Francesca's (D,T)
Gale St. Inn (D,T)
Gene & Georgetti (T)
Gibsons Steak (T)
Gioco (T)
Heaven on Seven (D,T)
Hema's Kitchen (D,T)
Japonais (D,T)
Joe's Seafood/Steak (T)
Keefer's (T)
La Sardine (T)
La Scarola (T)
La Tasca (T)
Le Colonial (D,T)
Lula (T)
L. Woods Lodge (D,T)
Maggiano's (T)
Meritage Cafe (T)
Mesón Sabika (T)
Mia Francesca (T)
Mirai Sushi (T)
Mon Ami Gabi (T)
Old Jerusalem (D,T)
Opera (T)
Orange (T)
Parthenon (T)
Penang (D,T)
Pierrot Gourmet (T)
Platiyo (T)
Poag Mahone's (D,T)
Potbelly Sandwich (D,T)
Red Light (T)
R.J. Grunts (T)
Rock Bottom Brewery (T)
RoSal's Kitchen (T)
Rosebud (D,T)
Salbute (T)
Saloon Steak (D,T)
San Soo Gab San (D,T)
Scoozi! (T)
Shaw's Crab House (D,T)
Smith & Wollensky (T)
Souk (T)
Sullivan's Steak (T)
Sushi Naniwa (D,T)
Sushi Wabi (D,T)
Swordfish (T)
Tarantino's (D,T)
Tizi Melloul (T)
Trattoria Roma (D,T)
Twin Anchors (T)

Village, The (D,T)
Volare (D,T)
Yoshi's Café (T)

Dining Alone

(Other than hotels and
places with counter service)
Ann Sather
Bar Louie
Bin 36/Bin Wine
Bite
Blind Faith Café
Blue Water Grill
Breakfast Club
Chicago Diner
Eatzi's
Eleven City Diner
Extra Virgin
Flat Top Grill
foodlife
Gold Coast Dogs
Heartland Cafe
Hot Doug's
Indie Cafe
Kaze Sushi
Kinzie Chophouse
Kizoku Sushi
Koi
Kroll's
Lula
Maiz
Manny's
Max & Benny's
Meiji
Mrs. Murphy & Sons
Nookies
Oak Tree
Penny's Noodle
Puck's at MCA
Reza's
Toast
Tsuki
Tweet
Viand Bar
Wiener's Circle

Entertainment

(Call for days and times
of performances)
A La Turka (belly dancing)
American Girl Cafe (musical/
 theater)
Cafe Bolero (Latin jazz)
Catch 35 (piano)

Chicago Chop Hse. (piano)
Chicago Prime Steak (jazz)
Chief O'Neill's Pub (Irish)
Costa's (piano)
Cyrano's Bistrot (cabaret)
Dover Straits (bands)
Edelweiss (German music)
El Nandu (guitar)
Emilio's Tapas (flamenco)
Geja's Cafe (flamenco guitar)
Green Dolphin St. (jazz)
Hackney's (varies)
House of Blues (blues)
Irish Oak (Irish/rock)
Kit Kat Lounge (varies)
Lalo's (DJ/mariachi)
La Strada (piano)
La Taberna Tapatia (DJ)
Lobby, The (jazz)
Lutnia (piano)
Mesón Sabika (flamenco guitar)
Mia Cucina (piano)
Myron & Phil's Steak (piano)
Nacional 27 (DJ/jazz)
Nick's Fishmarket (jazz)
Parkers' Ocean Grill (jazz/piano)
Philander's (jazz)
Philly G's (piano)
Pump Room (jazz)
Redfish (blues/jazz)
Ritz-Carlton Din. Rm. (piano)
Rock Bottom Brewery (karaoke)
Rumba (bands/DJ)
Sabatino's (piano)
Sayat Nova (DJ)
Shaw's Crab House (blues/jazz)
Signature Room (jazz)
Smoke Daddy (blues/jazz)
Souk (belly dancing)
Speakeasy (varies)
Sullivan's Steak (jazz)
Sushi Wabi (DJ)
Tizi Melloul (belly dancing)
Uncommon Ground (varies)
Webster's Wine Bar (bands)

Fireplaces

Andies
Ann Sather
Athena
Atwater's
Bêtise Bistro
Bistrot Margot
Boston Blackie's

Café la Cave
Carlucci
Carson's Ribs
Chen's Chinese
Chestnut Grill
Chicago Prime Steak
Clubhouse, The
Costa's
Courtright's
David's Bistro
Dee's
Don Roth's
Dover Straits
Edelweiss
EJ's Place
Enoteca Piattini
Entourage
Erie Cafe
Finley's Grill
Francesca's
Froggy's French
Gale St. Inn
Gene & Georgetti
Gibsons Steak
Greek Islands
Green Door Tavern
Hacienda Tecalitlan
Hackney's
Half Shell
Harbour House
Hecky's
Il Mulino New York
Japonais
John's Place
Keefer's
Koi
Les Nomades
Le Vichyssois
Lovell's/Lake Forest
Magnum's Steak
McCormick & Schmick
Melting Pot
Milk & Honey
Millrose
Mrs. Murphy & Sons
My Pie Pizza
Narcisse
North Pond
Park Grill
Prairie Grass Cafe
Red Star Tavern
Reza's
RL
Sai Café

Santorini
South Gate Cafe
Swordfish
Tallgrass
Tilli's
Tsunami
Uncommon Ground
Va Pensiero
Vie
Original Pancake

Game in Season

Alinea
Allen's
Ambria
Atwater's
Avenues
Bank Lane Bistro
Barrington Bistro
Bêtise Bistro
Bistro Banlieue
Bistro Campagne
Bistro Kirkou
Bistro 110
Bistrot Margot
Bistrot Zinc
BOKA
Brasserie Jo
Brett's Café
Buona Terra
Cab's Wine Bar
Café Absinthe
Café Bernard
Café des Architectes
Café la Cave
Café le Coq
Cafe Matou
Cafe Pyrenees
Campagnola
Carlos'
Charlie Trotter's
Chestnut Grill
Chez François
Chicago Firehouse
Chicago Prime Steak
CHIC Cafe
Cité
Coco Pazzo
copperblue
Courtright's
Crofton on Wells
Custom House
Cyrano's Bistrot
D & J Bistro

David's Bistro
De Cero
Emilio's Sunflower
erwin cafe & bar
Froggy's French
Frontera Grill
Gabriel's
Glunz Bavarian
Green Dolphin St.
Harvest
HB
Heartland Cafe
Hemmingway's
Hot Doug's
Isabella's Estiatorio
Jack's on Halsted
Jilly's Cafe
Karma
Kaze Sushi
Keefer's
Kevin
KiKi's Bistro
La Fette
la petite folie
La Piazza (Forest Park)
La Piazza (Naperville)
La Sardine
La Scarola
La Strada
La Tache
La Tasca
Le Bouchon
Le Français
Les Nomades
Le Titi de Paris
Le Vichyssois
Lovell's/Lake Forest
Meritage Cafe
Merlo
Michael
Mimosa
mk
Mrs. Murphy & Sons
Naha
Narcisse
North Pond
Oceanique
One North
one sixtyblue
Opera
Park Grill
Parlor
Philander's
Pump Room

Retro Bistro
Ritz-Carlton Din. Rm.
RL
Rushmore
Russian Tea Time
Salbute
Salpicón
Saltaus
Sapori Trattoria
Schwa
Seasons
1776
socca
Soiree Bar
South
Speakeasy
Stained Glass Wine
State
Tallgrass
Tarantino's
Think Café
Timo
Va Pensiero
Vie
Vivere
Volo

Historic Places

(Year opened; * building)
1847 Mesón Sabika*
1858 Don Roth's*
1865 Crofton on Wells*
1872 Green Door Tavern*
1880 West Town Tavern*
1881 Twin Anchors*
1884 Thyme Café*
1885 Red Lion Pub*
1886 Cold Comfort Cafe*
1890 Pasta Palazzo*
1890 Pizzeria Uno/Due*
1890 Sapori Trattoria*
1890 Webster's Wine Bar*
1893 Tavern*
1895 Club Lago*
1897 Tallgrass*
1900 Vivo*
1901 South Gate Cafe*
1905 Carnivale*
1909 Pompei Bakery
1911 Poag Mahone's*
1918 Drake Bros.' Steak
1920 Chef's Station*
1921 Margie's Candies
1923 Lou Mitchell's

1927 Francesca's*
1927 Village, The*
1927 Vivere*
1928 Philander's*
1930 Del Rio*
1930 Russell's BBQ
1930 Tufano's Tap*
1933 Bruna's
1933 Cape Cod Room
1934 Billy Goat Tavern
1935 Miller's Pub
1937 Café le Coq*
1938 Al's #1 Beef
1938 Pump Room
1939 Hackney's
1941 Gene & Georgetti
1942 Manny's
1945 Ann Sather
1945 Army & Lou's
1948 Superdawg Drive-In
1951 Papa Milano
1954 White Fence Farm
1955 La Cantina
1955 Pizzeria Uno/Due

Hotel Dining

Ambassador East Hotel
  Pump Room
Belden-Stratford Hotel
  Ambria
  Mon Ami Gabi
Carleton Hotel
  Philander's
Crowne Plaza Chicago Metro
  Hotel
  Dine
Crowne Plaza Hotel
  Karma
Doubletree Guest Suites Hotel
  Mrs. Park's Tavern
Doubletree Hotel
  Gibsons Steak
Drake Hotel
  Cape Cod Room
  Drake Bros.' Steak
Embassy Suites Hotel
  P.J. Clarke's
Fairmont Chicago Hotel
  Aria
Fitzpatrick Hotel
  Benihana
Four Seasons Hotel
  Seasons
  Seasons Café
Hard Rock Hotel
  China Grill

Herrington Inn
  Atwater's
Hilton Garden Inn
  Weber Grill
Holiday Inn Select
  Harry Caray's
Hotel Allegro
  312 Chicago
Hotel Blake
  Custom House
Hotel Burnham
  Atwood Cafe
Hotel Monaco
  South Water Kitchen
Hotel Orrington
  Narra
Hyatt Regency
  Stetson's Chop Hse.
InterContinental, Hotel
  Zest
James Chicago Hotel
  David Burke Prime
Margarita Inn
  Va Pensiero
Northshore Hotel
  Tapas Barcelona
Park Hyatt Chicago
  NoMI
Peninsula Hotel
  Avenues
  Lobby, The
  Pierrot Gourmet
  Shanghai Terrace
Pheasant Run Resort
  Harvest
Red Roof Inn
  Coco Pazzo
Renaissance Hotel
  Ruth's Chris Steak
Ritz-Carlton Hotel
  Ritz-Carlton Café
  Ritz-Carlton Din. Rm.
Seneca Hotel
  Saloon Steak
Sheraton Chicago
  Shula's Steak
Sofitel Chicago Water Tower
  Café des Architectes
Swissôtel
  Palm, The
Tremont Hotel
  Mike Ditka's

W Chicago Lakeshore
  Wave
Westin Hotel
  Grill on the Alley
Westin River North
  Kamehachi
W Hotel
  ristorante we
Write Inn
  Hemmingway's
Wyndham Chicago
  Caliterra B&G
Wyndham Northwest Chicago
  Shula's Steak

Jacket Required
Ambria
Carlos'
Charlie Trotter's
Spiaggia
Tru

Late Dining
(Weekday closing hour)
Agami (12 AM)
Al's #1 Beef (varies)
Andies (varies)
Artopolis Bakery (12 AM)
Athena (12 AM)
Avec (12 AM)
Ballo (12 AM)
Bar Louie (varies)
Bijan's Bistro (3:30 AM)
Billy Goat Tavern (varies)
Carmichael Steak (12 AM)
Carmine's (12 AM)
Chestnut Grill (1 AM)
Coast Sushi (12 AM)
Coobah (1 AM)
Cuatro (2 AM)
El Presidente (24 hrs.)
Emperor's Choice (12 AM)
Evergreen (12 AM)
Finley's Grill (1:30 AM)
Fixture (12 AM)
Flight (1 AM)
Gibsons Steak (varies)
Giordano's (varies)
Gold Coast Dogs (varies)
Greek Islands (varies)
Happy Chef Dim Sum (2 AM)
Hard Rock Cafe (12 AM)
Hugo's Frog & Fish (varies)

Itto Sushi (12 AM)
Izumi Sushi (12 AM)
Kamehachi (varies)
Kit Kat Lounge (12 AM)
Kuma's Corner (1 AM)
Landmark (2 AM)
Lao Sze Chuan (varies)
La Taberna Tapatia (12 AM)
Lou Mitchell's (varies)
Lux Bar (1:30 AM)
Margie's Candies (varies)
Melting Pot (varies)
Miller's Pub (2 AM)
Nancy's Stuffed Pizza (varies)
Narcisse (1 AM)
Nookies (varies)
Parlor (12 AM)
Parthenon (12 AM)
Pegasus (varies)
Penang (1 AM)
People Lounge (1 AM)
Pepper Lounge (12 AM)
Pete Miller Sea/Steak (varies)
Ping Pong (12 AM)
Pizzeria Uno/Due (varies)
Quartino (1 AM)
Reza's (varies)
Ribs 'n' Bibs (12 AM)
Rockit B&G (2 AM)
Roditys (12 AM)
Saltaus (12:30 AM)
Samah (12 AM)
San Soo Gab San (24 hrs.)
Santorini (12 AM)
Silver Seafood (1 AM)
Superdawg Drive-In (varies)
Tasting Room (12 AM)
Tavern on Rush (12 AM)
Tecalitlan (12 AM)
Tempo (24 hrs.)
Twisted Spoke (1 AM)
Webster's Wine Bar (12:30 AM)
Wiener's Circle (4 AM)

Meet for a Drink
(Most top hotels and the
following standouts)
Allen's
Avenue M
Ballo
Bandera
Bar Louie
Bijan's Bistro
Billy Goat Tavern

Bin 36/Bin Wine
Bistro 110
Blue Water Grill
BOKA
Brasserie Jo
Butter
Cab's Wine Bar
Café des Architectes
Canoe Club
Carnivale
Catch 35
Chicago Prime Steak
Chief O'Neill's Pub
China Grill
Coobah
Cuatro
del Toro
Dine
Di Pescara
Enoteca Piattini
Entourage
Extra Virgin
Finley's Grill
Fleming's Steak
Flight
Frontera Grill
Fulton's
Gibsons Steak
Goose Is. Brewing
Green Door Tavern
Grotto
Harry Caray's
Japonais
Joe's Seafood/Steak
Keefer's
Landmark
Lux Bar
Mambo Grill
Marché
McCormick & Schmick
Meritage Cafe
Mike Ditka's
Millrose
Miramar
mk
Nacional 27
Nine
NoMI
One North
one sixtyblue
Osteria Via Stato
P.J. Clarke's
Platiyo
Prairie Grass Cafe

Quartino
Red Light
Red Star Tavern
Rhapsody
RL
Rock Bottom Brewery
Rockit B&G
Rosebud Steak
Rumba
Saltaus
Scoozi!
Shaw's Crab House
Sidebar Grille
Signature Room
Smith & Wollensky
Soiree Bar
South Water Kitchen
Stained Glass Wine
Sullivan's Steak
SushiSamba rio
Tasting Room
Tavern on Rush
Ted's Montana Grill
312 Chicago
Timpano Chophouse
Tizi Melloul
Trattoria No. 10
Twisted Spoke
Volo
Wave
Webster's Wine Bar
X/O Chicago
Zapatista

Microbreweries
Goose Is. Brewing
Millrose
Piece
Rock Bottom Brewery

Noteworthy Newcomers
Agami
Aki Sushi
Avenue M
Berghoff Cafe
Birch River Grill
Block 44
Brazzaz
Brioso
Carnivale
Cereality Cereal
Chiyo
Comida Bebida
copperblue

Cuatro
Custom House
David Burke Prime
del Toro
Devon Seafood Grill
Dine
Di Pescara
Eatzi's
Eleven City Diner
Emilio's Sunflower
Entourage
Extra Virgin
Finley's Grill
Fixture
Fleming's Steak
Fonda del Mar
Fulton's
Fundajo Grill
Great Lakes Fish
Hachi's Kitchen
Harbour House
Haro
Harvest
HB
Il Mulino New York
Julius Meinl Café
Kohan Japanese
Kroll's
Kuma's Corner
Lake Side Café
Landmark
La Piazza (Naperville)
Luna Caprese
Lux Bar
Maiz
Max & Benny's
May St. Market
Michael
Mitchell's Fish Market
Mizu Yakitori
Montarra
Mrs. Murphy & Sons
Narra
Olé Olé
Pancho Viti's Mex.
Parlor
Parrot Cage
People Lounge
Quartino
Riccardo Trattoria
Sabor do Brasil
Sage Grille
Saltaus
Schwa
Sidebar Grille

Soiree Bar
Sola
State
Sushi Ai
Tagine
Ted's Montana Grill
Terragusto Cafe
Texas de Brazil
Timo
Timpano Chophouse
Tony Rocco's
Trattoria D.O.C.
Trucchi Italian
T-Spot Sushi
Zapatista

Outdoor Dining
(G=garden; P=patio;
S=sidewalk; T=terrace;
W=waterside)
Allen's (P)
Arco de Cuchilleros (P)
a tavola (G)
Athena (G)
Atwater's (P)
Bijan's Bistro (S)
Bistro Campagne (G)
Bistro 110 (S)
Bistrot Margot (S)
Blackbird (S)
Brasserie Jo (S)
Cafe Ba-Ba-Reeba! (P)
Carmichael Steak (G)
Carmine's (P)
Chez Joël (P)
Coco Pazzo (P)
Cyrano's Bistrot (S)
Edwardo's Pizza (P)
Feast (G)
Flight (P)
Frontera Grill (P)
Greek Islands (P,S)
Green Dolphin St. (P,W)
Isabella's Estiatorio (P)
Japonais (P)
John's Place (S)
Kamehachi (P,S)
Le Colonial (S,T)
Lucca's (G)
Maggiano's (P)
Mas (S)
Meritage Cafe (G)
Mesón Sabika (G,P)
NoMI (G)

Park Grill (P)
Pegasus (T)
P.F. Chang's (P)
Phil Stefani's (S)
Potbelly Sandwich (P)
Puck's at MCA (P,W)
RL (P)
Rock Bottom Brewery (G)
Rosebud (P,S,W)
Salvatore's (G)
Shanghai Terrace (T)
Smith & Wollensky (G,P,T,W)
South Gate Cafe (P,S)
SushiSamba rio (S)
Tapas Barcelona (G,P)
Tavern on Rush (P,S)
Timo (P)
Tuscany (G,P)
Twisted Spoke (P)
Va Pensiero (T)

Nine
NoMI
Opera
Osteria Via Stato
Quartino
Rosebud
Rosebud Steak
Saltaus
Scoozi!
Spring
SushiSamba rio
Tavern on Rush
Wave
Zapatista

People-Watching
Adobo Grill
American Girl Cafe
Avec
Avenue M
Bin 36/Bin Wine
Bistro 110
Blackbird
BOKA
Bongo Room
Brasserie Jo
Carmine's
Carnivale
Chicago Chop Hse.
Coobah
Cuatro
del Toro
Entourage
Gibsons Steak
Green Zebra
Harry Caray's
Il Mulino New York
Japonais
Keefer's
Landmark
Le Colonial
Lux Bar
Manny's
Marché
Mirai Sushi
Miramar
mk
Naha
Narcisse

Power Scenes
Alinea
Ambria
Avenues
Capital Grille
Catch 35
Charlie Trotter's
Chicago Chop Hse.
Coco Pazzo
Custom House
David Burke Prime
Entourage
Everest
Fulton's
Gene & Georgetti
Gibsons Steak
Hugo's Frog & Fish
Il Mulino New York
Keefer's
Le Français
Les Nomades
mk
Morton's Steak
Naha
NoMI
Ritz-Carlton Café
Ritz-Carlton Din. Rm.
RL
Ruth's Chris Steak
Seasons
Smith & Wollensky
Spiaggia
Spring
Tru

Private Rooms
(Restaurants charge less at off times; call for capacity)
Ambria
Athena

Ben Pao
Brasserie Jo
Caliterra B&G
Capital Grille
Catch 35
Charlie Trotter's
Chicago Chop Hse.
Club Lucky
Costa's
Edwardo's Pizza
Emilio's Tapas
Everest
Francesca's
Frontera Grill
Gabriel's
Gene & Georgetti
Gibsons Steak
Gioco
Goose Is. Brewing
Greek Islands
Joe's Seafood/Steak
Kamehachi
Keefer's
Mesón Sabika
mk
Naha
Nine
NoMI
one sixtyblue
Park Grill
Pasteur
Pete Miller Sea/Steak
Red Light
Rock Bottom Brewery
Rosebud
Russian Tea Time
Ruth's Chris Steak
Scoozi!
Shaw's Crab House
Smith & Wollensky
Spiaggia
SushiSamba rio
Tallgrass
312 Chicago
Tizi Melloul
Topolobampo
Trattoria Roma
Tru
Va Pensiero
Vivo
Wildfire

Prix Fixe Menus
(Call for prices and times)
Ambria
Arun's

Avenues
Bank Lane Bistro
Bin 36/Bin Wine
Bistro 110
Caliterra B&G
Carlos'
Charlie Trotter's
Chez François
Courtright's
Cyrano's Bistrot
D & J Bistro
Everest
Fogo de Chão
Froggy's French
Gabriel's
La Sardine
Le Français
Les Nomades
mk
Moto
North Pond
Oceanique
Pump Room
Red Light
Retro Bistro
Roy's
Sal & Carvão
Salpicón
Seasons
Spiaggia
Spring
Tallgrass
Topolobampo
Tru

Quick Bites
Aladdin's Eatery
Art of Pizza
Artopolis Bakery
Babylon Kitchen
Bagel, The
Bar Louie
Berghoff Cafe
Big Bowl
Bijan's Bistro
Billy Goat Tavern
Bin 36/Bin Wine
Cafe Selmarie
Cereality Cereal
Chicago Pizza
Cold Comfort Cafe
del Toro
Eleven City Diner
El Presidente

Extra Virgin
Flat Top Grill
foodlife
Gold Coast Dogs
Haro
Hot Chocolate
Hot Doug's
Lem's BBQ
Maiz
Manny's
Max & Benny's
Noon-O-Kabab
Oak Tree
Old Jerusalem
Pegasus
Penny's Noodle
People Lounge
Pierrot Gourmet
Pompei Bakery
Potbelly Sandwich
Puck's at MCA
Quartino
Russell's BBQ
Stained Glass Wine
State
Stir Crazy
Superdawg Drive-In
Tasting Room
Tempo
Uncommon Ground
Viand Bar
Webster's Wine Bar
Wiener's Circle

Quiet Conversation

Akai Hana
Aria
Arun's
a tavola
Bank Lane Bistro
Barrington Bistro
Best Hunan
Bêtise Bistro
Bistro Banlieue
Café Bernard
Café des Architectes
Café la Cave
Cafe Matou
Cafe Pyrenees
Cafe Selmarie
Café Spiaggia
Caliterra B&G
Cape Cod Room
Carlos'

Charlie Trotter's
Chicago Prime Steak
Chinoiserie
Cité
copperblue
D & J Bistro
Don Roth's
Dover Straits
erwin cafe & bar
Everest
Gale St. Inn
Gaylord Indian
Geja's Cafe
Hashalom
Itto Sushi
Jilly's Cafe
Kevin
Klay Oven
Kyoto
La Crêperie
La Gondola
Lawry's Prime Rib
Le Français
Le P'tit Paris
Les Nomades
Le Titi de Paris
Le Vichyssois
Lovell's/Lake Forest
Lucca's
Mimosa
North Pond
Oceanique
One North
Pierrot Gourmet
Pump Room
Rhapsody
Ritz-Carlton Café
Ritz-Carlton Din. Rm.
RL
Ron of Japan
Russian Tea Time
Salvatore's
Seasons
Seasons Café
1776
Shanghai Terrace
Shiroi Hana
Signature Room
Slice of Life
South Gate Cafe
South Water Kitchen
Takkatsu
Tallgrass
Tasting Room

Tavern
Trattoria No. 10
Tre Kronor
Tru
Va Pensiero
Village, The
Vinci
Vivere
Vong's
Zealous

Raw Bars

Blue Water Grill
Bob Chinn's Crab
Butter
Cape Cod Room
Cité
Davis St. Fishmarket
Fulton's
Half Shell
Hugo's Frog & Fish
Mitchell's Fish Market
Pappadeaux Seafood
Riva
Shaw's Crab House
Tin Fish

Romantic Places

Ambria
Avenue M
Avenues
Barrington Bistro
Bistro Banlieue
Bistro Campagne
Bistro Kirkou
Bistrot Margot
Bistrot Zinc
Block 44
BOKA
Butter
Café Absinthe
Café Bernard
Café la Cave
Cafe Pyrenees
Cape Cod Room
Carlos'
Charlie Trotter's
Chez François
Chez Joël
Chinoiserie
Cité
Coco Pazzo
copperblue
Courtright's

Crofton on Wells
Cuatro
Cyrano's Bistrot
D & J Bistro
Enoteca Piattini
erwin cafe & bar
Everest
1492 Tapas
Froggy's French
Fundajo Grill
Geja's Cafe
Gioco
Green Dolphin St.
Grotto
Il Mulino New York
Jacky's Bistro
Japonais
Jilly's Cafe
KiKi's Bistro
La Crêperie
Landmark
La Sardine
La Tache
Le Bouchon
Le Colonial
Le Français
Le P'tit Paris
Les Nomades
Le Titi de Paris
Le Vichyssois
Luna Caprese
May St. Market
Meritage Cafe
mk
Mon Ami Gabi
Nacional 27
Naha
Narcisse
NoMI
Oceanique
Pane Caldo
Pasteur
Pump Room
Rhapsody
Riccardo Trattoria
Rioja
Ritz-Carlton Din. Rm.
RL
RoSal's Kitchen
Rushmore
Seasons
1776
Shanghai Terrace
Signature Room

Soiree Bar
Sola
Souk
South Gate Cafe
Spring
Stained Glass Wine
Tallgrass
Tango Sur
Tasting Room
Tavern
Tizi Melloul
Topo Gigio
Tru
Va Pensiero
Vermilion
Vinci
Vivo
Vong's
Wave
Webster's Wine Bar
Wildfish

Senior Appeal

Andies
Ann Sather
Army & Lou's
Bacchanalia
Bagel, The
Berghoff Cafe
Bogart's Charhouse
Bruna's
Cape Cod Room
Carson's Ribs
Dave's Italian
Davis St. Fishmarket
Del Rio
Don Roth's
Dover Straits
Edelweiss
Francesco's
Gale St. Inn
Hackney's
La Cantina
La Gondola
La Strada
Lawry's Prime Rib
Le P'tit Paris
Le Vichyssois
Lou Mitchell's
Lutnia
Margie's Candies
Miller's Pub
Mirabell
Myron & Phil's Steak

Next Door Bistro
Nick's Fishmarket
Oak Tree
Original Pancake
Papa Milano
Pump Room
Rosebud
Russell's BBQ
Russian Tea Time
Sabatino's
South Gate Cafe
Tre Kronor
Tufano's Tap
Village, The
White Fence Farm

Singles Scenes

Adobo Grill
Bar Louie
BOKA
Café Iberico
Carnivale
Clubhouse, The
del Toro
House of Blues
Landmark
Lux Bar
Mike Ditka's
Narcisse
Nine
P.J. Clarke's
Red Light
Rock Bottom Brewery
Rockit B&G
Scoozi!
Stanley's Kitchen
SushiSamba rio
Tavern on Rush
Tilli's
Wave

Sleepers

(Good to excellent food,
but little known)
Amarind's
Amber Cafe
Bacchanalia
Balagio
Bite
Bruna's
Cafe Borgia
David's Bistro
Dorado
Fattoush

Heat
Izumi Sushi
Karma
Katsu Japanese
Kizoku Sushi
Kyoto
La Cucina/Donatella
La Piazza (Forest Park)
Lem's BBQ
Leonardo's
Le P'tit Paris
Les Deux Autres
Le Vichyssois
Lucia
Luna Caprese
Maiz
Matsu Yama
Montarra
Pacific Blue
Ringo
Schwa
Silver Seafood
Swordfish
Tavern
Tecalitlan
Thai Classic
Udupi Palace
Viand Bar
Wildfish

Teen Appeal

Ann Sather
Arco de Cuchilleros
Aurelio's Pizza
Bacino's
Bandera
Big Bowl
Cereality Cereal
Cheesecake Factory
Chicago Pizza
Eatzi's
Edwardo's Pizza
EJ's Place
Flat Top Grill
Giordano's
Gold Coast Dogs
Grand Lux Cafe
Hackney's
Hard Rock Cafe
Harry Caray's
Heaven on Seven
Hot Doug's
Hot Tamales
Ina's

Joy Yee's Noodle
Kroll's
Lou Malnati Pizza
Lou Mitchell's
LuLu's Dim Sum
L. Woods Lodge
Margie's Candies
Mity Nice Grill
My Pie Pizza
Nancy's Stuffed Pizza
Nookies
Original Gino's
Original Pancake
Penny's Noodle
Pizzeria Uno/Due
Pompei Bakery
Potbelly Sandwich
R.J. Grunts
Robinson's Ribs
Russell's BBQ
Stanley's Kitchen
Stir Crazy
Superdawg Drive-In
Tempo
Toast
Wiener's Circle
Wishbone

Trendy

Adobo Grill
Agami
Alinea
Avec
Avenue M
Bin 36/Bin Wine
Bistro Campagne
Blackbird
Block 44
Blue Water Grill
BOKA
Bongo Room
Butter
Café Iberico
Carnivale
China Grill
Coobah
Cuatro
Custom House
David Burke Prime
De Cero
del Toro
Follia
Fonda del Mar
Frontera Grill

Gibsons Steak
Gioco
Green Zebra
Hachi's Kitchen
Hot Chocolate
Hot Doug's
Il Mulino New York
Japonais
Landmark
Le Bouchon
Lux Bar
Marché
Mas
May St. Market
Mia Francesca
Mirai Sushi
Miramar
mk
Naha
Narcisse
Nine
NoMI
Olé Olé
one sixtyblue
Opera
Osteria Via Stato
Prairie Grass Cafe
Quartino
Red Light
Saltaus
Schwa
Scylla
Sola
Spring
SushiSamba rio
Sushi Wabi
Trattoria D.O.C.
Vermilion
Volo
Wave
X/O Chicago
Zapatista

Views

Atwater's
Avenues
Cité
Courtright's
Drake Bros.' Steak
Everest
Flight
Fulton's
Green Dolphin St.

Lobby, The
NoMI
North Pond
OPA Estiatorio
Park Grill
Pompei Bakery
Puck's at MCA
Ritz-Carlton Café
Riva
Rosebud
Seasons
Shanghai Terrace
Signature Room
Smith & Wollensky
South Gate Cafe
Spiaggia
Tasting Room
Tavern on Rush

Visitors on Expense Account

Alinea
Ambria
Arun's
Avenues
Blackbird
Bob Chinn's Crab
Brazzaz
Caliterra B&G
Cape Cod Room
Capital Grille
Carlos'
Catch 35
Charlie Trotter's
Chicago Chop Hse.
Coco Pazzo
Courtright's
Crofton on Wells
Custom House
David Burke Prime
Entourage
Everest
Gene & Georgetti
Gibsons Steak
Heat
Il Mulino New York
Joe's Seafood/Steak
Keefer's
Kevin
Lawry's Prime Rib
Le Colonial
Le Français
Les Nomades
Le Titi de Paris

Lobby, The
mk
Morton's Steak
Naha
Nine
NoMI
North Pond
Oceanique
one sixtyblue
Palm, The
Pump Room
Ritz-Carlton Din. Rm.
RL
Rosebud Steak
Roy's
Ruth's Chris Steak
Saloon Steak
Seasons
Shanghai Terrace
Shaw's Crab House
Signature Room
Smith & Wollensky
Spiaggia
Spring
Tallgrass
Topolobampo
Tru
Vivere
Wave
Zealous

Wine Bars

Avec
Bin 36/Bin Wine
Cab's Wine Bar
Café Bernard
Chestnut Grill
Cyrano's Bistrot
Fleming's Steak
Flight
Meritage Cafe
Osteria Via Stato
Quartino
Stained Glass Wine
Tasting Room
Volo
Webster's Wine Bar

Winning Wine Lists

Alinea
Allen's
Ambria
Arun's
Avec
Avenues

Bin 36/Bin Wine
Bistrot Margot
Blackbird
BOKA
Cab's Wine Bar
Campagnola
Capital Grille
Carlos'
Charlie Trotter's
Coobah
Courtright's
Custom House
Cyrano's Bistrot
Del Rio
del Toro
Everest
Fleming's Steak
Flight
Fogo de Chão
Gabriel's
Geja's Cafe
Green Zebra
Heat
Isabella's Estiatorio
Japonais
Landmark
La Sardine
Le Français
Le P'tit Paris
Les Nomades
Le Titi de Paris
May St. Market
Meritage Cafe
Miramar
mk
Moto
Naha
Narra
NoMI
North Pond
Oceanique
one sixtyblue
Pane Caldo
Rhapsody
Ritz-Carlton Din. Rm.
Salpicón
Saltaus
Seasons
1776
Signature Room
Smith & Wollensky
Spiaggia
Spring
Stained Glass Wine

Tallgrass
Tasting Room
Topolobampo
Trattoria No. 10
Tru
Va Pensiero
Vivere
Webster's Wine Bar
West Town Tavern
Zealous
Zest

Worth a Trip

Arlington Heights
  Le Titi de Paris
Evanston
  Campagnola
  Jacky's Bistro
  Va Pensiero
Highland Park
  Carlos'
Highwood
  Miramar

Hinsdale
  Salbute
Lakemoor
  Le Vichyssois
Lake Zurich
  Bistro Kirkou
  D & J Bistro
Lockport
  Tallgrass
Mt. Prospect
  Retro Bistro
Northbrook
  Prairie Grass Cafe
Tinley Park
  Tin Fish
Western Springs
  Vie
Wheeling
  Le Français
Willow Springs
  Courtright's

Milwaukee

Milwaukee's Most Popular

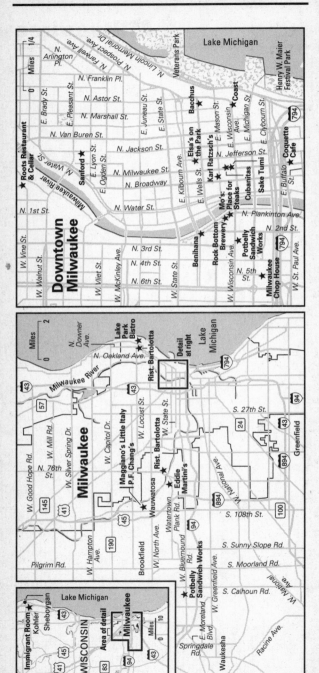

Top Ratings

Most Popular

1. Maggiano's
2. P.F. Chang's
3. Sanford
4. Lake Park Bistro
5. Potbelly Sandwich*
6. Bacchus
7. Coquette Cafe
8. Roots
9. Eddie Martini's
10. Mo's: Steak
11. Elsa's on Park
12. Ristorante Bartolotta
13. Rock Bottom Brewery
14. Benihana
15. Karl Ratzsch's*
16. Sake Tumi
17. Cubanitas
18. Coast
19. Immigrant Room
20. Milwaukee Chop Hse.*

Top Food

29 Sanford
26 Eddie Martini's
   Coerper's 5 O'Clock
   Immigrant Room
   Bacchus

25 River Lane Inn
   Coquette Cafe
   Riversite, The
   Osteria del Mondo
   Sake Tumi

By Cuisine

American (New)
29 Sanford
26 Immigrant Room
   Bacchus

American (Traditional)
25 Riversite, The
23 Jackson Grill
   Elsa's on Park

Asian (misc.)
24 Singha Thai
23 Pacific Rim
21 King & I

Eclectic
25 Tess
23 Pacific Rim
22 Bjonda

French
25 Coquette Cafe
   Lake Park Bistro
20 Elliot's Bistro

Italian
25 Osteria del Mondo
   Ristorante Bartolotta
23 Mangia

Japanese
25 Sake Tumi
24 Nanakusa
21 Hama

Pan-Latin
25 El Rey Sol
23 Cubanitas
21 Cempazuchi

Seafood
26 Eddie Martini's
25 River Lane Inn
23 Jackson Grill

Steakhouses
26 Eddie Martini's
   Coerper's 5 O'Clock
24 Milwaukee Chop Hse.

* Indicates a tie with restaurant above

Top Food

By Location

Downtown
26 Bacchus
25 Osteria del Mondo
    Sake Tumi

East Side
29 Sanford
25 Lake Park Bistro
    Tess

North Shore
25 River Lane Inn
21 Hama
19 North Shore Bistro

Outlying Areas
26 Immigrant Room
25 Riversite, The
23 Mr. B's: Steak

Third Ward
25 Coquette Cafe
24 Nanakusa
21 Palms

West Side
26 Eddie Martini's
24 Singha Thai
23 Jackson Grill

Top Decor

27 Bjonda
    Lake Park Bistro
26 Sanford
    Bacchus
    Immigrant Room

25 Coast
24 Sake Tumi
    Karl Ratzsch's
    Yanni's
    Eddie Martini's

Top Service

28 Sanford
26 Immigrant Room
    Bacchus
    Riversite, The
    Eddie Martini's

25 Dream Dance
    Lake Park Bistro
24 Mr. B's: Steak
    River Lane Inn
23 Sake Tumi

Bangs for the Buck

1. Potbelly Sandwich
2. Singha Thai
3. Cubanitas
4. Elsa's on Park
5. Edwardo's Pizza
6. Cempazuchi
7. El Rey Sol
8. King & I
9. Knick
10. Sake Tumi

Milwaukee
Restaurant Directory

Au Bon Appétit ☒
▽ 21 | 10 | 19 | $22

1016 E. Brady St. (Astor St.), 414-278-1233;
www.aubonappetit.com

You might not expect to find some of the "best chocolate mousse on the planet" in Milwaukee, but supporters insist it's waiting for you at this French-accented yet somehow still "authentic" East Side Mediterranean-Lebanese, adding "is there more delicious falafel outside Lebanon?"; as if that weren't enough, red toque–wearing chef Rihab Aris, with her "warm smile", makes "every guest feel welcome and wanting more."

Bacchus
26 | 26 | 26 | $56

Cudahy Towers, 925 E. Wells St. (Prospect Ave.),
414-765-1166; www.bacchusmke.com

"Milwaukee arrives" courtesy of this "snazzy" Downtown "in-a-class-by-itself" "jewel" that's "definitely a place to indulge" your taste for New American cuisine (it "doesn't get much better" than this) served within a "posh" setting; even admirers, though, assert that the "over-attentive staff just needs to relax a bit"; P.S. owners The Bartolotta Restaurant Group are planning a glass-enclosed conservatory space, opening onto the patio.

Barossa
20 | 17 | 19 | $35

235 S. Second St. (Oregon St.), 414-272-8466;
www.barossawinebar.com

"Fresh", "inventive organic creations" pleasing to "vegetarians and carnivores alike" (e.g. chicken Eos, a popular item at the "excellent" Sunday brunch) define this "lovely" New American in Walker's Point, a "hidden gem" "everyone wants to like" – in part because its "calm, warming" atmosphere makes it "great for social and business dinners"; still, some warn that it "can get pricey depending on what one orders."

Benihana
19 | 16 | 20 | $34

850 N. Plankinton Ave. (2nd St.), 414-270-0890;
www.benihana.com

See review in the Chicago Directory.

BJONDA ☒
22 | 27 | 23 | $51

7754 Harwood Ave. (Watertown Plank Rd.), Wauwatosa,
414-431-1444; www.bjonda.com

"Save up your dollars for a great night out" at this "classy", "aggressively hip" Wauwatosa Eclectic (No. 1 for Decor in Wisconsin) offering "downtown chic without the drive"; from the "amazing descriptions of the dishes that leave you wondering what delights your tongue is going to encounter" to the "adorable stools for women's purses", there's an "East Coast influence" (especially "welcome in the Midwest") that makes for a "fabulous dining experience"; P.S. don't miss the "romantic and private" Skylight Room.

Bosley on Brady — — — M
815 E. Brady St. (Cass St.), 414-727-7975;
www.bosleyonbrady.com
Offering a warm departure in the chilly Midwestern clime,
this Key West–themed newcomer sprinkles a Southern
coastal influence on its seafood-steakhouse theme, which
suits Brady Street's hodgepodge-of-edibles identity; visitors ease into the bright Floridian colors, piped-in smooth
jazz and breezy menu (yellowtail snapper, rib-eye steak,
sea scallops) like they're on holiday.

Carnevor ⊠ — — — M
724 N. Milwaukee St. (Mason St.), 414-223-2200;
www.carnevor.com
Chic meets red meat at this Downtown newcomer, a looker
that combines à la carte prime steaks (seafood too), trendy
tunes and a cutting-edge, three-level space on throbbing
Milwaukee Street; the staff pampers patrons with ultra-
attentive 'swarm service' and playful desserts (e.g. doughnut
holes with dipping sauces).

Caterina's ▽ 21 15 24 $35
9104 W. Oklahoma Ave. (92nd St.), 414-541-4200
Cat-fanciers of this "casual", "family"-friendly Southwest
Side spot insist "if it were Downtown or in the Third Ward
you'd never be able to get in", so enamored are they of its
"hearty Italian" fare ("as good a value as there is") and "old
supper club–style" decor; still, some find it "predictable",
with "nothing bad but nothing outstanding either."

Cempazuchi 21 20 20 $24
1205 E. Brady St. (Franklin Pl.), 414-291-5233
Lovers of "the freshest", "top-notch" margaritas (try the
flavor of the day) are in paradise at this "wonderful", *"muy
auténtico"* East Side Mexican, where "family recipes"
render "not-typical" dishes "bursting with complex
flavors" – "including several regional moles", the "best
fish tacos in town" and a shrimp sandwich that's "so good
[some] would consider it as a deathbed meal"; P.S. the
"festive" decor is nearly "as good as the food."

Coast 20 25 19 $42
O'Donnell Park Complex, 931 E. Wisconsin Ave. (Astor St.),
414-727-5555; www.coastrestaurant.com
"What a view!" is the consensus on this Downtown New
American, whose windows face Lake Michigan and the
Milwaukee Art Museum's nationally known Calatrava addi-
dition; the menu's coastal concept (for instance, "fresh"
Floribbean grilled grouper) is "imaginative and trendy" to
some, "hit-or-miss" to others, but crooners unite in wondering "who could resist those decadent, warm pop-
overs?"; P.S. the weather-dependent "outdoor seating is
the place to be."

COERPER'S 5 O'CLOCK CLUB ⊠   26 | 12 | 22 | $46
2416 W. State St. (24th St.), 414-342-3553
Clock-watchers "can't stop eating once [they] start" tucking into the "enormous portions" of "to-die-for" steaks at this Central City standby; its "kitsch", "time-warp-into-the-'50s" decor "will bring back memories of the classic steakhouse experience of days gone by", and "the servers will make you feel like you're visiting an older relative's house" – though some "don't like" the "required stop at the bar", where you "order a drink and dinner before getting to your table."

Coquette Cafe ⊠   25 | 21 | 23 | $36
316 N. Milwaukee St. (St. Paul Ave.), 414-291-2655;
www.coquettecafe.com
"Is this France?" local Europhiles ask about this "lively" "little bit of Paris" in the "newly hippified" Third Ward, "friendly and creative chef" Sanford 'Sandy' D'Amato's source for "hearty", "innovative" French cuisine "at affordable prices"; the "cozy", "casually elegant" atmosphere is "great for a pre-show meal" at one of the nearby theaters, and D'Amato's new adjacent Harlequin Bakery is "all it was promised to be."

Crawdaddy's ⊠   21 | 15 | 19 | $29
6414 W. Greenfield Ave. (National Ave.), 414-778-2228;
www.foodspot.com/crawdaddys
Better arrive early at this "always-packed hot spot", a "fun, fun, fun" N'Awlins "gem on the blue-collar" Southwest Side, or "be prepared to wait" for its "creative", "delicious" Cajun-Creole cuisine (think steak Diane with a Cajun twist) since the place "can get very busy" – especially "on weekends"; be warned, as well, that the "vibrant" setting strikes some as "conversational" but others as "uncomfortably noisy."

Cubanitas ⊠   23 | 21 | 19 | $23
728 N. Milwaukee St. (bet. Mason St. & Wisconsin Ave.),
414-225-1760; www.cubanitas.us
A "trendsetter on a fashionable" street that's become a "Restaurant Row" of sorts, this "welcoming, lively" Downtown Cuban (little sister of Italian Osteria del Mondo) attracts the "young, hip crowd" with "fantabulous" mojitos and "top-flight" food such as sweet or savory plantains served at "easy-on-the-wallet" prices in a "trendy", "modern" "comfortable oasis" of a space; N.B. expect counter service at lunchtime.

Dancing Ganesha   22 | 18 | 20 | $33
1692-94 N. Van Buren St. (Brady St.), 414-220-0202;
www.dancingganesha.com
"Innovative" and "delicious" "Indian food in a classier atmosphere than most" defines this East Sider that's run by mother-daughter team Usha and Ami Bedi; menu vets

know to order one of the inventive nightly specials (including fish and "veg options"), but novices needn't fear, as the "knowledgeable staff" will be happy "to explain it all"; N.B. there's also has a new casual bar menu.

Dream Dance ⊠   25   23   25 $59
Potawatomi Bingo Casino, 1721 W. Canal St. (16th St.),
414-847-7883; www.paysbig.com
They "treat you like royalty" at this "calming, romantic" Downtown "refuge" where the "amazing combinations" on chef Jason Gorman's New American menu (which uses venison from the Potawatomi's Red Deer Ranch, when possible) and "retail-priced wines" add up to a "foodies' heavenly experience, not merely a dream" – but detracting from the reverie, say some, is "having to go through the smoke-filled [Potawatomi Bingo] Casino to get there."

Eagan's   21   20   21 $32
1030 N. Water St. (State St.), 414-271-6900; www.pandls.com
A "winner all the way", this "cosmopolitan" "standby" with "interesting items" (such as the "fantastic" lobster BLT) on its seafood-focused Eclectic menu occupies a "wonderfully convenient" Downtown location that's close to concert and theater venues, meaning it's "easy to drop by for a [pre- or post-show] snack"; it's also a "great people-watching place", but unimpressed diners still size it up as "good – but nothing special."

EDDIE MARTINI'S   26   24   26 $54
8612 Watertown Plank Rd. (86th St.), 414-771-6680;
www.eddiemartinis.com
"It's back to the '50s" at this "real gem" of a West Side steakhouse "institution", a classic for "incredible" steaks ("my mouth is watering just thinking about them") and "unbelievable" martinis that's "popular with doctors" from the nearby medical complex and other "Milwaukee bigwigs"; its "sophisticated" "old supper club–like" interior has some convinced that "Frank and Dean are still with us", but remember that the "big drinks" are matched by "big tabs", so "bring extra cash."

Edwardo's Natural Pizza   20   10   15 $17
10845 Bluemound Rd. (Hwy. 100), 414-771-7770
700 E. Kilbourn Ave. (Van Buren St.), 414-277-8080
www.edwardos.com
See review in the Chicago Directory.

Elliot's Bistro   20   18   20 $37
2321 N. Murray Ave. (North Ave.), 414-273-1488;
www.elliotsbistro.com
"For the French bistro experience in Milwaukee", this "delightful" East Side "favorite" is "a definite must-do" "complete with an authentic [Gallic] chef", Pierre Briere, whose "traditional" cooking – from cassoulet to boeuf

bourguignon – "rivals that of many Paris bistros"; "great for a dinner date or meeting old friends", it's also a "perfect spot for weekend brunch."

Elm Grove Inn, The   ▽ 22 19 21 $40
13275 Watertown Plank Rd. (Elm Grove Rd.), Elm Grove, 262-782-7090; www.elmgroveinn.com
Offering a "good selection of [New] American favorites", this "quiet and inviting" Elm Grove Eclectic is "great for a special evening out"; its "historic location", a building dating to 1855, has a "cozy, romantic" atmosphere; some young folk find it all "rather staid", but that's a boon for seniors ("my grandmother loved it"), who also enjoy taking advantage of the early-bird menu – half-off the second entree from 4–5:30 PM.

El Rey Sol   25 14 21 $25
2338 W. Forest Home Ave. (Lincoln Ave.), 414-389-1760; www.foodspot.com/reysol
Ascend to "mole heaven" at this "friendly, casual" spot, the South Side home of "fresh", "authentic" "gourmet Mexican" fare (everything from Argentine steaks to enchiladas are "well presented") and "attentive yet relaxed service"; it may be "out of the way" for some, but most report a "great experience", part of which is the "wonderful" complimentary appetizers; P.S. paella Valenciana is served on weekends.

Elsa's on the Park ●   23 24 19 $24
833 N. Jefferson St. (Wells St.), 414-765-0615; www.elsas.com
"It doesn't get any better than" this "über-hip, trendy" "see-and-be-seen" American opposite Downtown's Cathedral Square Park feel fans who favor its "gussied-up versions of old favorites", including "outstanding burgers" and the "best pork chop sandwiches in town" (plus you "can't go wrong with the chicken wings"); P.S. the "lively" vibe and "awesome drinks" at its "amazing bar" also draw "huge crowds."

Envoy   – – – M
The Ambassador Hotel, 2308 W. Wisconsin Ave. (bet. 23rd & 24th Sts.), 414-345-5015; www.envoymilwaukee.com
A result of the exhaustive renovation of the art deco Ambassador Hotel, this Downtown New American offers a feeding frenzy from early in the AM into the evening; options range from the casual (a cheeseburger with applewood cheddar and pommes frites) to the fussy (Thai curried rack of lamb with green papaya salad and coconut cream), and a respectful late-night crowd gathers in the adjacent Envoy Lounge for cocktails and live jazz on weekends.

Gilbert's   – – – M
327 Wrigley Dr. (Center St.), Lake Geneva, 262-248-6680; www.gilbertsrestaurant.com
"When you want something different from the usual Lake Geneva family-style place", this New American – housed

in an 1875 Victorian house with 13 working fireplaces and a "marvelous view" of the water – is "worth the trip!"; work in the fare's largely organic status ("try the vegetarian tasting menu"), including ingredients from the edible garden in summer, and you just may have "one of Wisconsin's finest"; N.B. jacket suggested.

Golden Mast Inn ▽ 18 | 20 | 19 | $38
W349 N5293 Lacy's Ln. (Lake Dr.), Okauchee, 262-567-7041; www.weissgerbers.com/goldenmast
"On a balmy summer evening", a "spectacular" view of Okauchee Lake and a "relaxed" atmosphere "with a tinge of ritziness" will make you "feel at home" at this Weissgerber family–owned German-American; flatterers feel there's "nothing like" its "popular Friday [night] fish fry" that routinely "packs 'em in" (it's "one of the best in the area"), but grumblers grouse that the food overall is "hit-or-miss."

Hama 21 | 14 | 18 | $34
333 W. Brown Deer Rd. (Port Washington Rd.), 414-352-5051
Though there's "fresh" raw-fish fare on offer, some folks insist the "non-sushi entrees star" at this "inspired Japanese–Asian" fusion favorite "located in a strip mall" on the North Shore – "as do the spectacular desserts", such as banana fritters and Belgian chocolate mousse; still, some find the kitchen "uneven" and say the "limited space feels tight."

Heaven City ⓢ ▽ 24 | 25 | 25 | $40
S91 W27850 National Ave./Hwy. ES (Edgewood Ave.), Mukwonago, 262-363-5191; www.heavencity.com
Founding owner Scott McGlinchey no longer runs this Mukwonago New American reputedly set in gangster Al Capone's "haunted" "old hangout", but many still rank it a "superb" "must-visit" "with excellent food and service", as well as "great atmosphere" – indeed, clairvoyants claim that if you "close the bar, you might be treated to an unforgettable supernatural sideshow"; P.S. the long-running "Tapas Tuesday reigns supreme."

Holiday House – | – | – | M
525 E. Menomonee St. (Jefferson St.), 414-272-1122; www.holidayhousemilwaukee.com
Sib of East Side hangout Tess, this Third Ward Eclectic combines a low-key albeit elegant vibe and an accessible world-fusion menu created by chef-owner Joe Volpe; the window-framed dining room is just paces from Henry Maier Park (the mother of all city outdoor summer festival grounds), and when temps soar the planned sidewalk tables should be a paradise for people-watchers.

Il Mito ⓢ 21 | 19 | 21 | $34
605 W. Virginia St. (6th St.), 414-276-1414; www.ilmito.com
If you're as "passionate about food" as chef-owner Michael Feker, you'll "want to try everything" at this Fifth Ward

"hidden gem", a bastion of "creative Italian"-Med cuisine "in an overwhelmingly Latin restaurant district"; the "beautifully renovated" space – complete with exposed brick, a painted ceiling and an old bar with sliding step ladder – also offers guests the chance to "enjoy the vista of the Calatrava-like Sixth Street bridge."

IMMIGRANT ROOM & WINERY, THE ⌧
26 26 26 $64

American Club, 419 Highland Dr. (School St.), Kohler, 920-457-8888; www.destinationkohler.com

For "a fine-dining experience of the highest caliber", "gourmets" go to this "wonderful" "Wisconsin treasure" in Kohler's American Club resort, one of the "finest hotels in the Midwest", where the "elegant" New American fare comes with a "nice wine list" and "doting service" ("at these prices, it should be"); "now *this* is a place for romance and privacy" say fans of its six different dining rooms, which "take you back to the old days"; P.S. if the tab's too high, remember that "the prices on bottles and cheese in The Winery [next door] are extremely fair."

Jackson Grill ⌧
23 13 23 $41

3736 W. Mitchell St. (38th St.), 414-384-7384

"Don't go or it'll get too crowded" suggest selfish surveyors who "expect to wait" a while before slipping into this "little" South Side "hideaway" for its "small but incredible menu" of "excellent steaks", ribs and seafood; some complain that the "exterior looks like any neighborhood joint" and the interior is decidedly "bland" in the atmosphere department, but those who find it "homey and comfortable" insist it breathes "old-style Milwaukee."

Jake's Fine Dining ⌧
∇ 25 20 22 $39

21445 W. Gumina Rd. (Capital Dr.), Brookfield, 262-781-7995; www.jakes-restaurant.com

"You only have to go once" to this "nostalgic" Brookfield steakhouse – an "established presence on the West Side" since 1967 – "to feel like a regular" thanks to its "wonderful presentation" of "awesome" "comfort food" (filet mignon and signature onion rings) and "comfortable service"; "ask for a seat by" the "huge fireplace" ("a great place on a winter day") or belly up to the bar and "enjoy some fine brandy."

Karl Ratzsch's ⌧
24 24 23 $38

320 E. Mason St. (bet. B'way & Milwaukee St.), 414-276-2720; www.karlratzsch.com

"*Das ist gut!*" declare devotees of this "high-caliber" 102-year-old Downtown German, a "traditional favorite" where "authentic" Teutonic cuisine – "nothing says lovin' like schnitzel" or "great sauerbraten" – is served in an "appropriate setting" whose "old-world atmosphere" reminds travelers of "eating in Munich"; less enamored types say it's "heavy, heavy, heavy" (though "worth it once in a while"), but "where else can you get roast goose and a pianist [weekends only] playing *The Way You Look Tonight?*"

King & I, The 21 | 15 | 18 | $24
823 N. Second St. (bet. Kilbourn Ave. & Wells St.), 414-276-4181
"Yul Brynner would certainly have broken a sweat on some of these dishes", so "proceed with caution" when sampling the "delicious Thai food" at this "quick and easy" spot "tucked into an urban corner of Downtown"; its "convenient" location makes it a "great place for a pre-theater dinner" – even if the "old-school decor" is "in dire need of a makeover."

Knick, The ⬤ 22 | 20 | 21 | $27
Knickerbocker Hotel, 1030 E. Juneau Ave. (Astor St.), 414-272-0011; www.theknickrestaurant.com
"There's something for everyone" (from some of the "best appetizers" around to "great burgers" and "entrees that are good as well") on the "huge menu" at this "consistent" Downtown Eclectic that's "the place to be if you want to be seen"; it's "wonderful for Sunday brunch or a hearty lunch", and a "happy-hour favorite" too, with a "lively atmosphere" that attracts a "young and hip crowd" – no wonder the "terrace is a people watcher's dream."

LAKE PARK BISTRO 25 | 27 | 25 | $50
(aka Bartolotta's Lake Park Bistro)
Lake Park Pavilion, 3133 E. Newberry Blvd. (Lake Park Rd.), 414-962-6300; www.lakeparkbistro.com
"It's wonderful to sit by the windows" and revel in the "exquisite" Lake Michigan view (especially "heavenly" at sunset) at this "treat" located in Frederick Law Olmstead–designed Lake Park, where "lots of new twists on old classics" make the "ooh-la-la fabulous French cuisine" "worth every decadent calorie"; factor in a "romantic atmosphere" and staffers who "pay attention to all the details" and it adds up to a "great place for a special occasion" or "the perfect date."

MAGGIANO'S LITTLE ITALY 20 | 19 | 20 | $31
Mayfair Mall, 2500 N. Mayfair Rd. (North Ave.), Wauwatosa, 414-978-1000; www.maggianos.com
See review in the Chicago Directory.

Mangia 23 | 19 | 20 | $34
5717 Sheridan Rd. (bet. 57th & 58th Sts.), Kenosha, 262-652-4285
"Excellent for a casual spot", this "not-to-be-missed" "little treasure" in Kenosha, "midway between Chicago and Milwaukee", is an "oasis" of "authentic Italian cuisine", with a "wonderful menu" of "great pastas", "very good pizzas" and wood-roasted meats served in a "cozy dining room" – and "without ruining the family budget"; little sur-

prise, then, that it's considered a place of "proven worth in this rather desolate Downtown area."

MILWAUKEE CHOP HOUSE Ⓢ
24 | 22 | 22 | $50

Hilton Hotel City Ctr., 633 N. Fifth St. (bet. Michigan St. &
Wisconsin Ave.), 414-226-2467; www.milwaukeechophouse.com
"Bring your grandparents, grandchildren" and "everyone" in between to this "top-notch" steakhouse in Downtown's Hilton Hotel City Center, where the "excellent" steak-and-seafood fare is "cooked to perfection and served piping hot" by an "accommodating staff" in a "supper club–ish atmosphere"; some complain of "inconsistent" performance and suggest it's "a bit pricey for what you get", but most maintain it's "well worth" the expense, making it an "overall good place to go for a nice night out."

Mimma's Cafe
22 | 20 | 21 | $40

1307 E. Brady St. (Arlington Pl.), 414-271-7337;
www.mimmas.com
If you "want something that's not on the menu", ask chef and Sicily native Mimma Megna – "she'll do her magic and make an exceptional dish" at this "warm and inviting" Italian with a "classy" interior that "harkens back to the 1920s era"; many report it's "still a favorite" "must-stop" on the East Side, and a "pioneer" that deserves "credit for reviving Brady Street" since it opened in 1989, but others counter that it has "grown into a big", rather "run-of-the-mill" restaurant.

Moceans Ⓢ
21 | 20 | 22 | $50

747 N. Broadway (bet. Mason St. & Wisconsin Ave.),
414-272-7470; www.moceans.com
"Part of the 'Mo-pire'" that includes Mo's: A Place for Steaks, this Johnny Vassallo owned Downtown mecca (whose name rhymes with 'oceans') in Grenadier's old digs mates "great seafood" with "excellent service" "in a quiet romantic setting"; not all fin-feasters are fans, though, with some "disappointed" patrons reporting a "pretentious" vibe, "haughty", "heavy-handed" staffers and fare that's "way" "too expensive."

Mo's: A Place for Steaks Ⓢ
23 | 20 | 23 | $53

720 N. Plankinton Ave. (Wisconsin Ave.), 414-272-0720;
www.mosrestaurants.com
"You feel like you're in the big city to the south" at this "Chicago"-style steakhouse (and Moceans sibling), a "place to be seen" Downtown dining upon "juicy, tasty and enormous steaks" amid "hip decor" and a "lively" crowd; still, some de-Mo-ters detect some "attitude" and do "not like the à la carte menu", declaring they "need more than meat on the platter" for these "high prices" and dismissing the place as only "for the flashy spender" who doesn't mind "forking over lots of bucks."

Mr. B's: A Bartolotta Steakhouse   23 | 20 | 24 | $49
17700 W. Capitol Dr. (Calhoun Rd.), Brookfield, 262-790-7005;
www.mrbssteakhouse.com
Bringing "a bit of the Bartolotta touch" and "consistency"
to Brookfield, this cousin of Lake Park Bistro and Bacchus
is the "steakhouse of record" for many "locals", "wow"-ing
with "excellent", "personal service" from a "terrific staff"
that transports "mouthwatering" cuts and "great drinks"
in a "stylish yet casual" space; a word of warning from
vets to first-timers, though – "remember that this kind of
quality comes at a price."

Nanakusa   24 | 24 | 20 | $42
408 E. Chicago St. (Milwaukee St.), 414-223-3200
"Traditional Japanese" "meets urban chic" at this "beautiful, minimalist" Third Ward source for "top-quality sushi"
fashioned from "delicious" "fresh" fish, as well as "lovely
cooked dishes", all accompanied by "extensive wine and
saki offerings"; lauders "love" the "private" 16-seat tatami
room that contributes to the "Zen atmosphere", but some
say it's "really too bad" that the "service quality doesn't
match the quality of the food and decor", while others state
that "the high prices keep [them] from returning often."

North Shore Bistro   19 | 16 | 18 | $32
River Point Village, 8649 N. Port Washington Rd. (Brown Deer Rd.),
414-351-6100; www.northshorebistro.com
A "great place for get-togethers", especially "for a group
where everyone wants something different", this "reliable" "suburban hangout" is a "nice respite on the North
Shore", with "good", "consistent" New American fare and a
"friendly" staff; some, though, deem its cuisine "unremarkable", while others insist its "only failing" is its "pro-
saic" "strip-mall" setting.

Osteria del Mondo ⊠   25 | 22 | 22 | $48
1028 E. Juneau Ave. (Astor St.), 414-291-3770;
www.osteria.com
"Remaining solidly [near] the top of the ladder in
Milwaukee", this Downtown Northern Italian delivers
"outstanding meals" courtesy of chef/co-owner Marc
Bianchini, who "never ceases to amaze" with "elegant
fare" that's "inventive" "without being strange"; combined
with "wonderful service" and a "comfortable setting" (including "a great patio"), it amounts to a "fine-dining" experience that's "not to be missed"; N.B. a separate cigar
lounge and valet parking are available.

Pacific Rim   23 | 18 | 20 | $40
830 N. Old World Third St. (Kilbourn Ave.), 414-277-8100;
www.pacificrim-restaurant.com
"For a quiet but great dinner", fans find this "underappreciated" Downtown Eclectic "a great place to go" thanks to

a "unique menu" of Pacific Rim–inspired dishes evidencing a "fine fusion" of Hawaiian, Japanese, Thai and Western influences; even some who find the food "fantastic", though, fault the "lacking decor", declaring they'd "be inclined to return more often if the uninteresting dining space" received a "makeover."

Palms Bistro & Bar　　　　21 | 20 | 19 | $29

221 N. Broadway (bet. Buffalo & Chicago Sts.),
414-298-3000
"Lots of kudos" go to this New American in the Third Ward for its "excellent preparations" of "bistro-esque food" made from "fresh ingredients", its "simply elegant Cream City–meets-exotic"-"simian-themed" decor ("gotta love those monkeys") and its "just-right service" from a "friendly staff"; all told, it's a "nice stop for a quick, light bite"; P.S. there's "great outdoor seating in the summer", and the "expansive upstairs bar is also available for private parties."

Pasta Tree, The　　　　20 | 18 | 20 | $30

1503 N. Farwell Ave. (Curtis Pl.), 414-276-8867;
www.foodspot.com/thepastatree
"Pastaholics" who've "been dining here for years" praise this "casual" East Side Northern Italian for "imaginative" interpretations of their "favorite" "comfort food" delivered "piping hot" to the table; true, not everyone appreciates "practically sitting in the laps of the people next to you", but supporters defend the space as "romantic, comfortable" and "cozy (like eating in someone's living room)", swearing "you'll forget that the rest of the diners are even there."

P.F. CHANG'S CHINA BISTRO　　20 | 20 | 19 | $28

Mayfair Mall, 2500 N. Mayfair Rd. (North Ave.), Wauwatosa,
414-607-1029; www.pfchangs.com
See review in the Chicago Directory.

Pleasant Valley Inn　　　▽ 21 | 17 | 21 | $31

9801 W. Dakota St. (99th St.), 414-321-4321;
www.foodspot.com/pleasantvalleyinn
Though "hidden" on the Southwest Side, this American "gem" in an inn dating to the 1930s "gives you the feeling you're at a supper club in the North woods"; with its "great food and service", it strikes supporters as "a nice neighborhood" spot, but lukewarm sorts cite its "nothing-fancy" decor and "rather basic meat-and-potatoes" fare as evidence that it's "not bad" – but also "not spectacular."

Polonez　　　　　　　▽ 23 | 13 | 21 | $22

4016 S. Packard Ave. (Tesch St.), 414-482-0080;
www.foodspot.com/polonez
"Pierogi power!" proclaim dumpling devotees dedicated to this "true Milwaukee treasure", an "authentic" South Side Polish place proffering "made-from-scratch" fare that's "mm-mm-good" – and "one of the best values in

town"; true, it's "not a fancy place", but "the warm personality and service" of owners George and Aleksandra Burzynski puts sausage scarfers "at ease"; N.B. it also hosts a Friday night fish fry and Sunday brunch with live accordion music.

Potbelly Sandwich Works   20   15   18 $9
135 W. Wisconsin Ave. (Plankinton Ave.), 414-226-0014
17800 W. Bluemound Rd. (bet. Brookfield & Calhoun Rds.),
Brookfield, 262-796-9845
www.potbelly.com
See review in the Chicago Directory.

Ristorante Bartolotta   25   22   23 $46
2625 N. Downer Ave. (Belleview Pl.), 414-962-7910
7616 W. State St. (Harwood Ave.), Wauwatosa,
414-771-7910
www.bartolottaristorante.com
"You'll think you're in a big city" when visiting these "Italian favorites" – either the "wonderful" 'Tosa original or its "great sibling", a "welcome addition" to the East Side – as each is "a total star of a restaurant", featuring executive chef Juan Urbieta's "varied menu" of "incredible" cuisine ("the risotto is positively orgasmic!"), "excellent service" and "lovely", "cozy atmosphere"; P.S. "reservations are a must", though some suggest the "small venues always seem to be overbooked."

River Lane Inn 🖾   25   18   24 $37
4313 W. River Ln. (Brown Deer Rd.), 414-354-1995
"From [Wednesday] lobster night to the always-changing fish specials on the chalkboard", this "longtime favorite" (sibling to Mequon's Riversite) set in a turn-of-the-century building in an "off-the-beaten-path" North Shore location "still delivers" "consistently great" seafood ferried by "friendly servers" in a "low-key" setting – no wonder it continues to "attract a crowd" ("regulars love it").

Riversite, The 🖾   25   23   26 $46
11120 N. Cedarburg Rd. (Mequon Rd.), Mequon,
262-242-6050
"The always reliable, elegant sister to the River Lane Inn" on the North Shore, this "very popular" place in Mequon keeps dinner "creative" thanks to "artist"-chef Tom Peschong, whose Traditional American specialties are "superb"; "fabulous warm service" from a "stellar staff" that's "knowledgeable about" the "unbeatable wine list" and a "glorious setting" affording a "great view of the Milwaukee River" also make it "worth the drive."

Rock Bottom Brewery   16   15   16 $22
740 N. Plankinton Ave. (bet. Wells St. & Wisconsin Ave.),
414-276-3030; www.rockbottom.com
See review in the Chicago Directory.

Roots Restaurant & Cellar   25 | 23 | 21 | $37

1818 N. Hubbard St. (Vine St.), 414-374-8480;
www.rootsmilwaukee.com

A "class act all the way", this "wonderful place" on Brewers Hill "puts together delicious creations" of Californian-Asian "comfort food" (using some "organically grown local produce" from co-owner Joe Schmidt's nine-acre Cedarburg farm) in "surprisingly inventive combinations that really work"; "perched above the city", its bi-level location also offers "drop-dead views" of Downtown Milwaukee, so "whether upstairs or down" expect an "always-enjoyable" experience; N.B. the Cellar offers a less-formal menu.

Saffron Indian Bistro   ∇ 25 | 14 | 20 | $24

17395D-1 W. Blue Mound Rd. (bet. Brookfield & Calhoun Rds.),
Brookfield, 262-784-1332

"Your palate will thank you for the exotic trip" after a visit to this "unassuming and unpretentious" Brookfield strip-mall spot serving "lots of uncommon but delicious specialties from India" that offer an "innovative" respite from the "Americanized" offerings of some other subcontinental venues – indeed, the "food is much nicer than the appearance of the restaurant would suggest"; P.S. don't miss the "great buffet" offered daily at lunch.

Sake Tumi ⊠   25 | 24 | 23 | $34

714 N. Milwaukee St. (bet. Mason St. & Wisconsin Ave.),
414-224-7253; www.sake-milwaukee.com

"Don't let the corny", "*Laugh-In*–style name" "fool you into thinking this isn't a high-quality experience" advise addicts "hooked" on this "amazing" Asian, an "absolute must" Downtown whose "ambitious and well-executed menu has something for everyone" – from "trendy" fusion dishes to traditional Japanese and Korean BBQ fare; also, the "lively dining room" and "fun", "swanky" upstairs Buddha Lounge are "where the beautiful people go to eat sushi" and revel in a "cool vibe."

SANFORD ⊠   29 | 26 | 28 | $66

1547 N. Jackson St. (Pleasant St.), 414-276-9608;
www.sanfordrestaurant.com

"Words can't describe" the "world-class" experience at this "hits-on-all-cylinders" East Side New American "gem" that's definitely "in a league by itself" (as evidenced by the fact that it's ranked No. 1 for both Food and Service in Wisconsin); eponymous toque-owner Sandy D'Amato gets "all the details right" – from the "sophisticated" "gourmet" fare, to the "unbeatable" service provided by "friendly caring staffers" who can "feel your table's mood", to the "intimate", "ultramodern" dining room; P.S. "try the chef's 'Surprise'", an "especially fabulous seven-course" tasting menu.

Sebastian's ⊠　　　　– ｜ – ｜ – ｜ M

6025 Douglas Ave. (5 Mile Rd.), Caledonia, 262-681-5465;
www.sebastiansfinefood.com

A "way-off-the-beaten-path" setting adds to the "best-kept secret status" of this "friendly place" that's "worth the drive" to Caledonia for its "outstanding" New American cuisine and "surprisingly stunning dining room"; fans feel "it's unfortunate that this fine restaurant is disadvantaged by its location", as it "stacks up favorably against many in larger metropolitan areas."

Singha Thai　　　　24 ｜ 13 ｜ 18 ｜ $19

2237 S. 108th St. (Lincoln Ave.), 414-541-1234

Singha Thai II ⊠

780 N. Jefferson St., 414-226-0288
www.singhathairestaurant.com

"Delicious food" at a "good value" makes for a "great Thai" experience at this West Side "favorite" "hidden in a strip mall"; to be sure, the "uninspired", "no-ambiance" decor keeps some diners away, but folks who flip for the "authentic" fare ("their pad Thai is a favorite") insist the "picturesque" cuisine more than compensates; P.S. the Downtown branch opened post-*Survey*.

Social, The　　　　22 ｜ 21 ｜ 19 ｜ $30

170 S. First St. (Pittsburgh Ave.), 414-270-0438;
www.the-social.com

With "more room and better parking", the "new location" of this Fifth Ward spot that "recently moved into a remodeled factory" "is more ambitious" than its old Walker's Point digs, but its New American menu is "still very good" – including such "unique offerings" as its trademark "to-die-for macaroni and goat cheese", which "puts mom's to shame"; "you won't be as close to the kitchen as before", note social-ites, but "fun decor" and "more table choices make up for it."

Sticks N Stones　　　　20 ｜ 22 ｜ 21 ｜ $49

2300 N. Pilgrim Square Dr. (North Ave.), Brookfield, 262-786-5700;
www.sticksandstonesrestaurant.com

Supporters say there's "no need to throw sticks or stones" at this "glitzy" New American seafood emporium in Brookfield (a member of the DeRosa Corporation dynasty, along with steakhouse brother Eddie Martini's), as its "excellent" "fresh" fare, "attentive service" and "classy" interior make for a "great dining experience"; still, others opine that it's "not always as consistent as one would hope" and say it can be "a little loud when it's busy."

Taqueria Azteca　　　　▽ 21 ｜ 16 ｜ 21 ｜ $22

119 E. Oklahoma Ave. (Chase Ave.), 414-486-9447;
www.taqueriaazteca.biz

"Try the chalkboard specials", "amazing guacamole" and, of course, "those wonderful margaritas" at this "solid" source for "non-standard Mexican" fare whose "unique offerings" feature a fusion of European flavors; its "great patio" also helps make it a "treat", leading some to call it "the emerald of the South Side."

Tess　　　　25　17　22　$37
2499 N. Bartlett Ave. (Bradford Ave.), 414-964-8377
Savoring the "can't-miss" Eclectic menu of "excellent food" "from both land and sea" "while sipping a cocktail" at this "quiet, romantic bistro" adds up to the "perfect neighborhood night" for many East Siders; some say the decor of its "small, intimate" dining room is merely "so-so", but the "fabulous patio" "has the feel of a New Orleans courtyard" – too bad it's only open "in summer."

Third Ward Caffe ⊠　　　▽ 20　16　17　$36
225 E. St. Paul Ave. (bet. Broadway & Water St.), 414-224-0895;
www.foodspot.com/thirdwardcaffe
Caffe-klatchers who "enjoy" this "pleasant" Third Warder "time and time again" claim it's an "ideal place to go before the theater" or "for a pasta fix" anytime thanks to a kitchen turning out "good, quick" Northern Italian meals; others see it as "uneven" – but either way, it's "been around forever" (well, since 1982) so it "must be doing something right."

Three Brothers ⊭　　　23　15　20　$29
2414 S. St. Clair (Russell Ave.), 414-481-7530
"Bring an appetite" to this "delightful old-world tavern" in a former Schlitz brewery, a 56-year-old South Side "institution" (still run by the Radicevic family) that's "like hanging out at your grandma's kitchen table" – if, that is, your nana made "lovingly presented" burek, goulash and other "traditional" Serbian dishes; there's certainly "no pretense" to the "rustic and homespun" (some say "dumpy") interior, but most find it "fun and kitschy"– just "don't expect it to be fast."

Yanni's ⊠　　　22　24　21　$49
540 E. Mason St. (Jackson St.), 414-847-9264
This "cosmopolitan" Downtown steakhouse strikes supporters as a "great new restaurant" thanks to its "beautiful decor", "clubby atmosphere", "excellent steaks" and servers who "try very hard" to ensure a good experience; critics for whom "the jury's still out", however, say they "wouldn't rush back", calling it "too expensive for what it is" and insisting that the "over-attentive staff needs to relax a bit."

Zarletti ⊠　　　20　19　19　$32
741 N. Milwaukee St. (Mason St.), 414-225-0000
A real "find", this "solid" sophomore is a "great addition" to Downtown's Restaurant Row (aka Milwaukee Street), serving "inventive Italian" cuisine – "if you want sketti and meatballs, go elsewhere" – in a "surprisingly metro" "cappuccino-colored interior" that still manages to "feel like a neighborhood place."

Milwaukee Indexes

CUISINES
LOCATIONS
SPECIAL FEATURES

CUISINES

American (New)
Bacchus
Barossa
Coast
Dream Dance
Elm Grove Inn
Envoy
Gilbert's
Heaven City
Immigrant Room
North Shore Bistro
Palms Bistro & Bar
Sanford
Sebastian's
Social, The
Sticks N Stones

American (Traditional)
Elsa's on Park
Golden Mast Inn
Pleasant Valley Inn
Riversite, The
Rock Bottom Brewery

Asian Fusion
Hama
Roots
Sake Tumi

Cajun
Crawdaddy's

Californian
Roots

Chinese
P.F. Chang's

Creole
Crawdaddy's

Cuban
Cubanitas

Eclectic
Bjonda
Eagan's
Elm Grove Inn
Holiday House
Knick
Pacific Rim
Tess

French
Coquette Cafe
Lake Park Bistro

French (Bistro)
Elliot's Bistro

German
Golden Mast Inn
Karl Ratzsch's

Hamburgers
Elsa's on Park

Indian
Dancing Ganesha
Saffron Indian

Italian
(N=Northern)
Caterina's
Il Mito
Maggiano's
Mangia
Mimma's Cafe
Osteria del Mondo (N)
Pasta Tree (N)
Ristorante Bartolotta
Third Ward Caffe (N)
Zarletti

Japanese
(* sushi specialist)
Benihana*
Hama
Nanakusa*
Sake Tumi

Korean
(* barbecue specialist)
Sake Tumi*

Lebanese
Au Bon Appétit

Mediterranean
Au Bon Appétit
Il Mito

Mexican
Cempazuchi
El Rey Sol
Taqueria Azteca

Pacific Rim
Pacific Rim

Pizza
Edwardo's Pizza

Polish
Polonez

Sandwiches
Potbelly Sandwich

Seafood
Bosley on Brady
Eagan's
Eddie Martini's
Jackson Grill
Moceans
River Lane Inn
Sticks N Stones

Serbian
Three Brothers

Steakhouses
Benihana
Bosley on Brady
Carnevor
Coerper's 5 O'Clock
Eddie Martini's
Jackson Grill
Jake's Fine Dining
Milwaukee Chop Hse.
Mo's: Steak
Mr. B's: Steak
Yanni's

Thai
King & I
Singha Thai

LOCATIONS

MILWAUKEE

Brewers Hill
Roots

Central City
Coerper's 5 O'Clock

Downtown
Bacchus
Benihana
Carnevor
Coast
Cubanitas
Dream Dance
Eagan's
Edwardo's Pizza
Elsa's on Park
Envoy
Karl Ratzsch's
King & I
Knick
Milwaukee Chop Hse.
Moceans
Mo's: Steak
Osteria del Mondo
Pacific Rim
Potbelly Sandwich
Rock Bottom Brewery
Sake Tumi
Singha Thai
Yanni's
Zarletti

East Side
Au Bon Appétit
Bosley on Brady
Cempazuchi
Dancing Ganesha
Elliot's Bistro
Lake Park Bistro

Mimma's Cafe
Pasta Tree
Ristorante Bartolotta
Sanford
Tess

Fifth Ward
Barossa
Il Mito
Social, The

North Shore
Hama
North Shore Bistro
River Lane Inn

South Side
El Rey Sol
Jackson Grill
Polonez
Taqueria Azteca
Three Brothers

Southwest Side
Caterina's
Crawdaddy's
Pleasant Valley Inn

Third Ward
Coquette Cafe
Holiday House
Nanakusa
Palms Bistro & Bar
Third Ward Caffe

West Side
Eddie Martini's
Edwardo's Pizza
Singha Thai

OUTLYING AREAS

Brookfield
Jake's Fine Dining
Mr. B's: Steak
Potbelly Sandwich
Saffron Indian
Sticks N Stones

Caledonia
Sebastian's

Elm Grove
Elm Grove Inn

Kenosha
Mangia

Kohler
Immigrant Room

Lake Geneva
Gilbert's

Mequon
Riversite, The

Mukwonago
Heaven City

Okauchee
Golden Mast Inn

Wauwatosa
Bjonda
Maggiano's
P.F. Chang's
Ristorante Bartolotta

SPECIAL FEATURES

(Indexes list the best in each category. Multi-location restaurants' features may vary by branch.)

Brunch
Eagan's
Elliot's Bistro
Golden Mast Inn
Knick
Palms Bistro & Bar
Polonez
Tess

Buffet Served
(Check availability)
Eagan's
King & I
Polonez
Saffron Indian

Business Dining
Bacchus
Bjonda
Carnevor
Coast
Coquette Cafe
Eagan's
Eddie Martini's
Elm Grove Inn
Envoy
Il Mito
Jake's Fine Dining
Karl Ratzsch's
Knick
Lake Park Bistro
Milwaukee Chop Hse.
Mo's: Steak
Mr. B's: Steak
North Shore Bistro
Pacific Rim
Ristorante Bartolotta
River Lane Inn
Riversite, The
Roots
Saffron Indian
Sticks N Stones
Yanni's

Celebrity Chefs
(Listed under their primary restaurants)
Au Bon Appétit, *Rihab Aris*
Jackson Grill, *Jimmy Jackson*
Mimma's Cafe, *Mimma Megna*
Osteria del Mondo, *Marc Bianchini*
Riversite, The, *Tom Peschong*
Sanford, *Sandy D'Amato*

Child-Friendly
(Alternatives to the usual fast-food places; * children's menu available)
Benihana*
Bjonda*
Caterina's
Cempazuchi
Coast*
Edwardo's Pizza*
El Rey Sol*
Gilbert's*
Golden Mast Inn*
Hama
Il Mito
Karl Ratzsch's*
Knick
Lake Park Bistro*
Maggiano's*
Mangia*
Mimma's Cafe
Palms Bistro & Bar
Pasta Tree
P.F. Chang's
Pleasant Valley Inn*
Potbelly Sandwich*
Ristorante Bartolotta
River Lane Inn
Rock Bottom Brewery*
Sticks N Stones
Taqueria Azteca*
Tess
Third Ward Caffe

Cigars Welcome
Bjonda
Carnevor
Elm Grove Inn
Elsa's on Park
Gilbert's
Golden Mast Inn
Heaven City

Osteria del Mondo
Yanni's

Delivery/Takeout
(D=delivery, T=takeout)
Benihana (T)
Bjonda (T)
Cempazuchi (T)
Crawdaddy's (T)
Dancing Ganesha (T)
El Rey Sol (D,T)
Elsa's on Park (T)
Hama (T)
Il Mito (T)
Knick (T)
Maggiano's (T)
Mimma's Cafe (T)
Nanakusa (T)
North Shore Bistro (T)
Palms Bistro & Bar (T)
Pasta Tree (T)
Polonez (T)
Potbelly Sandwich (D,T)
River Lane Inn (T)
Rock Bottom Brewery (T)
Roots (T)
Singha Thai (T)
Taqueria Azteca (T)
Third Ward Caffe (T)

Dining Alone
(Other than hotels and
places with counter service)
Benihana
Bjonda
Cempazuchi
Coquette Cafe
Cubanitas
Hama
Lake Park Bistro
Nanakusa
North Shore Bistro
Potbelly Sandwich
Rock Bottom Brewery
Singha Thai

Entertainment
(Call for days and times
of performances)
Coast (varies)
Elm Grove Inn (classical guitar)
El Rey Sol (guitar)
Gilbert's (jazz)
Golden Mast Inn (jazz)

Immigrant Room (piano)
Karl Ratzsch's (piano)
North Shore Bistro (jazz)
Rock Bottom Brewery (karaoke)

Fireplaces
Bjonda
Coast
Elm Grove Inn
Gilbert's
Golden Mast Inn
Heaven City
Jake's Fine Dining
Sebastian's

Game in Season
Barossa
Bjonda
Coast
Coquette Cafe
Dream Dance
Eddie Martini's
Elliot's Bistro
Elm Grove Inn
Gilbert's
Golden Mast Inn
Heaven City
Holiday House
Immigrant Room
Jake's Fine Dining

Historic Places
(Year opened; * building)
1855 Elm Grove Inn*
1875 Gilbert's*
1875 Third Ward Caffe*
1890 Elsa's on Park*
1890 Three Brothers*
1900 Ristorante Bartolotta*
1900 River Lane Inn*
1904 Karl Ratzsch's
1918 Immigrant Room*
1927 Envoy*
1930 Pleasant Valley Inn*
1948 Coerper's 5 O'Clock

Hotel Dining
Ambassador Hotel, The
  Envoy
Hilton Hotel City Ctr.
  Milwaukee Chop Hse.
Knickerbocker Hotel
  Knick

Jacket Required
Immigrant Room

Late Dining
(Weekday closing hour)
Elsa's on Park (1 AM)
Knick (12 AM)

Meet for a Drink
(Most top hotels and the
following standouts)
Bacchus
Barossa
Bjonda
Bosley on Brady
Carnevor
Cempazuchi
Coast
Coquette Cafe
Crawdaddy's
Cubanitas
Dancing Ganesha
Eagan's
Eddie Martini's
Elsa's on Park
Envoy
Holiday House
Il Mito
Jackson Grill
Knick
Lake Park Bistro
Mo's: Steak
Nanakusa
North Shore Bistro
Osteria del Mondo
Palms Bistro & Bar
Rock Bottom Brewery
Sake Tumi
Social, The
Sticks N Stones
Taqueria Azteca
Tess
Yanni's
Zarletti

Microbreweries
Rock Bottom Brewery

Noteworthy Newcomers
Bosley on Brady
Carnevor
Cubanitas
Envoy
Holiday House

Sake Tumi
Yanni's

Outdoor Dining
(P=Patio; S=Sidewalk;
W=Waterside)
Coast (P)
Eagan's (S)
Edwardo's Pizza (P)
Golden Mast Inn (P,W)
Il Mito (P)
Knick (P)
Maggiano's (P)
Mangia (P)
North Shore Bistro (P)
Osteria del Mondo (P)
Palms Bistro & Bar (S)
Pasta Tree (P)
P.F. Chang's (P)
Potbelly Sandwich (P,S)
Ristorante Bartolotta (S)
River Lane Inn (P)
Riversite, The (P,W)
Rock Bottom Brewery (P)
Roots (P)
Taqueria Azteca (P)
Tess (P)
Third Ward Caffe (S)

People-Watching
Bacchus
Bjonda
Carnevor
Coast
Coquette Cafe
Cubanitas
Eagan's
Eddie Martini's
Elsa's on Park
Envoy
Il Mito
Knick
Maggiano's
Mimma's Cafe
Mo's: Steak
Nanakusa
North Shore Bistro
Palms Bistro & Bar
Pasta Tree
P.F. Chang's
Ristorante Bartolotta
River Lane Inn
Rock Bottom Brewery
Sake Tumi

Sanford
Sticks N Stones
Three Brothers
Yanni's

Power Scenes
Bacchus
Carnevor
Eddie Martini's
Envoy
Lake Park Bistro
Mo's: Steak
Mr. B's: Steak
Yanni's

Private Rooms
(Restaurants charge less at
off times; call for capacity)
Bjonda
Coast
Coquette Cafe
Eddie Martini's
Edwardo's Pizza
Elm Grove Inn
Gilbert's
Golden Mast Inn
Hama
Heaven City
Immigrant Room
Maggiano's
Mangia
Mimma's Cafe
Mr. B's: Steak
Nanakusa
Osteria del Mondo
Pacific Rim
Polonez
River Lane Inn
Riversite, The
Rock Bottom Brewery
Sebastian's
Sticks N Stones

Prix Fixe Menus
(Call for prices and times)
Bjonda
Elliot's Bistro
El Rey Sol
Gilbert's
Immigrant Room

Quick Bites
Cubanitas
Edwardo's Pizza

Elsa's on Park
Hama
Knick

Quiet Conversation
Au Bon Appétit
Barossa
Bjonda
Bosley on Brady
Dream Dance
Eddie Martini's
Elliot's Bistro
Elm Grove Inn
Envoy
Golden Mast Inn
Il Mito
Jake's Fine Dining
Karl Ratzsch's
Milwaukee Chop Hse.
Osteria del Mondo
Pacific Rim
Pasta Tree
Polonez
Riversite, The
Sanford
Third Ward Caffe

Raw Bars
Benihana
Eagan's
Moceans

Romantic Places
Dancing Ganesha
Golden Mast Inn
Heaven City
Il Mito
Immigrant Room
Lake Park Bistro
Mimma's Cafe
Osteria del Mondo
Pasta Tree
Ristorante Bartolotta
Riversite, The
Third Ward Caffe
Three Brothers
Zarletti

Senior Appeal
Elm Grove Inn
Envoy
Golden Mast Inn
Immigrant Room

Jake's Fine Dining
Karl Ratzsch's
Pleasant Valley Inn
Polonez
Riversite, The
Three Brothers

Singles Scenes
Barossa
Bjonda
Carnevor
Crawdaddy's
Cubanitas
Eagan's
Elsa's on Park
Holiday House
Knick
Mo's: Steak
Nanakusa
Palms Bistro & Bar
Rock Bottom Brewery
Sake Tumi
Social, The

Sleepers
(Good to excellent food, but little known)
Elm Grove Inn
El Rey Sol
Heaven City
Jake's Fine Dining
Polonez
Saffron Indian

Teen Appeal
Edwardo's Pizza
Maggiano's
P.F. Chang's
Potbelly Sandwich
Rock Bottom Brewery

Trendy
Bacchus
Barossa
Bjonda
Carnevor
Cempazuchi
Coast
Cubanitas
Dancing Ganesha
Eddie Martini's
Elsa's on Park
Il Mito

Knick
Lake Park Bistro
Maggiano's
Mo's: Steak
Palms Bistro & Bar
P.F. Chang's
Ristorante Bartolotta
Sake Tumi
Sanford
Social, The
Zarletti

Views
Bacchus
Coast
Gilbert's
Golden Mast Inn
Heaven City
Knick
Pleasant Valley Inn
Riversite, The
Sebastian's

Visitors on Expense Account
Barossa
Coquette Cafe
Cubanitas
Eagan's
Edwardo's Pizza
El Rey Sol
Il Mito
King & I
Knick
Maggiano's
North Shore Bistro
Polonez
Rock Bottom Brewery
Saffron Indian
Singha Thai
Social, The
Taqueria Azteca

Wine Bars
Barossa
Immigrant Room
Osteria del Mondo
Pasta Tree

Winning Wine Lists
Bacchus
Barossa
Carnevor
Coquette Cafe

Dream Dance
Lake Park Bistro
Mangia
Milwaukee Chop Hse.
Osteria del Mondo
Ristorante Bartolotta
Sanford

Worth a Trip
Caledonia
  Sebastian's

Kenosha
  Mangia
Kohler
  Immigrant Room
Lake Geneva
  Gilbert's
Mukwonago
  Heaven City
Okauchee
  Golden Mast Inn

Wine Vintage Chart

This chart is designed to help you select wine to go with your meal. It is based on the same 0 to 30 scale used throughout this *Survey*. The ratings (prepared by our friend **Howard Stravitz,** a law professor at the University of South Carolina) reflect both the quality of the vintage and the wine's readiness for present consumption. Thus, if a wine is not fully mature or is over the hill, its rating has been reduced. We do not include 1987, 1991–1993 vintages because they are not especially recommended for most areas. A dash indicates that a wine is either past its peak or too young to rate.

	'85	'86	'88	'89	'90	'94	'95	'96	'97	'98	'99	'00	'01	'02	'03	'04
WHITES																
French:																
Alsace	24	–	22	27	27	26	25	25	24	26	23	26	27	25	22	–
Burgundy	26	25	–	24	22	–	28	29	24	23	26	25	24	27	23	24
Loire Valley	–	–	–	–	–	20	23	22	–	24	25	26	27	25	23	–
Champagne	28	25	24	26	29	–	26	27	24	23	24	24	22	26	–	–
Sauternes	21	28	29	25	27	–	21	23	25	23	24	24	28	25	26	–
German	–	–	25	26	27	25	24	27	26	25	25	23	29	27	25	25
California (Napa, Sonoma, Mendocino):																
Chardonnay	–	–	–	–	–	–	–	–	–	–	24	25	28	27	26	–
Sauvignon Blanc/Sémillon	–	–	–	–	–	–	–	–	–	–	–	27	28	26	–	
REDS																
French:																
Bordeaux	24	25	24	26	29	22	26	25	23	25	24	28	26	23	25	23
Burgundy	23	–	21	24	26	–	26	28	25	22	27	22	25	27	24	–
Rhône	–	–	26	29	29	24	25	22	24	28	27	27	26	–	25	–
Beaujolais	–	–	–	–	–	–	–	–	–	–	24	–	25	28	25	
California (Napa, Sonoma, Mendocino):																
Cab./Merlot	27	26	–	–	28	29	27	25	28	23	26	22	27	25	24	–
Pinot Noir	–	–	–	–	–	–	–	–	24	24	25	24	27	28	26	–
Zinfandel	–	–	–	–	–	–	–	–	–	–	26	26	28	–	–	
Italian:																
Tuscany	–	–	–	25	22	25	20	29	24	28	24	26	24	–	–	
Piedmont	–	24	26	28	–	23	26	27	25	25	28	26	18	–	–	
Spanish:																
Rioja	–	–	–	–	26	26	24	25	22	25	25	27	20	–	–	
Ribera del Duero/Priorat	–	–	–	–	26	26	27	25	24	26	26	27	20	–	–	

On the go.
In the know.

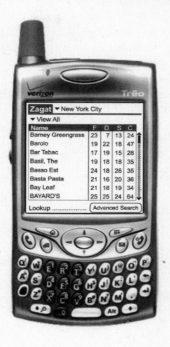

ZAGAT TO GO^{SM}